"Sam Trust had the fortuitous timing of building a career in music publishing during an era when the business was run by fantastic Damon Runyon characters rather than by corporate suits. He emerged from that era with a trove of fascinating stories. To his reputation as a longtime music insider and visionary spanning from his time with the Beatles catalogue to his founding of Killer Tracks and beyond, he can now rightfully add another credit: master storyteller."

    Scott Martin, Deputy General Counsel,
    Paramount Pictures

"Sam is one of my favorite people. We shared a number of worldwide hits."

    Russ Regan, President: UNI Records, President of Twentieth Century Records, (retired)

"Sam is one of the most honorable premier music publishing executives in the music industry."

    Cliffie Stone, Country Music Hall of Fame icon, producer, manager, music publisher.

"A man of honesty and integrity. One of the most knowledgeable, gifted music publishers of our generation."

    Terry Slater, EMI Music producer, music publisher and EMI Music Director, 1969-1982

"A powerhouse music publishing innovator during some of
the glory years of American songwriting. He taught me
many valuable lessons about both the music business and
plain old street smarts. Trust me, Sam Trust is a brilliant
and dryly funny man, with some fascinating stories to tell.
Don't miss this one."

    Harry Shannon, novelist, songwriter, music supervisor

"I have always loved music, knew a little about how singer -
songwriters were produced, how a singer could have a hit one
day only to see it lost the next. The world brought to life in
this book is the world behind the scenes of music making,
deals made and some lost. Sam Trust's stories will amuse,
inspire and inform you with his first hand accounts from
that competitive arena."

    Sean Dwyer, writer, editor

Would You Trust this Man with Your Songs?

A Life in Music Business

By Sam Trust
with Mary Jane Fraser

Drawings by Eileen Melia
Cover design by Norman L Green
ISBN 978-0-692-14444-2

TABLE OF CONTENTS

Foreword

This book, which is actually a collection of short stories, came about at the insistence of Mary Jane Fraser, who listened to a few of my stories at dinners with her then gentleman friend, who had been a writer at ATV Music. She had frequently journeyed from Bellingham, Washington to visit him in Carmel, where my wife and I reside.

Mary Jane requested that I write down these stories. I scoffed at the request, insisting that they were nothing more than dinner conversations. She was quite insistent and on her next trip showed up with a tape recorder. I reluctantly agreed to dictate a few, but after hearing the results, told her to erase them.

I decided that I could write better than speak, and took a shot at writing a story. She was delighted at the result, as were a few close friends from the business. So, I started at the beginning of my career in the music industry, and kept going. This book is in no way a personal "memoir," but rather a story of my learning and progressing in the business, leading to some interesting events I was a part of, including some household industry names, with whom I interacted.

Though Mary Jane did not write or co-write any of these stories, this book would not have been accomplished without her appraisals, constant urging and suggestions of which stories should or shouldn't be included, as well as her pursuit for publication.

It should be kept in mind that these stories deal with a time prior to iPods, file-sharing, downloading, YouTube and streaming. It is also my feeling that it was also a time of a little more humanity in the industry, than currently exists. Yes, there were gripes about recording deals, short accountings, etc. but overall it just seems to me a more colorful time. The business had characters with names like, "Happy," "Smiley," "Juggy," "Cookie," "Snuffy" "Lucky" and "Moish." It was also a time during which some of the world's greatest recording artists and songwriters were developed. I had the pleasure of dealing with some of these names who, even today, produce a disproportionate amount of royalties.

I hope these industry stories are enjoyable, and to some extent, educational as to the music business then and now. To that end I've included, for reference, a glossary of music business terms used during that time and now.

Mary Jane Fraser is a free-lance writer and arts education consultant. She travels the world but the great Pacific Northwest is her home.

CHAPTER 1
What Now?

Nothing could have prepared me for what was about to happen. As the time for the concert approached, all seats including the boxes appeared to be filled, except the box to my immediate left. Suddenly the auditorium went black, and a wide spotlight covered that box, spilling over to ours. The Queen entered, on the arm of the velvet-caped Lord Mayor of London as the orchestra majestically played "God Save the Queen." To the right of the Queen, entering simultaneously, accompanied by two lovely young ladies, was Prince Philip. When the ceremony concluded Prince Philip reached across the upholstered common barrier to shake my hand, and announced that he was looking forward to this concert. As we chatted, the Queen, wearing a silver and diamond tiara, leaned over the box to see to whom the Prince was talking, smiled at me and waved. Frequently, Prince Philip would bend my way to comment on a particular performance with, "That was a really good one!" Remembering my humble and unlikely beginnings in the music industry, I couldn't help but marvel at where I found myself.

It began on my ninth birthday when my dad bought me a bugle I had been longing for. As it was during World War II and metal was scarce, the bugle was made of plastic in the color army khaki. Nevertheless, I was thrilled and even put it in my bed the first night to guard it. In less than a week I could play a respectable version of Taps. A few years later I was able to save enough money to buy a second hand cornet. Sadly, as the war ended, I was often called upon by the local American Legion to perform Taps, wearing my Boy Scout uniform and standing at the gravesite of returning soldiers killed in the war. Looking back to that time, I realized, perhaps, that was what put me in the predicament I was then experiencing.

I persisted in my involvement with music throughout school, college, and my military service, where I served close to two years, most of which was aboard Aircraft Carriers, as lead trumpet in the Admiral of carriers of the 7th Fleet's Flag band, sailing throughout the Pacific.

In late September of 1957 I was mustered out of the U.S. Navy at the old Treasure Island Naval Base in San Francisco Bay. Now it was time to get real. How was I, at age 24, about to make a living? How was a Bachelor of Music degree going to help me achieve this? I had disdained a Music Education degree that, of course, was more practical, but I had considered it a "cop out."

Rather than go straight home, I decided I needed time to unwind and think (much to my parent's displeasure). I decided to take advantage of an offer from a friend I met while stationed in San Diego, who had a beach house just north of that city. After spending several days there, I hopped a bus to San Antonio, Texas to visit my former college roommate, Gary, also a trumpeter, who was playing with the 4th Army band stationed there. From there it was a long Trailways Bus trip to my hometown of Pittsburgh, Pa. My parents met me at the station. While my mom was thrilled, my dad was very cool and hardly spoke. He was still sore, because I had refused to come straight home and accompany them on a trip to Atlantic City (the last place I wanted to be at that time).

After a short time at home, I knew I had to make some money and it wasn't going to happen there. Before being drafted into the service, in Cincinnati, where I had graduated from the Conservatory of Music, I had gone to work at WCPO-TV, a local TV station that happened to originate an ABC Network show from their studios, "The Dottie Mack Pantomime Hit Parade." Having been employed there full-time prior to military service, they legally had to offer me my job when I was discharged. So, I picked up a 1940 Plymouth for $100 and off I went, back to Cincinnati.

The station was none too pleased to see me, as the job I had as a commercial set-up man, (remember, those were the days of "live" TV) had been satisfactorily filled but they knew they had to re-employ me, so they put me in charge of the prop room. I worked the 4:30 PM to 1:AM shift.

After about 2 months the stagehands insisted I join their union. I told them I had no intention of doing so. From then on they put the "chill" on me and made me generally uncomfortable. I knew it was time to go. So, off I went, back to Pittsburgh to again consider my future. All that time I tried to continue to practice my trumpet, though irregularly.

In a mood of disgust, my father said "Well, I guess I could get you a job as a counter man at Steel City Automotive," the company where he was a salesman.

That did it. I was tapped out, but knew the only place for me to possibly get a trumpeter's job was New York City. I called my dad's younger brother "Itz" (Irwin), who was a long distance truck driver and asked him if he needed a helper on his next trip to New York, and he said he was leaving the next day. Itz and I always had a great relationship; I always thought of him as the big brother I never had. So started my life in New York.

Fortunately, I had cousins who worked in the city offer me the use of their apartment and a couch to sleep on until I could get on my feet financially. I contacted another trumpeter from college, a New Yorker who was able to get me a few jobs after I got my #802 union card. It quickly became obvious that I couldn't support myself on these odd jobs so I took the Civil Service Exam to get a job as a librarian at the music division of the New York Public Library on East 58th Street, which had an opening. My first day of work was February 14th, 1958--Valentine's Day, a day I would long remember and celebrate. That position, which paid 28 dollars per week, was fortuitous for me in several ways. It allowed me to move out of my cousins' apartment and into the Union Settlement House on East 103rd St. and 2nd Avenue, behind the then location of the Manhattan School of Music. I was given free rent in a room, the size of three telephone booths, and free dinner so long as I agreed to give free individual trumpet lessons to Puerto Rican children. The area of the Union Settlement House was referred to as "Spanish Harlem," which apparently never slept. It allowed me to practice my trumpet at all hours. Between the rumble of trucks on 2nd Avenue, seemingly constant sirens, and hell raising on the streets, my practicing seemed to fit right in. This was an experience I will never forget. The library job allowed me to benefit from my conservatory training since it dealt mainly with serious, i.e., classical music. Most importantly, it introduced me to one Joan Van Genderen, a music theory major who was completing her degree at the Mannes School of Music, while working at the same place. The library insisted that we address all persons formally, so I was always "Mr. Trust" and because of her long last name, I would address her as "Miss Van G." (That lasted only until June of 1959 when she became "Mrs. Trust.")

While working the front desk at the music library, a young lady with the name of Glantz wished to take out a piece of music. I mentioned that she had the last name of the great first trumpeter of Toscanini's orchestras, The New York Philharmonic and The NBC "Symphony of The Air." She said "Oh you mean Uncle Harry." I was "floored," and told her I was a trumpeter who greatly admired him. I knew it was almost impossible to get to be his student and added that it would be an honor to be able to take lessons from him. To present my credentials I advised her that I played trumpet with the Cincinnati Symphony during my senior year at the Cincinnati Conservatory of Music. She said that she would speak to him and get back to me. Several weeks later she stopped by the library and gave me his telephone number. She said he would find room for me on his schedule. I was overjoyed. Harry Glantz was a legend to trumpet players, and a wonderful teacher. I learned much from him for my 10 dollars per lesson. (A chunk out of my $28 per

3

week, but worth it.) One day he said to me "Sam, I know you're looking for work, so I could call my cousin Saul Caston, who conducts the Denver Symphony, to fit you in there. What do you think?" I said that I'd greatly appreciate it, flattered that he could recommend me.

I had no idea that Caston was his cousin. Saul Caston was also a well-known great trumpeter as first chair, for many years, of the Philadelphia Orchestra. Unfortunately, at my next lesson he advised that Saul told him he was retiring and would no longer be with the orchestra.

During this period I met a good friend and former trumpeter and arranger from the conservatory, Art Decenzo, who was also living and struggling in New York. He was referred to by friends as "The Deetch." Art was not much of a trumpeter, but worked mainly as an arranger. The Cincinnati Symphony in fact, played some of his arrangements. He was in search of an apartment and offered to share with me if a good inexpensive one could be found. I immediately agreed, remembering what a fabulous cook he was as well as a great buddy.

Once again, good luck came into play by way of my library job. Joan Bennett, a flutist from the conservatory, appeared at the library. She had been in town for auditions, and successfully was accepted by the Chicago Symphony Orchestra. I inquired as to where she was living and she told me was staying at a wonderful apartment on Claremont Avenue, a block from Julliard. (Julliard moved to Lincoln Center some time later.) She would be keeping her apartment until she needed to move to Chicago but mentioned an available one on the 5th floor (with no elevator). It was a two-bedroom apartment, just what Deetch and I were looking for. The rent was $95 per month, which we figured we could handle.

In late spring of 1958 we moved into that sparsely furnished apartment. I, of course, had to relinquish my lessons with Glantz in order to pay my share of the rent. My library job plus some occasional playing as a "ringer" with community orchestras provided me with enough to survive. That summer I learned that the Buffalo Symphony had an opening for second trumpet. Auditions were to be held at Steinway Hall on 57th Street. The well-known conductor, Josef Krips, was to preside over the auditions. The prospective trumpeters were to play the beautiful solo passage from Wagner's "Parsifal." I submitted my name and, of course, practiced that music prior to the audition. To my surprise, 29 candidates showed up. The job paid $90 per week for a 19-week season. The rest of the year you were, apparently, on your own.

I was scheduled to be number 4 on the list. I stood outside of the small stage and listened to the first two candidates and thought, "Well, I can play that as well as them." The third applicant, a short, thin player, then stepped onto the stage and literally "sang" through the passage with a wonderful tone. I was "blown away." It immediately struck me -- if I had to play better than him to get 2nd chair in an orchestra that paid that little for such a short time, I was simply not in contention. When the conductor called my name to audition, I said, "Maestro, I'm not prepared." I put my horn back in its case and left the building. I, in effect, left that profession as a career, as well.

When I returned to the apartment I realized that I had made a life-changing decision, but knew I wanted, somehow, to stay in music. I talked it over with Deetch. We both decided to check newspaper-classified sections, as a starter, to try to find work in music. About a month later as I was returning to the apartment from the library, approaching the flight of stairs to the fifth floor I looked up to see Deetch standing in front of our apartment holding a newspaper high in his hands and saying, "Here it is, your job!" When I got up the stairs he read *The New York Times* ad to me.

"Wanted: music clerk, must have knowledge of popular and classical music,
Prior library experience preferred."

Both he and I felt that it practically had my name on it. Deetch had recently gone to work at Corelli-Jacobs film and music editors. His job was to work at a movieola machine spotting and applying music to mostly industrial and educational companies' films from the DeWolfe Music libraries. DeWolfe was one of the early companies (from the UK) that pioneered music library usage.

I prepared a résumé and mailed it to BMI, a company I had only a slight recognition of. Broadcast Music Inc. is a performance licensing organization similar to ASCAP. These organizations, via licenses from music writers and publishers, collected revenue from mainly radio and TV stations, (during that time) but also other non-broadcast venues, for music performed or created by their writer and publisher affiliates. The revenue collected is accounted to the affiliates in the form of royalties. BMI was launched in 1940 by the radio broadcast industry to supply music to the then 500 radio stations who were victim to the ASCAP refusal to license songs to stations due to a standoff in rate negotiations. Until that time, ASCAP was the sole music-licensing agency. BMI hurriedly hired arrangers who updated Public Domain standards and tried enticing writers and publishers to join their new "performing rights society." Early on, works by Stephen Foster became hits as well as music with lyrics applied to Tchaikowsky, Chopin, and Rachmaninoff melodies, all of which were in the Public Domain.

Within a week I received a response with an interview date. The Assistant Director of Logging, Julian Weissgold, interviewed me. He noticed on my résumé that I was a Navy veteran and inquired where I had gone to boot camp. We learned that we were both at Great Lakes at the same time, he as a young officer, an ensign, and me a "boot." After a pleasant discussion, he advised that he would get back to me as he had other candidates to interview. I simply wouldn't let that stand. I responded, "What for? You know I'm perfect for this job. You know it, and I know it. You won't find anyone better. Let's just settle it now." He became flustered and said it was his duty to interview the others. I finally let up on him and left. Three days later he called to advise me I got the job starting the following Monday. My new career in the music industry was about to commence.

CHAPTER 2
Have A Chair At BMI

On September 22, 1958 at 9:AM I arrived at BMI for my first day of work. BMI was then located at 589 Fifth Avenue at 48th Street. It was catty-corner to Rockefeller Center, home of NBC, and a short four blocks from CBS, then on Madison Avenue. ABC was across Central Park on 60th St., which was a short taxi ride. In those days each network had their own staff orchestras. CBS had Alfredo Antonini with a full symphony orchestra, NBC had Arturo Toscanini and "The Symphony Of The Air," and ABC had about 38 players including a trumpet section with both Billy Butterfield and Bobby Hackett. All of this, as well as practically all the important music publishers were located within this area, which I would come to know in a short time.

BMI occupied the 7th and 8th floors of the building. The 7th floor housed Index, Logging, (song identification and crediting) Accounting, Editing, the "machine room" (data processing) and the mail-room. You could say it was the "grunt" floor. The 8th floor was, basically, the executive floor. It contained Legal, Publisher Relations, Writer Relations, Station Relations, Non-broadcast Relations, the President's office, the various vice presidents offices, and the conference room. Naturally, I was on the 7th floor as part of the Logging Department.

The Logging Department was one large room. At one far corner of the room was a well-carpeted office, presided over by Israel (aka Ike) Diamond, Director of Logging. At the other far corner was a small enclosure occupied by the previously mentioned Julian Weissgold, Assistant Director of Logging. Directly between them were desks where workers dealt with foreign repertoire, expert loggers (whose jobs I will shortly explain) and another desk for odd jobs. Research card files of songs in wheeldexes occupied the rest of the area, aside from a small portion used as a royalties section near Weissgold's cubicle. There was one huge electrically controlled, rotary file, filled with the reference cards, which was more easily handled, since the section needed could be found by pushing a button. The card containing the title requested

7

would come directly to the clerk. That file contained titles A through F. The rest of the files were in giant hand spinning wheeldexes spread across the room. I was assigned the wheeldexes S to Z. Directly in front of these files and occupying the rest of the space to the windowed hall, were vertical racks of pre-punched cards containing the titles of the most frequently played BMI songs, as well as those in the top one hundred charts of trade magazines. Again the files were manned, or I should say, in this case, run by women positioned alphabetically at stations. Each week this section was updated with the latest popular BMI titles. It must be kept in mind that I'm discussing a time more than a half-century ago. Processing files was almost wholly accomplished by IBM keypunch cards.

At the outset of BMI, the founding 500 radio stations agreed to submit Station Logs with all music performed for one full month of each year. Naturally, as stations were added they would also comply as would their eventually related TV outlets. As the burden of the additional logs increased, the reports were then limited to 2 weeks and eventually 7 random days. The selection of the stations was by an objective statistical group headed by Dr. Paul Lazarfield of Columbia University that took into consideration geography, population, per capita income, etc. BMI had no idea as to who would be picked. There could be no possibility of collusion between BMI and publishers or writers to tip off which station was about to be logged.

As station logs were received they were registered, put into folders and given to the expert loggers (there were three at the time of my initial employment.) These experts were veterans of BMI who knew the "standard songs" controlled by BMI's publisher affiliates, and kept up on all BMI weekly chart activity, which was constantly increasing for BMI affiliates. The experts had special double-sided pencils, red on one end, blue on the other. The information on these preprinted logs provided for the song title, publisher, record company and serial number. Often this full information was not included. A blue line was used for non-BMI songs, (almost always ASCAP) and a red for BMI. The experts identified about 85% of the titles and the logs were forwarded to the ladies at vertical pre-punched cards for crediting. The unmarked songs were then passed to the wheeldex operators for research and song code assignments. When all was complete, those titles were sent to the keypunch operators in the machine room for processing and final royalty statement preparation.

About one month after I started, one of the expert checkers decided to leave. This meant that only two remained to deal with a job that barely three could handle, and often called for overtime to keep up with the constant receipt of station logs. The two remaining checkers were Ed Lecomte, who had been with the company for many years after a career as an actor, and "Murray." Ed was very good at his job, but Murray was a strange individual, to say the least and was obsessed with his quest to be the fastest checker.

I don't ever remember Murray wearing anything but a wrinkled white shirt, black pants and sneakers. He would often sit at his desk during his lunch hour with a sandwich at his side while he continued log checking. On occasion, I saw him leave for the men's rest room with a station log tucked under his armpit. Murray spoke in short clipped sentences, and may well have been autistic.

Knowing the critical situation that resulted from the loss of a checker, and armed with figures showing that he was the fastest checker, Murray requested a meeting with Mr. Diamond. At that meeting, he demanded a large raise in salary or he would quit. Diamond was rather short and bald, but quite muscular, well educated, and articulate. He had been in his position for many years, but obviously frustrated to not have risen to the 8th floor. Diamond would not accept his threat, so Murray, convinced that he would be asked back on his terms, quit. The next day Weissgold called me into his office and asked if I would be interested in having the job as a checker. I asked what it paid. (I was being paid $65 per week.) He said $70 and I replied I'd take it. I made one further request. I had been sitting in a straight-back chair working at the wheeldex files and asked for an upholstered leather-like swivel chair similar to the one in his office. They must have been desperate, as Weissgold assured me that it was no problem. He would order one right away.

Armed with a familiarity of the fakebook* titles from my dance band days, which were predominantly ASCAP, and studying the standards from BMI's former renegade ASCAP publishers such as E. B. Marks, M.M. Cole, and Peer Music, (as examples) I started as an expert checker the next day. Ed Lecomte and I went immediately on overtime daily from 5 PM until 9. As regular working hours were 9 to 5 with an hour off for lunch, amounting to a 35-hour week, our first 5 hours were at regular pay, then the rest at "time and a half." This amounted to over $100 per week. After $28 per week, and living on a diet of scotch broth (a thick soup of barley, mixed vegetables and some meat) using only a little water to keep it thick rather than the full additional can as directed, this payday was a fortune to me. When I started at BMI I weighed 144 lbs. By the end of the year I was close to 170.

9

After two weeks I felt that I was hitting my stride at this position and breaking through with Ed, who had always been quite reserved. However, I still hadn't received my promised upholstered swivel chair. Early one morning I walked into Weissgold's office and replaced his chair with mine. Ed got a kick out of this. When Weissgold arrived, he was confused and started searching the premises. He spotted me sitting in his chair and said, "Sam, I think you're sitting in my chair." Julian Weissgold was very pleasant, bald like Diamond, but good looking and about two years older than me. You had the feeling that every time he addressed you he seemed to be apologizing. He was definitely groomed to be an organizational man, in fear of rocking any boat.

I replied, "No, Mr. Weissgold, this is the chair you promised me weeks ago."

He was flustered and said, "This one is mine, yours is being ordered." I suggested he take it when it arrived, and told him I had no intention of giving him the chair.

He said, "We'll see about that" and marched directly into Mr. Diamond's office. He was there for quite some time. Eventually Diamond came to see me. I confirmed that I was keeping the chair. He then walked in Weissgold's cubicle and that was the end to it. Later that week I noticed a similar chair in Weissgold's office. The matter was never mentioned again.

Ed Lecomte, the elderly senior checker, and I became pals. He even found a condominium in his neighborhood outside of New Brunswick, New Jersey for us, which took us out of Brooklyn. He confided to me that during his "lean days" as an actor, he was spotted by a sculptor and asked to be a model. As he needed the work, he took the job. He was considered by the sculptor to be perfect to pose for a statue of Thomas Jefferson. During the modeling, he and the sculptor became fast friends. The sculptor told Ed that he would put something of Ed into the statue. Ed pointed out the thumb on one hand had an overgrown joint. Ed said if you ever get to Washington and go to the Jefferson memorial, I could check it out.

*Fakebooks were un-authorized lead lines and chords to familiar songs, which might be requested by patrons of venues that had small bands. The sheets were usually in three-ring binders, which could be opened to rest easily on music stands. Much later many publishers decided to authorize these printed editions, providing royalty rates for the sales.

CHAPTER 3
A Touch Of Class

I stayed at the checker position for about 10 weeks piling up overtime pay, finally able to enjoy some time with Miss Van G. It became clear to all that we were definitely an "item," and as such enjoyed the company of two other CCM grads, recently married, Chuck and June Magruder who had come to New York about a year earlier. They were both fine musicians and sought-after vocalists who quickly became established on the New York scene. They were part of the Ray Charles choral group on The Perry Como TV show, did commercials as "The Honey Dreamers" and were first call for the most vocally challenged spots on TV and radio.

Meanwhile, Deetch was also doing well financially, and decided that with so many CCM graduates in the city, we should do some entertaining. We had only a small Formica top table that couldn't work for entertaining so Deetch came up with a plan. One day he arrived with a bedroom door that he purchased from a lumber company. Together we attached a 2 by 4 to a wall about 2 1/2 feet from the floor. We then placed hinges from the purchased door to that base, with magnets on the wall near the ceiling and the top of the door, and, Voila! With a tacked on cloth covering, we had a folding dining room table. Oh, did we entertain! With Deetch's fine cooking and a minimum contribution from all attending, dinners were great! There was Chuck and June, Gene Hessler who was in the pit orchestra at Radio City as a trombonist, Buzz Brusletten, recently returned composer from a fellowship grant in Europe, Bill Bryan a writer/composer working at CBS TV, Maurice Burns, member of the Metropolitan Opera chorus, Alex Chavich, a blind pianist working on his Masters degree at the Manhattan School of Music, Joan (Miss Van G,) me, and Margaret "Hinky" Harr," with her latest beau, and any other CCM grad who happened to be in town.

Directly in front, and to the right of my desk at BMI sat the classical music checker, a very quiet and obviously well educated Sy Ribakove, who also kept a low profile. BMI's Logging Department always had a

11

"grab bag" as part of its Christmas party. Unbeknownst to me, Sy had picked my name out of the bag. After I received my gift, a beautiful set of cuff links, (which I still use) I came over to thank him, and an interesting conversation ensued. Though we were always friendly, acknowledging each other's greetings, Sy said he always wanted to get to know me. In the course of our conversation, he advised me that he intended to leave at the end of the year and spend more time as a writer. He had several of his pieces published in national magazines and this was the direction he intended to pursue. He asked whether I would be interested in taking his position, an offer I couldn't possibly refuse. He said that he would recommend me to Diamond. I was ecstatic!

In early 1959, I gave up my job as expert checker to become the classical music expert in the Logging department, a position far more interesting and challenging. Programming of classical music then, as now, occupied a miniscule portion of the broadcast media. Despite this fact, Carl Haverlin, then president of BMI was devoted to the perpetuation and preservation of this music. Early on, BMI became associated with an American publishing company that had the U.S. rights to major European classical music publishers. These publishers included B. Schotte Soehne, Enoch & Cie, G. Ricordi of Milan, and Durand to name a few. At that time, some late works by Richard Strauss, Puccini, and other familiar names were still protected by U.S. copyright. That U.S. representative was Associated Music Publishers (AMP.) Their offices were across the street from BMI near the corner of 47th and 5th Avenue. In addition, BMI underwrote the American Composers Alliance, (ACA,) presided over by composer Robert Ward at the time. BMI represented such American composers as Walter Piston, Roger Sessions, Alan Hovhaness, Daniel Pinkham, Ulysses Kay and Elliot Carter to name a few. Probably the most popular of the BMI represented composers, at that time was Paul Hindemith.

In order to acknowledge what little serious music programming did take place on classically formatted stations, which were few and, at the time only on AM frequencies, a classical music universe of stations was created at BMI. The universe consisted of some 14 stations throughout the U.S. whose performing rights payments were very low as most of the music performed was already public domain. However, some contemporary, serious music was also offered. Each of these stations, such as WQXR in New York and WGMS in Washington D.C. produced weekly or monthly program guides listing titles with composer names. These guides were regularly submitted to BMI instead of the station logs required from Pop Music stations. All listings of BMI licensed composers were logged and given multiple credits. (These works were much longer than pop songs.) Much to my shock and disappointment, all classical titles in our wheeldexes were mixed in with the pop song titles rather than by composers. So, if a symphony was performed you would have to sort through all the "S" files of symphony to find the right composer. Add to that problem, a station may have reported it as "sinfonia," so that title had to be checked. The same problem existed for chamber music also known in German as kammermusik, Sonata as Sonate, Concerto as Konzert, and so on. The files were choked with these multiple coded titles for the same work. Apparently, Sy Ribakove had a fantastic memory and didn't bother to urge Mr. Diamond to correct the files. Diamond was unquestionably an empire builder for which each added file enhanced his importance. I set out to correct this problem and advised Diamond, who seemed disinterested in the project. I told him it would take some time and might require some overtime, which he disproved of as unnecessary. I decided to attack the problem, overtime or not. I noticed that there was some open space on the very last wheeldex, my old station. I therefore, started at the A's and pulled out every serious music title I could find. I placed each under the proper composers name in the file I created in the spaces available in that last wheeldex. As these multi-coded works were removed throughout all the files, the contents of each wheeldex shrunk somewhat, so some of the contents of the next wheeldex files were moved to the previous one. By the time I was finished one of the huge wheeldexes was completely empty with the shiny metal wheels glistening. Mr. Diamond was unhappy to see his empire shrink, and had that file immediately removed.

Sy had advised me that I would have to conduct a yearly Concert Music Questionnaire using the 14 stations of the classical music universe. This was a pet project of Mr. Haverlin. I, therefore, had the opportunity to visit his office and introduce myself. Haverlin was a veteran of the broadcasting industry who had served as President of BMI almost from inception. Carl Haverlin was articulate, intelligent, an earnest supporter of the arts. He was also an historian. His particular interest was Lincoln and, in fact, he was referred to as a "Lincolnian." I had even seen him walk the office halls with Carl Sandburg as his guest. He was medium sized but, whether sitting or standing, he had the bearing of a West Point Cadet. When he spoke, you could swear the room had been acoustically modified to enhance his voice. We discussed the project and I left with trepidations concerning my ability to satisfactorily deliver the report.

The questionnaires, sent out to the 14 stations, were returned to me. I analyzed the contents, and came up with my comments and conclusions in a 4-page report and submitted it to Mr. Haverlin. This was the first report I had prepared since my sophomore year in college, so I was naturally hesitant. After about a week I received a note back from him: "Excellent report, Sam. Keep up the good work." I breathed a sigh of relief and, of course, pride. I can only assume Mr. Diamond received a copy of that note, as events followed that would, once again, lead me in new directions.

Now that the challenge of the Concert Music Questionnaire was over, I continued with my job as classical music expert. My desk was located directly in the Foreign Logging area presided over by Leo Cherniavsky, a fine concert violinist, who arrived in this country from Germany just in time. After performing with various orchestras, he decided to accept a position with BMI as head of Foreign Logging. While he was located in the Logging Department, he actually reported to Jean Geiringer, Vice President of Foreign Relations. Geiringer, from France, was a well-respected expert on international copyright. In the early days of BMI, ASCAP threatened any foreign publisher who assigned rights to any of their songs to a BMI sub-publisher would be blacklisted by ASCAP. Further, they stated when BMI went out of business they would not accept the company back.

BMI was, therefore, unable to represent any works outside of North and South America. In desperation, they sought out Geiringer, who was well connected throughout Europe, to join the BMI executive staff as VP of Foreign Relations, with a very lucrative salary and almost complete autonomy. Geiringer quickly fixed the problem by offering foreign publishers the exact same rates as a BMI publisher. Usually rates for works from a foreign publisher were split 50-50 between them and their sub-publisher. As BMI domestic rates, at that time, were roughly the same as ASCAP's, this amounted to double payment. The doors were kicked open. Leo Cherniavsky's job was to assure that foreign songs performed on U.S. stations were accurately credited. There were, and continue to be, stations that cater to the German market (mostly polka formats) French, Polish, and various other European languages. German, at the time seemed to be the most active. The German Performing Rights Society, GEMA, retained a Dr. Plage (pronounced Plahgah) as their U.S. agent. Plage was short, no more than 5 feet 2, but wiry and certainly grim-faced. He was about 67 years of age, ran several miles each morning at 4:30 AM, regardless of the weather, ate a Spartan breakfast and then off to work. He would visit BMI once per month to examine station logs that performed German music. Leo told me that he had worked for German Intelligence in World War I and served them as well in World War II in Japan, Germany's Axis partner. For good reason he intimidated Leo, who obviously experienced the many hardships of the German Jews while he lived in Germany. Dr. Plage would take my desk for the hours of his visit, as it was next to Leo's, so Leo could keep an eye on him. If per chance he found an error, he would pounce on it and yell at a frightened Leo in German. Once when Leo was to be gone when Plage was to visit, Leo advised me to keep my desk locked as was his, and to not work on anything while he was there. He advised that Plage was trained to read everything upside down as well. I kept my eyes on him and grunted back to him when he left. The name Plage, unfortunately always created fear in Leo. Leo and I became close friends through our love of serious music, but constantly ribbed each other over our instruments. He would hold his nose while nasally humming the opening bars of Haydn's Trumpet Concerto, while I constantly reminded him that fiddlers were a dime a dozen. It was during this time, in late spring of that year, when another surprising event occurred that would again change the course of my work to another area of music, for which I was to become a specialist.

CHAPTER 4
TV Time

One day in early May as I was working at my desk, I noticed a tall extremely well dressed gentleman enter Diamond's office. My desk abutted his outside wall so I had a good view. Approximately 15 minutes later, they both came to my desk.

Diamond introduced me to Richard Kirk, VP of BMI's West Coast Operations as follows: "Dick, I want you to meet our Director of Television Logging, Sam Trust." In a state of shock, but trying not to show it, I shook hands with Kirk. Diamond had insured him that television background music crediting was in good hands.

Dick Kirk was about 6 ft. 2", always immaculately dressed in a tailored suit and high starched collar, with a beautiful tan. The one most significant feature, for that time, was his totally baldhead, penciled in eyebrows, and thin mustache. He was referred to around the office as "Mr. Clean." (a perfectly bald strongman featured in a cleaning product ad at the time) I was later to learn that he had lost all hair on his body to alopecia resulting from a traumatic wartime disaster. While serving on a destroyer in the Pacific, his ship was destroyed by a Japanese torpedo attack that he barely survived.

After Kirk left, I went into Diamond's office and said, "What was that?" Diamond explained that Kirk wanted to transfer all television logging to the west coast office, as the majority of music scoring for television was located there. Diamond was to have no part of seeing his empire diminished and came over vamping, at my desk. I asked what I was supposed to do and he replied, "Gather all the material needed to credit background music and scoring, and to forget about concert logging." As I would soon learn, this would be an enormous project.

BMI had not paid for background music on radio. When TV came along background music was, again, never logged. With the advent of background music libraries, token non-logging payments were awarded yearly to these entities. They, or their representatives, usually lawyers, would supply what proof they could find from distributor sales figures, or any other sources to substantiate broadcast performances. The total of these payments was insignificant. ASCAP was no better. While they claimed to pay for background music, payment was computed at 1/100 of a credit, and that was for works that they could identify. The "recognized works" category continued to dominate their payments. Songs performed on Network were no problem as they were clearly indicated for both organizations. Though local TV stations were still on a sampled basis, network-logging reports were daily. Every program broadcast on ABC, CBS, and NBC was reported indicating the songs performed. No one anticipated how TV would develop after its debut at the end of the 1940's and early 50's. It was thought that a great deal of music would be performed on Variety Shows and that there would be programs featuring the big bands such as Tommy Dorsey from the Roosevelt Hotel, the Harry James' Band, etc. Though early on there were a number of variety shows featuring music, such as Dinah Shore, Perry Como, and other popular song artists, programming didn't develop as anticipated. Featured song performances eventually stopped appearing in prime-time hours. Instead, situation comedies and 1/2 hour drama series became popular. Most of them used pre-recorded music to drop in where needed, and there wasn't that much needed. Music cue-sheets for these programs were often haphazardly prepared, showing titles for the cues and composers, but not the duration of the performances. BMI files contained no music cue-sheets. So, I had a huge mountain to climb. I started first at the music clearance departments at each network, where I had to introduce myself and make a huge request for copies of the music cue sheets they had on file for their current programming and, secondly, copies for past programs, which I knew would probably end up in syndication. This was asking a big favor of them I knew, but I had to have them and offered to compensate them for their efforts. As time moved on I entertained these music clearance directors on a regular basis.

Two months earlier, my engagement to Joan had taken place and we planned our wedding for the end of June. We were to honeymoon on the west coast, where I would hook up with some of my old navy buddies who were living there, as well as relatives of Joan's and mine. Now that I was in the middle of this huge project, I advised Diamond of my plans. He said to work at the west coast for some extra days, if I needed. It was a chance to learn of, and meet some of the music directors at the studios. Dick Kirk and I broke the ice re: East Coast vs. West. He and his assistant, Gordon Messner, were very helpful. During the early part of that trip we stayed with my navy buddy, Neal Brooks, at his and his wife's home in Pacific Grove on the Monterey Peninsula. One day he took us to Carmel, a neighboring town. Both Joan and I were very taken with it and I vowed that we would get back there, someday.

When we returned, I was told by the network clearance departments that I could borrow music cue sheet files, duplicate, and return them. We used the latest duplicating equipment at that time, Xerox, a process involving placing the cue sheet next to the copy, then pulling them through a wet tray, allowing time to dry, and then separating them. I stood at a Xerox machine for hours at a time, before telling Diamond that it simply wasn't a one-man job. As a result, an assistant was hired and we were given space in another location nearby as part of the music editor's area. My time was also occupied with correspondence with the heads of music at the west coast studios, and still dealing with the TV Network and TV local station logs. Radio network programming was quickly phasing out, so TV Networks were becoming the most important source of revenue.

Systems had to be developed to account for TV theme and background usage. The prevailing rates for songs identified as "background" on television were based on network and local radio rates at the time, and merely reduced by 50%. This was a makeshift system that would drastically change over the course of the next 18 months.

During my time at BMI the ASCAP antagonism towards BMI remained strong. In 1953 some 30 ASCAP writers, with the support of ASCAP, had filed a lawsuit against BMI, its then stockholders NBC, ABC, CBS and some 500 stations, claiming that BMI had conspired to eliminate the traditional ASCAP standard songs from broadcast performance. Those stockholders were, in fact, never paid a dividend and only had banded together to form an alternate performing rights organization so they would not be held hostage to one group's demand, as was the case in 1939. The fact was, at that time, only an exclusive group of writers were allowed membership into ASCAP. They did not license country music, folk, or what was then referred to a "race" (R & B) music. Since this was not part of their repertory, the broadcasters requested "per program" licenses as they wished to not pay ASCAP for music they did not represent. ASCAP denied, and demanded a doubling of their fees. The ASCAP "writers" (in 1953) went through various courts. New bills were presented to congress. All failed. The action was finally terminated in 1968 "with prejudice." Ownership of stock of BMI by the broadcasters was eventually eliminated. However, though ASCAP continued to smart from this decision, they still favored owners of standard repertoire as part of their recognized works crediting. In years to come, by necessity, their horizons expanded to welcome all writers and address non-standard songs more equitably.

At the time I became involved with TV and film background music, ASCAP virtually controlled the West Coast studios. The studios publishing companies, most of which were purchased from well-known east coast publishers, such as Famous Music by Paramount, Witmark Music and Remick by Warners, and Robbins, Feist & Miller Music by MGM, were created before the advent of BMI. These publishers were well represented on the Board of Directors of ASCAP. Usage of BMI songs in films was rare, if at all. BMI film composers were virtually non-existent.

BMI acknowledged that its repertoire of music on the television networks represented less than 33%. However, with the dwindling use of featured music, an opening was found. Through Dick Kirk's effort on the west coast, film score composers were found who were willing to leave ASCAP for, what can only be called guarantees of better earnings from BMI. Luring these writers wasn't that difficult since ASCAP still had not raised their rates for this type of music. Probably the first to sign was Lionel Newman working at 20th Century Fox. Earle Hagen came early, bringing the Sheldon Leonard produced programs into the BMI fold. The largest scoop of ASCAP composers was accomplished by Kirk, with the assistance of lawyer Abe Marcus, of Zissu, Marcus, and Stein who represented a great many of them. Almost as a group, the following composers jumped ship: Fred Steiner, Jerry Goldsmith, Hugo Friedhofer, Bernard Hermann, Herschel Burke Gilbert, Arthur Morton, Kenyon Hopkins, Leith Stevens, Emil Newman and John Williams. Gradually BMI became the performing rights choice of film composers until ASCAP finally awakened some time later and acknowledged the importance of film music writers. Until that happened, BMI continued to draw top names. Most of those film composers turned to television scoring, which was absorbing more TV network music usage in prime time than featured popular songs, justifying BMI's strategy in acquiring these composers.

Sidney Kaye, founder, and Chairman of the Board, demanded a crediting system to justify the significant payments that had been made to these writers. By that time, we had accumulated substantial music cue-sheets and were now receiving them regularly from the contacts that I had made. Makeshift payments during that period, based on existing radio song performance rates, were 2 cents per cue for local, 3 cents for network with the theme rate at 6 cents for opening theme plus 6 cents for closing theme. These themes were considered worth more as they identified the program. With the edict laid down by Sidney Kaye, an overhaul was due for which I was to spend many hours and endure initial severe criticism, but later, praise.

CHAPTER 5
The Old Ball Game

The remainder of 1960 was taken up with establishing files for crediting TV theme and background music using the per cue basis. Royalty statements had to be created to accommodate this crediting, rather than just songs as had been done since the inception of BMI. I continued examining TV Network and Local station logs, as well as constantly trying to improve the reference cards in the wheeldex files. Eighth floor executives became aware of my work and often called me to meet with them regarding the TV performances of various writers and publishers. At the time Bob Sour was VP of Writer Relations and Thea Zavin Assistant VP (soon to become VP) of Legal and Publisher Relations. Both began contacting me directly, much to Mr. Diamond's dismay.

One day in October of that year I was called into Mr. Diamond's office during our coffee break. Diamond, who was a short man, had a slight rise under his desk chair, so that if you were sitting next to him, he would be looking down at you. He would have a beautiful coffee mug and pastry on his desk and would slowly sip, pause for a tasty bite and articulately choose his words, while I sat with my paper coffee cup. He spoke of his long years of service at BMI, and then came to the point concerning my trips upstairs without contacting him. He took a long sip and came out with: "Now, Sam, if you were in my place and you had an employee act in the manner you have, what would you do?"

I took a long pause; I stood up to leave and replied: "Mr. Diamond, if I was in your place and you were working for me, I would have fired you long ago for the quality of your work, and the condition of the files, which has been your responsibility as Director of Logging." He was clearly shocked as his coffee cup came down noisily on his glass-top desk. He admitted, clumsily, that perhaps that because he had been passed over for promotion so often during his employment that it might have caused his interest to slacken off somewhat.

About 90 minutes later he appeared at my desk. "Sam, I know you are an ardent Pittsburgh Pirate fan, here's two tickets to this afternoon's World Series game. Take off the rest of the day." I was flabbergasted, since I knew the game was sold out. My Dad was in town with a "standing room only" ticket. I called him so we could meet. To our delight, the Pirates beat the Yankees 4 to 3.

CHAPTER 6
What's The Big Idea?

Robert J. (Bob) Burton was the most powerful, if not feared, executive at BMI at this time. He stood at 5 ft.7, was built stocky, but leaning to excess. His white hair was in a crew cut. He had a ruddy complexion, and his head seemed to come straight down to his shoulders with no detectable neck. He wore broad-framed glasses that were almost coke bottle thick. He was always nattily dressed. He supervised all vice presidents, save one, Jean Geiringer of Foreign Relations. (this was a sore point with Burton) It was Burton who handled negotiations with the TV networks regarding payments to BMI. Hence, the effort to increase the BMI share of performances was vital to him. TV background and theme usage via the acquisition of the new writers was his ace in the hole.

Burton had recently been given a judgeship in his town of New Rochelle, NY and enjoyed being addressed as Judge Burton. In order to accommodate Sidney Kaye's insistence on a system, which would justify the huge advances given to the new TV and Film writers, Burton scheduled a meeting to be held at Kaye's famous Lotos club, at 66th St. and Fifth Avenue. I had attended an earlier meeting there and had been introduced to all the executives, and had the pleasure of meeting Sidney Kaye, the founder of CMI and a lawyer I learned to revere above all others. I also saw how domineering Burton could be at that earlier meeting.

As that date approached, which was on a Monday, Dick Kirk was in New York and tried to approach me on the Friday before. Diamond saw him coming towards my office, cut him off, and showed him to the hallway. He came back later and, through the hallway window, motioned for me to meet him upstairs after work. Burton had apparently given Kirk the responsibility of devising the requested system. Kirk was extremely nervous and asked me to have dinner with him at the Oak Room of The Plaza Hotel that evening. As I had come to

23

work with an open neck shirt, I hurriedly bought a tie and met him there. He was already waiting at a reserved table.

After some small talk and ordering dinner, he came right to the point. The all-important meeting was the next Monday. Sidney Kaye was to attend and review the presentation of the system. Despite wracking his brain, Dick simply couldn't come up with anything. He hurriedly gave me the details of the amount of payment that was advanced and pleaded with me to find a system that would justify it, or in other words, follow the dollar. He talked of Carl Haverlin's imminent retirement, and suggested himself as a candidate to replace him. If I could pull this rabbit out of the hat, he would never forget me. I ignored this, as it was obvious that Burton would be the natural successor. We finished dinner and he gave me the telephone number of his hotel and asked me to contact him, if I could come up with anything over the weekend. We parted, and I took the subway back to our apartment in Brooklyn, my mind spinning all the way.

That Saturday morning I was up early, with a pad and pencil, making notes and experimenting with formulas. Our first born, Jenny, was also up, demanding attention while propped on the kitchen table, my makeshift desk. I had come up with a scheme based on TV Network station counts, but couldn't possibly work out the calculations from our apartment. What I needed was the Monroe calculator in Logging's royalty section. It should be remembered these were the days prior to the invention of the hand or pocket calculator. The office was, of course, closed. I knew that the only one to have a key was Diamond, so I searched the telephone directory, knowing that he lived in Forest Hills in Queens. I found his number, called and requested that he meet me in front of the office at noon. He was reluctant, but when I told him the report was needed by Judge Burton on Monday, he readily agreed.

The TV Networks supplied station counts for all their programming on a weekly basis. These counts listed all the stations picking up shows originating from the network. Naturally, the most popular shows had the most stations and often were picked up by independents, as well as their affiliates. I studied the counts over a number of months during the height of each season. In those days programming was predominantly in 30 minutes segments. A popular filmed series ran 39 weeks, with a 13-week hiatus. By finding the average station count for these filmed series and matching this count against the total amounts advanced to the writers, it came to a type of algebraic formula that could be worked out, even when using the per cue and theme crediting system. By 6 PM I had proved it out to my satisfaction, using a lined yellow page tablet, with the assistance of the well-punched Monroe calculator. I returned to our apartment exhausted and called Kirk at his hotel on Sunday and arranged to meet him at 9 AM at the Lotos club to explain the system to him. The formal meeting was to start at 10 AM, with Mr. Kaye due at 10:30 AM.

I met Kirk at 9 on Monday morning. We found an empty parlor and I explained the system to him. He studied it until he understood it completely. At 10:00 the meeting commenced as planned with Burton opening with some humorous chatter.

He then turned to Kirk and said: "Dick, what do you have for me?"

Kirk stood up, walked over to the head of the conference table, handed the system to Burton, saying "Bob, here's what we've worked out. It's really quite simple and logical." He then proceeded to explain it in detail to Burton, who "got it" immediately. Burton studied it, put on the table quite pleased just as Sidney Kaye entered the room. Greetings were made all around to the Chairman who arrived smiling as usual. He turned to Burton and reminded him why he was here.

Burton immediately responded, "Sidney, I think you're going to like this. Here's what I've come up with." Kaye understood it, and confirmed instituting the formula into our TV Logging system. I also, now, understood how big business worked.

Subsequently, new TV Theme and Background Music statements were created and in use in the Logging department and I continued to gain insight into this new area of the music industry. At the same time, I was also overseeing the wheeldex files to insure that when feature songs were performed in TV shows they were properly credited. Logging had long been the whipping boy of Writer and Publisher Relations when complaints were made of missing credits. I could recall one day while sitting at my wheeldex file, as a clerk, an elderly gentleman standing over me about to light a small cigar asked, "What'll you give me if I toss this match in there?" I replied, "Please do! If I could afford it, I'd give you a week's pay." Thus, began a relationship with George Marlo, perhaps, the most memorable and lovable man I ever met.

That event, however, indicates the lack of respect given to the Logging department at the time. As Logging questions developed, Thea Zavin, now VP of Publisher Relations and Bob Sour, VP of Writer Relations, would call on me the get the answers, as they had not been satisfied with the explanations given to them by Mr. Diamond. Diamond, apparently, now accepted this situation without protest, and if he asked, I would apprise him of what I was doing.

Major Motion Picture studios were now moving into production of TV Series, and I observed that their music departments were now supplying more detailed music cue sheets. All were now providing not only the cue titles or serial number, but also actual timings and descriptions of usage. BMI was still paying on a per cue basis, without regard to the length of the performance. After comparing payment of the per cue method against actual timings, it was evident that a change based on timing was much more equitable to all concerned. I believed the change to be inevitable as both writers and publishers would soon complain of the inequities.

I sent a memo to Judge Burton calling to his attention an inequity in payment, using a "Twilight Zone" episode as an example. I also copied Sidney Kaye, as he was interested in the launch of our TV Theme and Background statements. In that particular episode Bernard Hermann had, aside from his famous theme, a total of 28 seconds of background music all derived from 7 four-second cues. The background scorer, Jerry Goldsmith, had a total of 6 cues derived from 16 minutes of scoring. Hermann, on our per cue method, would earn more than Goldsmith. It seemed to me that a change must be in order. Burton's reaction shocked me. In his reply to me, and Mr. Kaye, he belittled my request, stating that Mr. Kirk had far more experience in this area. He further stated that this was an anomaly. Kirk had confirmed to him that the average one half hour show totaled about 18 minutes of music with about 20 cues, and there was no need to recognize my findings. While I liked Dick Kirk, this information was simply incorrect. I was steaming, and could not let the matter stand. I prepared a reply and, in fact, showed it to Diamond. Diamond said,

"If you send that to him, you'll be finished at BMI."

I replied, "If that's the case, I wouldn't want to work here, anyhow."

In my reply, I had set a trap and Burton stepped right into it. I had sent him another example similar to the first using the TV show "Line-up," starring Karl Malden and Michael Douglas. Burton, once again belittled me by pointing out the show contained 17 minutes, 59 seconds-- almost the exact timing that Mr. Kirk approximated.

My one line reply was: "I call your attention to the fact that this is a one hour program."

Kaye followed up with: "We will immediately make preparations to convert to a timing method of crediting as Mr. Trust has suggested. Further, Mr. Trust will meet with me regularly to create a definitive schedule of crediting for the various types of usages."

The next day I received a call from Judge Burton's secretary. "The

Judge would like you to come to his office immediately." When I arrived, Burton was pacing his office with a cigarette in the middle of his lips, as was his style.

He said, "Sit down," pointing to his couch. "I guess you think you're a smart son of a bitch!" I simply shrugged my shoulders, palms up and grinned. He continued pacing, then stopped and looked directly at me. "Tomorrow there will be an engineer in your office installing a direct line to my office. It will buzz and it will always be me, so pick it up!" "Another thing. Any memo I get from Dick Kirk will be forwarded directly to you for comment." With that, I left his office and a close relationship with Burton was established.

CHAPTER 7
A Great Man

As directed by Sidney Kaye, meetings were scheduled for Wednesday afternoons at 3PM at the law firm Rosenman, Kaye, Colin, Petschek and Freund, one of the most prestigious and sought-after in New York. Judge Samuel I. Rosenman was the key speechwriter for Franklin Roosevelt, and is credited with the term "New Deal." I was honored to meet "one on one" with Mr. Kaye. Meetings were held in the firm's large conference room, just the two of us. Sidney Kaye was of medium height, with a full head of graying hair. He wore somewhat thick silver-rimmed glasses, which somehow did not block out laughing eyes, which seemed to appear when answering an argument in a homespun manner while smoothly disposing his opponent.

In addition to the conversion of credits to a timing system, every conceivable usage of music in TV and films was examined, discussed and debated. If Mr. Kaye felt my recommended definition of a usage of music was questionable we'd debate it, and sometimes argue. If I questioned his definition, the same would happen. The closest description I can make for these sessions would be two rabbis arguing Talmudic law. For example: I would define a Visual performance as "the main focus of audience attention." Mr. Kaye would think about it, and come back with "why not actors attention." and the discussions would begin.

Other points of examples: How to deal with partial visual performances. How many seconds were needed to accord it full credit? If partial, what rate should be assigned? How should we credit recognized songs used as background since that song relates to the action on screen as opposed to just cueing? Should there be a limit on payment of scores being paid on the timing basis, since producer/publishers would now have incentive to pack the film with "wall to wall" music? (This actually occurred with one company) Should the rates for prime time shows also be assigned to daytime serials? If reduced, what adjustment? After each meeting I would print out the definitions we agreed upon and enter it into what would become a rather lengthy syllabus.

These meetings went on for about 8 months. Finally, the syllabus was almost complete. At the very last meeting, which was merely to put on the finishing touches, a point was raised by Mr. Kaye. I thought it was inconsequential and said, "Well, OK, you're the boss."

Mr. Kaye stood up looked down at me and exploded, "WHAT? WHAT? You dare say that to me? Why do you think you're here? I depend on you to tell me like it is! You've been the only one in this company not afraid to do so, and you say 'you're the boss!"

I was shocked and said, "OK, OK, I get it! I think you're wrong on this point."

He sat back down, settled himself and finally said, after a great pause. "Well, I've given it some thought and think my phrasing is better." Those meetings were a wonderful experience. I learned a great deal from a great man.

CHAPTER 8
The Bad And The Good

During the time I was spending with Mr. Kaye, Thea Zavin and Bob Sour were assigning more and more responsibility to me. I would be called upon to determine if advance payment requests by writers and publishers, or for the most part, their lawyers were justified, based on my findings from a more corrected Logging department. They were now also aware of reports I was now receiving from my distributor contacts of TV shows.

I recall one encounter in Mrs. Zavin's office with a well-known lawyer, who, over time, had handled a number advance requests on behalf of his writers and publisher clients. In this case he was representing a British writer/publisher named Jeff Kruger who did the music and theme to a TV series entitled "Man From Interpol." Kruger was at the meeting with him. The lawyer delivered an assessment of the number of stations that were picking up the show, and suggested we get started with a minimal advance of $25,000.

Mrs. Zavin looked at me and said "Sam, what do you think?"

I paused and replied, "Pinch me!"

Thea smiled and replied, "What do you mean?"

I said, "I must be dreaming. This show is only on a fraction of the number of stations he claims, and it's not doing that well on those."

"Well, what do you think would be a reasonable advance?" I suggested $5,000 as a favor based on her past relationship with the lawyer.

Naturally, the lawyer was livid, but Thea stuck with it and said, "If the show picks up, we can discuss it again." I walked out to the elevator, and the lawyer caught up with me.

"Do you know who I am?"

I confirmed that I did and then replied, "Now you know who I am, so don't come in here with your bullshit figures anymore." Needless to say, he and I never dealt with each other after that meeting

On a more pleasant note, one day I saw a thin old man wearing a tattered overcoat walk into Diamond's office. Diamond stepped out, came down to my office and asked me to handle this man who had been a pest to him for years. Arthur Kleinert entered my office meekly and sat down across from me. He was quite frail and spoke with a soft German accent. He said he had been coming here for several years complaining that he hears his music on television every day, but he's never been paid. He had been earning a meager living playing piano behind silent pictures at The Museum of Modern Art. I asked him the time he hears his music and he thought it was in the morning between 8:00 and 9:00. I promised him that I would look into it and get back to him. I checked through station logs to determine which shows with music were on in New York at that time. The one show that was a constant was "Captain Kangaroo." I went to the CBS-TV Network logs and came up with nothing until I noted a sheet of a daily show segment called "Picture Book Parade." The sheet reported no music, just episode numbers. I decided to watch the show at home one morning, and come to the office a little later. There it was, the segment entitled "Picture Book Parade." A large picture book containing a story narrated, as each page was turned. Accompanying the story was delightful piano music in the background. As soon as I got to the office I called my friend Duke Poklitar, director of music clearance at CBS. He was surprised and said he'd get back to me. That afternoon, he called back very upset. He advised that the film department never bothered to send music cue-sheets for clearance. He would get them to me and apologized profusely.

After I received 5 years worth of cue-sheets I called Mr. Kleinert and arranged for him to meet me at my office. He arrived, wearing the same overcoat and hesitantly sat down. I explained the situation and apologized for the previous lack of action. I then reached across my desk and handed him a check for 10,000 dollars. He was shocked. Tears came to his eyes as he grabbed my hand with both of his thanked me. I told him this was just an advance against past overdue royalties, and as long as the show would be on the air he would receive regular payments. He begged me to come to his silent movies performances at the Museum. I again thanked him for his patience. Unfortunately, I never managed to get to the Museum.

Later that year I was officially named Director of Logging, replacing Mr. Diamond who was sent to the other side of the building to work in another newly named effort.

CHAPTER 9
A Wonderful Trip

A highlight of the year occurred in late June when Bob Sour asked me to join him on a trip to the West Coast to visit the film studios. This would be an opportunity for me to meet the people with whom I'd been corresponding. He was also interested in meeting a number of West Coast songwriters, particularly those who were candidates for songs in films. Bob had founded the BMI Theater Workshop in an effort to develop Broadway show writers, an area totally barren to BMI at the time. He urged bonusing works written for movies at triple rate, which was put into effect with great success, but, unfortunately, it became a financial burden later, due to that success. (1)

Bob Sour was one of the original employees at BMI as a songwriter. As few publishers were available to BMI during their founding years, there was little choice, but to create a BMI Publishing company. Bob enjoyed that company's first hit, "We Could Make Such Beautiful Music Together." Back in 1930, he was a co-writer of one of the great standards of all time, "Body and Soul," but was refused membership into ASCAP's elite society of members. On the trip to Los Angeles I asked him about this loss of revenue.

He smiled and said, "That song still put my sons through prep school and college." One of the great paradoxes occurred, when Bob was later made president of BMI and still had his most popular song in ASCAP, at the same time that Stanley Adams, president of ASCAP, had his most famous song, "What A Difference A Day Made," licensed through BMI. (via E.B. Marks who was one of the first companies to switch to the then new BMI) Both writers, however, were now being credited through newly created "writer assignments."

Bob had taken me under his wing, (as did Thea Zavin) encouraging me to study SPA (early writer contracts i.e., Songwriters Protective Association, which later became AGAC) (2) agreements. Much to, my surprise, Thea Zavin had arranged for BMI to send me to law school. I thanked her but, to her surprise, I asked if I could take business courses instead, since all I had was a Bachelor of Music degree from Cincinnati Conservatory of Music. She reluctantly agreed. Since we were living in New Brunswick, New Jersey, home of Rutgers University, I signed up for several night classes. One of these courses, in fact, became extremely useful later on, by virtually saving the company that I had founded.

Bob Sour was a proud graduate of Princeton, just down the road from New Brunswick and had me as his guest at the Princeton/ Rutgers football game that year. We both knew that those two teams were the first to play college football, starting in the 1860's.

I made the most of our west coast trip visiting Universal, Columbia, Twentieth Century, Warners, Paramount, Desilu, and Four Star TV. The best was yet to come at Disney. Bob had arranged for the Sherman Brothers, Bob and Dick to meet us at BMI's office in Beverly Hills, which had a piano. They offered to play songs from their forthcoming film "Mary Poppins." Their experience was, of course, chronicled in the recent film starring Tom Hanks and Emma Thompson, "Saving Mr.Banks." They had gone through a few of their songs and then did a rousing performance of "Supercalafragelisticexpealidosis." You must keep in mind that Bob Sour was a student of the carefully crafted song. So, despite their explanation of the song, during Dick's singing Bob leaned over to me and whispered, "Did you ever hear such a piece of shit in your life?" I'm sure he later regretted that remark. Afterwards, we went to the Disney lot where the Sherman brothers hosted a luncheon for us. It was a great joy when Walt Disney came by and asked if he might join us. What a thrill to listen to him discuss some history of the company.

1) In 1962 the film "Mondo Cane," produced in Italy was released. You will recall that Jean Geiringer, in order to attract foreign publishers to release through BMI offered, in effect, double payment. With the approval of triple payment for songs first released in a motion picture, each performance of the song "More" received 6 times the normal payment. "More" became one of the most performed songs of that year and the years to follow, earning far more than was ever anticipated, or even budgeted for, causing BMI to re-think the problem of too much success.

2) American Guild of Authors and Composers

CHAPTER 10
Re-shuffling The Deck

When I arrived back at my office I started a renovation of the Logging files and personnel. I was determined to end the blame that had constantly been foisted on the department. I had each clerk at the wheeldexes and rotary files seek out duplicate cards with different code numbers for the same identical song. Through the years, new coding systems were installed without removing cards containing the previous code numbers. In order for the clerks to realize that I knew the system, I would, at random, sit down at a file while the clerk was at lunch, and do the same work assigned to the clerk. That way I could discuss any problems that would come up, as one of them. The other problem that I was determined to solve was the constant late submission of statements. Though the goal was to render statements 6 months after performance, statements were being sent out 10 to 11 months after.

One of the innovations that I came up with was subscriptions to all TV Guides. This produced what amounted to census performance of TV series in syndication. I had realized "sampling" local TV stations for these usages, as was the practice for Radio, simply couldn't provide the information that was capably supplied by TV Guide. After a few months, morale improved, and statements were being submitted when scheduled i.e., six months after performance.

An edict was established allowing no card to be removed from a file by anyone without a blue card, signed by the requestor, inserted in its place. One day Judge Burton brought a well-known writer to the department and requested a card from one of the file clerks. He was refused unless he would sign a card. He demanded, "Do you know who I am?"

The clerk replied, "Yes sir, but I work for Mr. Trust and if I give it out, he could fire me." Burton came steaming into my office complaining. I asked him to point out the clerk.

He did, and I said, "I think I'll give him a raise for his courage." I reminded him that executive personnel doing what he had requested was what got Logging into the mess that I inherited, and I wasn't going to let that happen again. He cooled down and the matter was settled.

In mid 1964, Mrs. Zavin offered me the position of Executive Director of Publisher Relations. It was hard to refuse an invitation to the Eighth Floor, the "Executive" floor. When I arrived, I was given a rather small office and a secretary. I felt out of place, and missed the tumult of activity of the Logging department and Machine room, as well as the twenty-some employees I supervised. Mrs. Zavin realized this and laid as much work on me as I could handle. Soon I was given a larger office and two additional employees.

There is usually a general misunderstanding of the term "music publisher." One tends to think their work is the printing of music. At one time, long ago, when printed music was their sole source of income, that was the case. Today that is a mere minor facet of his operation, which is almost always jobbed out to a print company who will handle the sales and distribution. Today, the main focus of the music publisher is finding a talented writer or writer/artist to develop and promote his or her music to a producer or record company. In some cases the publisher even produces the recording that may be purchased or leased to a record company. The resulting success is a copyright that is owned by the publisher and is an asset to his overall music catalog, producing income from additional "cover" recordings, performances, film usage, print, permissions, and any other existing or future forms of transmission for the period of copyright protection. The maximum period of copyright protection in the United States is now 95 years. To extend protection and exploitation throughout the world, the publisher can assign his rights to a comparable publisher in a foreign territory for a limited term.

Theodora Zavin was a brilliant executive, a "go to" person for the unsolvable problem. When my son Ben was born in 1963, she sent a beautiful miniature tea set to our three-year-old daughter Jenny, congratulating her on the arrival of her brother. Brilliant, and insightful!

One thing I insisted upon was the delivery of TV Network logs delivered to me monthly, so I could keep up with programming. This proved invaluable even in this new position, and would soon help to resolve a network problem brought on by ASCAP claims.

CHAPTER 11
Gaming The System

Just prior to my move upstairs, I was presented with a problem involving the, now legendary, Jazz trumpeter Clark Terry. Terry was a member of the trumpet section, along with Doc Severinsen, in Skitch Henderson's Tonight Show orchestra. Clark had developed a routine called "mumbles," whereby he would mumble some jibbersh, a la scat singing style, to a riff-like composition he had created. This act went on for a number of months, but performances were apparently never reported to Terry. So, Clark came in to see me. Having been a trumpeter, I was overjoyed to meet him and talk trumpet.

I promised I'd look into it and get back to him. My research into this matter also opened the door to further problems involving the Tonight Show. The station logs did, in fact, show the performances, but not the writer, and attributed the works to an ASCAP publisher owned by Skitch Henderson. I filed a complaint to my clearance contacts at NBC. They found that the associate producer had reported the usage incorrectly. They apologized, re-submitted the reports, and I was able to re-capture the performances for a very grateful Clark Terry.

Sometime later, actually in 1965, Bob Sour contacted me stating that NBC received a report from ASCAP claiming an inordinate amount of feature song performances compared to BMI. TV Network negotiations were coming up soon, so we were very much concerned. Sour asked me to check out this claim. As I continued to receive TV Network logs, despite leaving Logging, I was ready.

As referred to earlier, featured song performance usage had shrunk as a result of the plethora of TV series on the networks. So, I checked those NBC shows that could possibly contain feature song performances. The Tonight Show, being a nightly show, with a large orchestra was an obvious choice. What I discovered turned out to be scandalous.

With knowledge of the ASCAP system of crediting, I found an inordinate amount of "Visual Instrument" performances. ASCAP paid any Visual-Vocal or Visual-Instrumental performance at the feature song rate, which was, and is far higher than background or cue music. As this was a "live" show, music cue-sheets were not prepared, only the listings of the songs. Two ASCAP publishers appeared to have most of these usages, which indeed had these song titles. I had a theory of what was taking place and related it to Bob Sour. Sour called a senior Vice president at NBC to arrange a meeting. I requested that the head of Music Clearance, whom I regularly dealt with, also attend. The meeting was held in General David Sarnoff's conference/dining room. I explained my suspicion, and requested "air checks" take place, unbeknownst to anyone involved with the show. Jim Stabile, the NBC vice president, agreed and Peter Zalantis, my music clearance contact, was to audit the show, in the back of the control room studio and clock and describe the usages. The air checks confirmed my suspicions. Every time the show broke away for a commercial, a camera panned the band playing a transition riff of a title cleared as a "song" at ASCAP. When the commercial ended the band was panned again prior to returning to Johnny. The total performance time for each play was less than 5 seconds. In those days the Tonight Show ran 90 minutes. You can imagine the number of "feature plays."

The publishing companies were owned by Skitch Henderson, a longtime ASCAP member who knew how to "game" the system. Later, NBC advised me that the lead cameraman was cut in on the deal. It was not long afterwards that Doc Severinsen took over the band and kept that leadership until Johnny Carson's retirement.

CHAPTER 12
Your Table, Sir

One of the benefits of my move to the eighth floor was meals and entertainment. While heading the Logging department I hosted many a luncheon for Network music clearance executives, as well personnel of film distributors in order to receive music cue sheets. Being given a limited budget, I had to be creative in finding suitable restaurants. I found that by looking at the second floors and basements of buildings there were many, different, inexpensive, yet delightful eateries. As a result, I developed a list that represented virtually every style of cooking from Peruvian to Filipino. The conditions for being posted on this list were:

1. lunch could cost no more than $1.50.
2. food must be tasty and memorable.
3. the establishment must use tablecloths and cloth napkins.

This list contained almost every country imaginable. To my surprise, for years later, I was getting telephone calls from network and ad agency personnel asking me where they could find a good Brazilian, Chilean, or Spanish or any number of restaurants. Today, of course, most of these are gone, having their locations replaced by steel and glass structures. Becoming Executive Director of Publisher Relations availed me to being a guest of many publishers, or their lawyer representatives at mostly posh restaurants. Those occasions also went a long way in my learning the music publishing business.

On one unforgettable occasion, however, I was the host of a rather huge dinner at the Four Seasons. The publisher was Roosevelt Music owned by Hal Fein. Hal came to my office with a new recording by Frank Sinatra of "Strangers In The Night" by Bert Kaempfert. He was, of course, excited and predicted it would go to Number one. I told him I liked the record, but as Sinatra hadn't had a number one in over 10 years, I doubted this would do it. He became very excited as well as somewhat upset, and said he'd bet me it would go to the top. I said, "OK, what's the bet?" He said, "Dinner at the Four Seasons," which at that time was one of the most expensive restaurants in New York. After I agreed, as it was a rather substantial bet, I reported what I'd done to Thea Zavin.

She smiled and said, "I hope you lose." Hal and Thea were good friends and she looked forward to meeting Bert Kaempfert.

As it turned out the song did make it to number one. Thea and I hosted a great evening at The Four Seasons, attended by Hal his wife, Jerry Brown and wife, (Hal's associate) Bert Kaempfert and wife, Thea and her husband, Joan and me. It was a terrific evening, celebrating Roosevelt Music and BMI's number one. Thea said it was the best "sucker" bet ever made.

CHAPTER 13
Business With A Heart

Much of my work now involved negotiating advance payments to publishers. At the time they were many independent companies. They are now mostly found listed, if at all, on the stationery of large vertically integrated Mega-entertainment corporations such as Sony, Universal, and Warner Brothers.

I particularly enjoyed dealing with the real professionals of the business who dealt with me directly, without counsel of a lawyer present. The "artist/writer/publishers" rarely appeared at these meetings, only their lawyers. Some of my most enjoyable meetings were with Al Gallico, who I can only describe as a genuine Damon Runyon character. Al knew the business inside and out with an ear for a hit. He came from the stable of Lou Levy's Leeds Music, which seemed to produce half the successful music publishers in New York. Al and I became life-long friends, even after I left BMI.

One day I was sitting in his office before our lunch date and saw a framed five-dollar bill hanging on his wall above his desk, and asked him what that was all about. Al related a story I'll never forget. It basically was his introduction to the business.

When Al was a teenager he got a job, after school, delivering sheet music in Manhattan for G. Schirmers, Music Publishers. One day a delivery brought him to a brownstone in the West Fifties. Outside the door he heard music playing. Lou Levy came to the door for the music, but had to go back inside for the money. Al poked his nose inside and saw three girls singing accompanied by a rather bald pianist... The girls were the Andrew Sisters and the pianist, Phil Silvers.

When Levy returned, Al said "I want to work for you."

Levy said, "Get lost, kid I don't need anybody." Al persisted until Lou finally said, "What does Schirmer's pay you?"

Al replied, "Eight dollars a week."

Lou then said, "I'll give you five." Al took it even though Lou, who couldn't afford it at the time, never paid him. Later, Al was drafted, but got assigned to a post near New York City and continued to plug songs for Lou during that time and after the war. (with pay.)

After Lou Levy sold his company (Leeds Music, ASCAP and Dutchess Music, BMI) to MCA, which is now Universal, he sent a five dollar bill to Al apologizing for the late payment. Al framed it. Lou and his wife, one of the Andrew Sisters, named their son Leeds, who would become a successful music executive and head Universal Music, following its first chief of Universal Music, Sal Chianti --another Lou Levy alumnus. Leeds and I continue a longtime friendship.

I first met Al after he left Shapiro-Bernstein Music, where he encouraged that company, an early ASCAP stalwart, to open a BMI affiliate. Oddly enough, that company continues to exist as one of the few independents. Though a thorough New Yorker, Al struck gold in Nashville with his new company. He was an anomaly as most Nashville publishers were residents of the town. Somehow Al charmed everybody there and struck up relationships with some of Nashville's hottest producers, which turned into mutually profitable business associations.

Naturally, Al became a regular traveler to that town through his almost monthly visits, and was a well-accepted oddity by the music community. Al had numerous country hits "Stand By Your Man" (Tammy Wynette) "Almost Persuaded" (David Houston) are just some examples. The story of Al's Bobby Goldsboro hit "Honey," will always remind me of the heart of the music publishing business at that time. Everyone at Columbia Records could sense that it would be a smash. They asked Al what he wanted on the B-side of the recording. To everyone's surprise, he told them that his buddy George Pincus had a recording on the album and to use that one. George was having a rough time, so Al simply wanted to give him a free ride.

Another example occurred when I negotiated a new deal for Al at BMI. Al was having meteoric success in his performing royalties. After his initial years of success, he qualified for a 25% bonus. A year later he qualified for a 50% bonus. Then came the year of the new negotiation. The highest rate we could offer was as a "guarantee" which would be available based on his quick rise in performances. I offered it to Al, who was somewhat skeptical since his earnings were quite good at the 50% bonus. I mentioned to him that the amount I was offering him was a guarantee, which gave him stability in the event he wasn't so successful during the next term. After some thought he said "OK, draw it up." The following week I received a call from Sal Chianti, President of Universal Music requesting a lunch date. Sal was looked upon as the dean of music publishing and would soon become the first full-time president of The

National Music Publishers Association. I was delighted to have lunch with Sal, but was surprised by the subject. Sal wanted to go over my offer to Al to make sure it was the best deal he could get. We went over the numbers, and he was OK with them. Can you imagine?---a competitor looking out for the competition. I later, as a music publisher, served 14 years as a director of the <u>NMPA</u>, mostly under Sal's leadership.

CHAPTER 14
Of Thea, Sing!

In 1965 Judge Bob Burton died as a result of his smoking in bed, while attending a BMI Board of Directors meeting at a hotel in Vancouver, B.C. The entire suite was destroyed. He had been made president of BMI the previous year. Burton joined BMI in the 1940's as legal counsel, moving to VP of Publisher and Writer Relations, then Senior VP. His funeral, in New Rochelle, N.Y. was widely attended by many writers and publishers, as well as personalities from the business. In October of 1965 Bob Sour was made President.

I can't continue without relating an event at a meeting involving Burton, Thea Zavin, and Dick Kirk, as well as other senior executives that took place at the Lotos Club in 1964.

Our biggest concern was the upcoming rate negotiations with CBS. Much like my analysis of NBC, I was asked to prepare a report of featured song usage on CBS. Again, there was little usage due to the glut of film series. My findings showed that almost one half the usages on that network were from one show---Captain Kangaroo. Everyone was, of course, surprised. A discussion ensued on how we could get more songs in that show.

Burton at the head the table suddenly addressed Kirk, "Dick, can't you fix up the Captain?" inferring that Kirk had some experience in "procurement."

Kirk responded, in an effort to be humorous, "Bob, how can I do that? You know the kangaroo is a unisexual animal."

Burton replied, "What? There's no such thing as a unisexual animal!" Then came the best response I have ever heard from, of all people, Thea Zavin who was sitting to the left of Burton.

"Bob, you must be wrong."

Burton turned his whole body to the left to face her, "What are you talking about?"

"Well, Bob, what about those publishers you'd tell to 'go fuck yourself'?" Burton became beet red as the rest of us roared.

43

CHAPTER 15
The Jersey Bounce

I previously mentioned that most professional music publishers met with me directly, but seldom did artist/writer-owned companies. They always seemed to be represented by lawyers, some of whom appeared arrogant based on their representation of a famous name(s). Such was the case of the representatives of the Four Season's (Jersey Boys) catalog, Seasons Four Music.

Martin (Marty) Machat was a hard-driving dealmaker who represented major artists. His previous dealings were with Mrs. Zavin. For this deal, he sent in his new young associate, Eric Kronfield. Having learned from Marty, he approached me in the haughty, tough talking image of his boss. The Four Seasons were just starting to approach fame and, Eric playing on this demanded a rather heavy advance of $25,000. I checked the logging figures to date and told him the best I could offer was $9,000. I informed him that the company was on its way to a 25% bonus category, and once it was reached I could offer him more. He was furious and told me I could keep the $9,000 as it was an insult, and stormed out of the office. About three months later I found the performances had indeed increased and sent a short note to Eric, enclosing a 25% bonus award for his signature. It was accepted and returned, and Eric called shortly after for another appointment. When he arrived he gloated and told me how wrong I was. I advised him that I could now move the advance up to his request for the $25,000.

He sneered at me and said, "Are you kidding? I now want $50,000!" I rejected him, and he walked to the door, turned around and said, "That's it, our deal is up as December 31st. I'm taking the company to ASCAP!"

Before he could get out the door, I shouted, "Eric, I don't think so!" He turned around as I said, "You'd better sit down; you're not going anywhere!" He came back and sat down. I reached into my desk and showed him the copy of the 25% bonus agreement he had signed. Aware that the term of the agreement was coming to an end shortly, I specifically inserted a short clause extending the term by three years. He obviously had not read it, and routinely signed. He was furious accusing me of dealing underhanded. I simply told him that it was HIS job to read agreements of behalf of his clients.

He turned and walked out shouting, "This isn't over."

The next morning I received a call from Bob Sour requesting that I come to his office, advising that Marty Machat was with him. Bob was now president, sitting at the same desk as had Bob Burton and Carl Haverlin before him. He said, "Marty tells me that when you drew up the 25% bonus agreement for Seasons Four Music, you slipped in a three year extension. Is that correct?" I answered that I did, noticing the basic term was about to expire. I added that it wasn't that unusual, and I had done it before without protest. I also stated that Machat's associate had the opportunity to read the agreement before he signed it.

Sour smiled and said "Good work, Sam. I think you deserve a raise!" He then turned to Machat and said: "I think it's time for you to leave Marty!" And so it ended.

CHAPTER 16
The Marvelous Mr. Marlo

Aside from the promotion to the executive floor, the greatest benefit and joy to me was the proximity of my office to George Marlo's. Despite the fact that BMI had a compulsory retirement policy at age 65, George in his eighties, was still a fixture in Writer Relations at this time, and with good reason. He had spent his entire life in the entertainment industry and most of it in music. He was a raconteur extraordinaire telling stories of his experiences. George was a snappy dresser with his grey hair in an ivy-league haircut. He wore his tie straight down from his collar with no knot, a small, thin Italian cigar, either in the corner of his mouth or in his hand, and always a twinkle in his eye with a smile. All the women adored him, yet he stayed a bachelor all his life, keeping his residence at the swanky Astor Hotel. George and I became fast friends, and I was an avid listener to his stories.

Just before joining BMI he was Tommy Dorsey's manager. He was close to many of the Big Band leaders of that era. Before that, he was many things, including a music publisher with a number of hits to his credit. In 1940 he was asked by Sidney Kaye to organize the professional department of BMI's publishing company, and continued on after it was eliminated, in Writer Relations.

My favorite story, which he documented in a BMI employee newsletter, was his career in silent movies. In those early days major movies were being produced in Brooklyn. At the time George owned an auto called the Amsbury Special, which was spotted by a casting director who wanted to use it for a film. As these were special cars, owners were reluctant to allow other drivers to drive them. George was offered $25 per day for the use, but he stated, "It comes with the driver." Hence, his debut in motion pictures. George was to drive the car, with the leading lady, to the door of a mansion with the camera shooting at a distance. The leading man would then slip into the car before the close-up shot; however, the cameraman didn't stop rolling the film. The next day the director saw the rushes of the footage and decided George was the new face he was looking for. George became a "leading man" and was featured several pictures including "Man Without A Country."

George had a devilish sense of humor and was famous for his practical jokes, some I witnessed, others I learned about. One of his victims was BMI's music editor, Milton Rettenberg. Rettenberg retained his position during the time I was employed even though his position became gradually less important. Early on, all musical submissions were examined to determine their authenticity. In cases, where public domain melodies were used, determinations were made as to the percentage of credit to be allowed. ASCAP's counterpart was an editor named Sigmund Spaeth, who was known as the "tune detective," to the general public. This irked Rettenberg no end, as he felt he was just as good. George and Milton's offices were close together. George was always the first in. Each day as Milton would arrive George would ask "How are you today, Milton?" Rettenberg was considered by many to be somewhat of a hypochondriac, and each day he'd complain of a malady. "My throat is so sore," one day "I've got swollen glands," the next, and on and on. George grew tired of the complaints and created a "Milton Rettenberg daily health report" paper tablet, with the following categories on each sheet:

Date......

Please check the following:

I had a --good --fair—poor-- bowel movement

My throat is --raw – scratchy—inflamed

My back is sore –aching –stiff

And so on for other maladies.

The tablet was placed on the receptionist's desk with instructions to forward it to Mr. Marlo's office each day when complete. So ended the complaints.

I personally witnessed an event at the expense of a young temporary worker in George's department. George was known to the children of all BMI employees as "the candy man." In his desk's double drawer he installed a clear plastic box with a lid, which filled the entire area. In this plastic box was every conceivable type of candy imaginable. Any visiting child's first stop (including ours) was to the "candy man."

A young lady "temp" noticing George's small thin cigars he used daily, asked him where he got them. George simply replied, in all seriousness, "I breed them, and smoke them when they're new, and at they're very best." She said "No, that can't be." George replied, "Ah, but it is, my dear. In fact, I plan to breed some this evening in my incubator. I'm a bit busy right now, but before you leave tonight, I'll be happy to show you the process." George then went into his office for an alleged important telephone call and closed the door. He then stepped out and purchased two large stogies and returned. While he was in his office, he had removed the candy and cleaned his "incubator." At the end of the day he called in the young female temp-worker and showed her his incubator. He placed the stogies close together and advised that if all went well there might be a newborn by morning. He shut the box tightly and said, as she looked at him strangely, "Good evening, see you tomorrow," and they both left the office. George was always the first one at work every day, but the next day, he was particularly early, sensing the young lady might get there early to check the box. He put one of his little cigars between the stogies, turned off lights, and left. Sure enough, the clerk came in opened his desk and found the "newborn" just as George was arriving. She was excited and shouted to George that he was right, there was a newborn cigar. The rest of his department, knowing of the hoax, roared with laughter as George tried to comfort her embarrassment.

Writers loved George. He welcomed them all. There were times when some were badly in need of an advance, but there was nothing in their account that could justify a payment. George would often reach into his pocket and pull out a few bills to "keep them going." He thought nothing of it.

One morning I arrived early in a very serious mood, as I was dealing with a complex publishing matter. George looked me over and said, "Why so serious?" I told him that I was struggling over "this damn situation" and simply not in a very good mood. He said, "Sam, if you were with me every morning, you wouldn't be feeling sorry for yourself." I asked, "Why so?" George told me that before he gets to the office each day he visits a hospital for crippled children and tries to "cheer them up." He said if you'd see them, you'd never feel sorry for yourself again.

George knew he was getting up in years and vowed that he'd never end his life in a hospital. He said that his last days would be spent at his apartment at the Astor hotel with the comfort of a good-looking nurse.

At the end of 1968, I accepted an offer to become president of Capitol Records Music Publishing division in Hollywood California. I left the first two weeks in January of 1969, and then returned to pack up my family for the move. I learned that George was seriously ill and taken to the hospital. I couldn't get the name of the hospital, so decided to call the Astor. Sure enough, a nurse picked up the telephone. She advised me of George's condition, which was grave. She was able to get the phone to George, who greeted me, reminding me of his vow. He knew of my leaving BMI and said, "Congratulations, Sam, you're going to do well, I know it." He passed away some ten days later and left a mark on anyone who ever met him.

CHAPTER 17
Canadian Capers

During my later years at BMI I was appointed to oversee and examine BMI's subsidiary BMI Canada, with offices in Toronto and Montreal. Two Canadian brothers headed these offices, Harold Moon in Toronto, and Clyde Moon in Montreal. It was the feeling that these operations were not producing enough revenue. As rate proceedings with the CBC (Canadian Broadcasting Company) were scheduled within a year, both Judge Bob Burton, president of BMI, and Theodora Zavin, Senior Vice President of Performing Rights wanted my findings. As most of my visits were to Toronto, Harold Moon and I became friends. I would bring his favorite cigars from New York (they weren't available in Canada) and return with a side of Canadian bacon. Harold was a big man whose goal seemed to be to please everyone.

At that time, Canadian composers and writers had the choice of being affiliated with CAPAC, which was represented by ASCAP in the United States, or BMI Canada, which was represented in the U.S. by BMI. Conversely, U.S. ASCAP publishers and writers were represented in Canada by CAPAC, and BMI publishers and writers by BMI Canada. Obviously, these two organizations would vie for the most revenue from the CBC. Notwithstanding this rivalry, John Mills, president of CAPAC and I became good friends. CAPAC was the first to give testimony at the rate proceeding, which took place in Ottawa. While one of their executives was in the witness box, he was being attacked regarding a CAPAC claim for a Symphony Number 13. The CBC interviewer sneered that Beethoven had written only 9, and while Mozart and Haydn had written many more, there was no contemporary he knew of who had composed 13. There was a moment of silence, when I leaned over to John Mills and told him that it was Shostakovich who had written the 13th. He was protected in the U.S. and Canada through an MCA (Sal Chiantia) deal negotiated with the Russian organization, Mishkanega, that CAPAC made the claim. John immediately stood up and repeated it. The CBC representative backed off, much chagrined. John could not thank me enough. It seems my experience as a classical music checker in the Logging department was paying off.

During the proceedings, I was the chief witness for BMI Canada, while standing for three hours in the witness box. I was well prepared and, as a result, income for BMI Canada was adjusted from a ratio of 1 to 6 with CAPAC to 1 to 2 1/2. This worked out to be an increase in BMI income from the CBC of better than 100%. Unfortunately during my testimony, which became quite heated, Harold Moon, who was very friendly with CBC executives, passed out, and had to be rushed to the hospital. It was a panic attack and a recess was called. Harold was a "hail fellow, well met" who had cautioned me to be very courteous, and sensitive to the CBC. As I was known to be "outspoken," some of my attack testimony apparently got to him. After a short hospital stay, he was, of course delighted to learn of the outcome.

During my short, regular trips to Canada I became aware of the birth of the music industry in that country. Up until then Canada really had no growth...but then I realized something was being ignited, particularly in the Yorkville section of Toronto. That knowledge would serve me well when I would soon leave BMI to enter the field of music publishing.

Mrs. Zavin always thought I came back from my Canadian trips with fresh ideas. She attributed it to the gentle click-clack of the train wheels. Whenever she would have a large project or a problem she would say, "Don't you have a trip to Canada soon?" "I would find a reason, gather up her papers to be analyzed, and book a roomette cabin for sleep and study. She was, of course, right. I somehow, did my best thinking and work to the accompaniment of the train's wheels.

CHAPTER 18
Me, A Publisher?

As I gained experience in Publisher Relations, my direct dealing with publishers and lawyers became an everyday occurrence, either in my office or at luncheons. I can still remember the names of the publishers and their companies, but won't bother mentioning them, as the majority has been devoured by vertically integrated entertainment conglomerates. Needless to say, it was a different time.

On several occasions during such meetings it was suggested that I consider getting into music publishing by joining their company. On one such luncheon the publisher insisted that afterwards we go to his office, which was nearby, to see how it was newly decorated. I took the "tour" which ended up in the owner's office. He was so proud of his new chair that he insisted I try it out. I sat down and complimented him on its comfort. He leaned over the desk and said, "Good! It's your chair and office as president of our company." I quickly got up and said, "No thank you," and started to leave. He ran after me asking how much I wanted to take the job. I responded with an outrageous figure. He said, "wait, wait--how much is that per week?" I said if he had to ask, I was not a candidate and hurriedly left.

In 1968, two others repeatedly approached me. Lou Teicher, a vice president of all CBS's music, called me and invited me to lunch to, more or less, get acquainted. Obviously, he knew about me from his music clearance employees, and perhaps my surveys of CBS' music content used by BMI for negotiating rates. We lunched at his favorite dining place, Toots Shor's. He was welcomed by Toots and introduced me to Toots as he showed us to our table. Lou was one of the classiest gentlemen I ever encountered in the music business. He was handsome, immaculately dressed, spoke slowly and eloquently, and gave the impression of being interested in everything I said. We simply talked music, theatre, the arts in general, and sports. He was an avid tennis player and took lessons from Pancho Segura when he visited the west coast. It was a very enjoyable lunch and I was pleased to meet him. From time to time we met for more of these interesting luncheons.

The other gentleman who urged me to consider music publishing was Joe Abend, an employee of Pickwick Records. Pickwick had recently made a deal to represent all of Capitol Records re-issues. The deal was very profitable to both parties. Abend would travel frequently to the west coast to meet with Stanley Gortikov, recently appointed president of Capitol Records, and the newly formed Capitol Industries. Gortikov was interested in growing Capitol's music publishing entity, Beechwood Music. Beechwood was pretty much a "<u>drop-in</u>" publisher of works created by their artists for which they were able to capture publishing rights in their initial agreements. Most of the company's strongest copyrights were a result of Capitol's former president, Alan Livingston, backing a failed Broadway musical, "Sky Scraper," produced and financed by the music publisher E. H. Morris. As collateral, Morris put up "Autumn Leaves," "Witchcraft," "Five Minutes More," and "S'posin" among others well-known songs. The show failed and Capitol's music publishing entity got 50% ownership the songs.

Joe Abend constantly urged me to consider this position as he had already recommended me to Gortikov. I was reluctant, but promised that I'd meet Gortikov, at his request, when he was next in New York. About a month later, Stan Gortikov called me from the Sherry Netherlands hotel and asked if I could meet him there after work. I met him, and found him to be smiling, very gracious, and intelligent. We had a fine chat, but I told him that it was not for me. He asked me why? I told him that I had some experience on the Hollywood film scene, and found that people seemed to be judged by the model of their car, size of their swimming pool, and their lawyer. He argued that it wasn't the case at Capitol. I told him I was flattered to be offered the position, but couldn't accept. Later, Joe Abend called again asking me to reconsider to no avail.

That summer our family vacationed in Nantucket. It was probably the best vacation we ever had as a family. In the midst of it Stan Gortikov telephoned me at our vacation house. How he got the number, I'll never know. Again, he asked me to reconsider. I told him we were having a great time on the east coast, and wouldn't dream of leaving. I thought that was the end of it.

The BMI Country Music Awards were, as usual, held in Nashville that October. I had greatly enjoyed attending them in the past and was looking forward to it once again. On one occasion I chaperoned Hank Williams' widow, Audrey, and on another, Cindy Walker, composer of "You Don't Know Me" among others. So, I was disappointed when Thea

Zavin informed me that she wanted me to stay behind to oversee the office this time. As fortune would have it, once again Stanley Gortikov arrived in New York at just that time, and invited me to meet him at his hotel for a drink. At that point, I was still smarting from being left behind and thought, why not?

Once again, I met a smiling Gortikov. He had a proposition for me. He suggested that I have an all-expense paid visit, with my wife, to Hollywood for a visit. We would fly first class, have a limousine at our disposal, stay at the brand new Century Plaza hotel, be his guest for dinner and a concert by the Los Angeles Philharmonic, and then visit the Capitol Tower, with no obligations. I thought it over, called Joan and said it was a great offer. Her parents could watch over our children and we'd have a nice break. So, as I had some vacation time available, we decided to go in early November.

When we arrived, as promised, a car was waiting. The next day Stan and his wife picked us up for dinner and the concert. It was a lovely evening despite the fact that Stan was embarrassed at losing his way back when the concert was over. I ribbed him about being a native Angeleno who couldn't find his way home. The next day he picked me up for a visit to the Capitol Tower. Having worked some ten years in the shadow of Rockefeller Center, I was shocked when we arrived and he announced, "Here it is, the Tower." It was simply a round 13-story building.

I said, "Stanley, you're kidding me...this must be a mock up, where's the real Tower?" He said, smiling, "This is it, let's go." I proceeded to take the tour and meet various executives. He then introduced me to the head of Personnel, Tom Trout who imparted information about employment, medical benefits, pension, and advantages of living in Los Angeles. He even discussed housing and offered to show us availabilities. He had found a home in his area, Woodland Hills, which he considered a "steal." The owners were going through a divorce and wanted a quick resolution. Joan and I visited the home, which indeed impressed us. It was beautifully built and situated, with terrazzo flooring in the entranceway, two impressive fireplaces, and landscaped beautifully with a row of citrus trees in the backyard. We met the husband, who showed us all the amenities. The elementary school was just a short walk from the house. Joan and I had a lot to consider. We told Tom we'd get back to him.

In the interim, I discussed with Gortikov my main reason for resisting working for Capitol. I couldn't abide being a supplier reporting to a user. I didn't want to be shackled with the necessity of running by Capitol any song or artist/writer on a first refusal basis. I wanted the freedom of placing material where best suited, regardless of label affiliation. Stan explained that this was no problem as he was chairman of Capitol Industries, which was comprised of Capitol Records, Audio Devices, and now Music Publishing. I would, therefore, report directly to him, not the record company.

Joan and I discussed everything that this decision entailed. I had been employed for 10 years at BMI, so my pension was vested. It could easily cover the down payment for the house. The salary was quite a bit more than I was presently earning plus it was under a three-year contract. Joan's family would be three thousand miles away, which was a negative. I was in a good, but limited, position at BMI, which was a non-profit company. We had to give it a lot of thought. In the end, we decided to go for it. Our decision was made.

I got back to Tom Trout to advise him of our decision. During our conversation I seemed to detect a Western Pennsylvania accent and asked him where he was from.

He smiled and said, "Pittsburgh."

I then asked what section. He responded, "Swissvale."

I said, "That's next to where I lived, Squirrel Hill."

He then said, "You don't remember me, do you?"

I said, "Should I?"

"Sam, I replaced you as the punter on the Allderdice High football team when you graduated."

The contract was in the process of being drawn and would be sent to us for approval. Now, we faced the most difficult part of our decision when we returned to New York.

CHAPTER 19
Transition

When I arrived back at the BMI offices after our West Coast jaunt I was quite apprehensive knowing what I must do. The first person to let know of my decision would be Mrs. Zavin. Thea Zavin had been largely responsible for my elevation in status. I was one of three executives she called as "Her boys." The others were Neil Anderson, director of Writer Relations, and Ron Anton, Legal, who would eventually succeed Neil in Writer Relations. We would often meet in her office around 4PM for tea (many varieties) and discuss recent problems, in a relaxing atmosphere. I arrived in her office and sat down across from her, and let her know of my decision. She was stunned, and tears welled up in her eyes. I told her the salary I was offered, and felt it was time for a change. She said she had tried to get a larger salary and a vice presidency for me, but was turned down by the Board of Directors who felt that I was too young. I felt terrible, but the deed was done.

Bob Sour, who was another champion of mine, had recently retired from the presidency of BMI, having reached mandatory retirement at age 65. Edward Cramer, a member of Sidney Kaye's law firm, who had liasoned between the firm and BMI, replaced him. He was therefore acquainted with BMI personnel and systems, so he was the next one to inform. Although I didn't reveal this information to many people at BMI, it obviously started to be picked up.

Several days later Joan and I were invited, as part of a BMI group of executives, to the premier of the New York City Opera at Lincoln Center, starring Beverly Sills. After the performance we attended a small reception that included the BMI executives. While standing with Joan and talking with Alan Becker, who was in charge of the BMI theatre workshop, Sidney Kaye (Chairman of the Board) and his wife Muriel smilingly joined us.

Alan, not known for his tact blurts out, "Mr. Kaye, congratulations are in order for Sam. He's leaving to become president of Capitol Records Music Publishing." Kaye, lost his smile, put his drink down and walked away, followed by his wife Muriel. I hadn't yet told Mr. Kaye, and was furious with Alan for blurting it out, and let him know it. After a short interval Kaye returned and apologized for his abrupt departure. He explained that he was shocked, and simply said something I will never forget.

"You see, Sam, you were being groomed." He then said, "Naturally, I wish you every success," and walked away. Needless to say, it provoked much thought.

The following week, word was out everywhere, and I received an unexpected call from Lou Teicher of CBS suggesting another luncheon. He, of course, was aware of my decision, and asked if I had signed my contract yet. I advised him it was still being drawn. He then suggested that I consider coming to CBS, implying that he would soon be retiring and looked upon me as a possible successor. I told him, though I was flattered, I couldn't possibly consider this, as I had prepared BMI for so many rate negotiations against CBS, I could be looked upon as a turncoat. He smiled and said he could understand my attitude, but didn't see it that way. He wished me good luck and hoped we'd keep in touch. He then did me a favor, which was literally lifesaving for my wife Joan. He suggested that if I ever got into a situation requiring immediate medical help, that I contact his brother Joe, who was chief of medicine at the University of Southern California. A life-threatening situation actually did occur with Joan while I was working at Capitol Records, and in desperation I contacted Dr. Joseph Teicher, who was quick to call the best diagnostician he knew and arrange an immediate appointment, which most probably saved her life.

I had about four more weeks to work, before departing for Hollywood, and tried to make the best of them. Beechwood Music was somewhat of a one-dimensional catalog, devoid of the country hits that Capitol Records was producing. I was aware of the owners of Central Songs, a catalog that contributed to an inordinate amount of Capitol's country hits, and decided to look into it, as a possible acquisition. I had mentioned it to Stan Gortikov when I was in Hollywood. He asked me to gather information about it. I knew that this would be an excellent acquisition, considering Capitol's success in both Nashville and Bakersfield.

Cliffie Stone, a name I was familiar with, was listed as the owner of Central Songs, so I tried to get as much information about him as possible. I found that Central Songs also had an office in Nashville. I remembered attending a show prior to the Country Music Awards in Nashville, and hearing a recent hit from that catalog, the title of which I could never forget, "May The Bird of Paradise Fly Up Your Nose," performed by Little Jimmy Dickens.

Ed Cramer was now president of BMI. As previously mentioned, he was liaison between BMI and Sidney Kaye's law firm. In that capacity I got to know and respect him. On one occasion, he brought the famous Senior Partner, Judge Samuel I. Rosenman, to meet me. Rosenman, advisor and speechwriter for FDR was quite well known and credited with creating Roosevelt's moniker, "New Deal." I was impressed with his stature. He was rather short, with a full head of white hair combed in wavy pompadour. He wore silver rimmed glasses, had a reddish complexion, and a hint of jowls. He was everything I could have imagined as a judge, including a quick grasp of situations.

Ed asked me to prepare a report for him, of all my thoughts and suggestions for improvements, before my departure. I spent a good deal of time on this project and delivered it to him on my final day.

I then spent the next week in Hollywood before returning to pack up our family for our move to the west coast.

During that time I visited Cliffie Stone at his offices in Hollywood, which were only two blocks from the Capitol Tower. I told him of my interest in acquiring the company for Capitol, and he seemed pleased, but also alerted me that Wesley Rose, owner of the very successful country music publishing company, Acuff-Rose was intent on purchasing Central, with an initial offer of 1.2 million dollars. He invited me to visit Central's Nashville office on our drive to the west coast, which we did.

Before leaving, BMI treated me to a farewell luncheon, arranged by Thea Zavin with the Performing Rights staff. BMI was a great experience. It helped me prepare for my next step in the music industry,---—music publishing.

CHAPTER 20
Westward, Oh!

We had an enjoyable auto trip to Los Angeles with our family, only to arrive just after a huge rainstorm, which had done damage to many homes. Fortunately, our home was intact. We were, however, to face a number of un-expected storms, both personally and career-wise shortly thereafter.

New offices had been arranged for Beechwood Music, across the street from the Capitol "Tower," at Argyle and Yucca. They were quite spacious and provided free parking on the same level as the offices. While my designated office was quite spacious, much to my surprise, the person that I assumed I was replacing, Herb Hendler, the former general manager with whom I had negotiated Beechwood agreements, while at BMI, was still in place in a large office nearby. I immediately called Gortikov for an explanation. He said, "Herb's been here for a while and I didn't have the heart to fire him. I'll leave that up to you--perhaps he can be helpful?" I told him in no uncertain terms there could only be one boss. If I find he interferes, I'll fire him on the spot, and you will support me. He agreed. It didn't take long. Herb was dead-set on producing a rock musical, which was the current rage at that time. I went over the script, heard a few songs, and was not impressed. He presented a budget to me for approval, and I turned him down. He said he'd go "over my head" for approval. I said, if he chose to do that he could, and then proceed out of his job. He went straight to Gortikov, who informed him that he needed my approval. When he returned to the office I fired him. Later Gortikov called me to ask what happened. I informed him that I had fired him.

Gortikov seemed shocked, and said "just like that?"

I replied, "Yes, just like that! The way you should have before I got here!" With that out of the way, I needed to get on with building this company. One of the first letters I received was from Ron Anton of BMI, one of Mrs. Zavin's "boys." It was a good-natured thank you note to me for leaving, which resulted in Ron getting appointed Vice President within two weeks of my departure.

Aside from getting to know my existing employees and their particular jobs, I had to allay any fears that I was "The Angel of Death." I knew I had risked the possibility of employees leaving out of loyalty to Herb Hendler and his dream for a Broadway musical. As it turned out, only one clerk departed.

My first order of business was following through on the Central Songs acquisition. Wesley Rose was still in the "catbird" seat with his offer of $1.2 million. Now that Central Songs office was located only two and one half blocks away from Beechwood's, I started spending time with Cliffie and his staff. They were quartered in a wonderful building owned by Central Songs, complete with a demo studio and, oddly enough, a banana tree just outside the back of the building. It was obvious that Cliffie, a large man pushing close to 300 lbs., had a great rapport with his staff and writers.

This company had everything I was looking for, and Capitol needed. I was able to get all the financial figures that were needed, and started on an analysis and justification for the acquisition.

In the meantime, Gortikov asked me to do an analysis of Capitol's licensing division. Licensing dealt with royalty payments to publishers and he felt that, with my experience, I might be helpful. That department was under the supervision of Robert Karp, head of Legal. I had met Karp earlier and felt a rather cool reception. I asked him, who was the director of licensing, so I might meet with him, and he gave me the name. I visited the department and was told that person had died two years before. So much for Bob Karp's supervision. My investigation disclosed a chaotic department. I prepared my report and sent it to Gortikov. He immediately called for a meeting in his office with me and Bob Karp who, as expected, was seething. Bob had been with Capitol for many years, far more than Gortikov. Gortikov reviewed my criticisms to us, which I confirmed, and Bob denied. I claimed that the information in the files was substantially out of date. Bob, again, denied it and asked for an example. I, of course, had one ready. I asked him to check the status of one particular song. He called down to licensing and was told that it was in file correctly and the parties had been regularly paid. Bob gleefully reported this information to us. Gortikov looked at me for my response. I said, "That's great Bob, but, unfortunately, that song went public domain three years ago." Though being correct, I created an enemy for the rest of my stay at Capitol.

CHAPTER 21
The Big Acquisition

While observing successful publishing companies at BMI was helpful, creating one was another matter. Beechwood was a one-dimensional company having no exposure in television, films, or country music, and no known contracted writers. To me, the acquisition of Central Songs would be the first step in broadening Beechwood's horizon. I, therefore, spent much time learning about that catalog and its writers. My report was quite thorough and I thought my analysis to be convincing. The report was submitted to Stan Gortikov, who went through it and decided to submit it to the full board of directors for their approval at their up-coming meeting. I was invited to that meeting and asked to briefly discuss the merits of the acquisition. There were approximately ten gentlemen seated around the conference table. At one end seated next to me was Glen Wallichs, the founder of Capitol Records and Chairman of the Board. At the other end of the table were Len Wood, Chairman of Music and Records of EMI, which owned 71% of Capitol Records. Gortikov was in the middle taking charge of the meeting. After my short talk Gortikov had some further comments and asked each Board member for their views. Unfortunately, to the left of Gortikov sat Bob Karp who blasted the acquisition stating Capitol could make better use of their money. That set the tone of negativity that went round the table. The fifth member actually said that he didn't recognize even one title.

I shot back that it wasn't his place to evaluate the catalog based on his taste in music, but my expertise on the value. "Otherwise, why was I hired?" That silenced the room until he finally said: "Well I'm not for it!" Not one director gave it a positive until Glenn Wallichs looked across the table to Len Wood and asked, "Len, what do you think of it?" Len was very English, soft-spoken, and conservatively dressed. He simply said, "Gentlemen, I'm shocked. I went over Mr. Trust's report with the boys back in London and they think he's brought it in "spot on." There was a short silence. Then Gortikov, after a quick unseen signal from Wallichs, raised his voice saying, "Gentlemen, let's bring this to a vote, I for one, am for it." He then called for ayes and nays. There were no nays. After the meeting I went up to Len Wood to introduce myself. He was complimentary and asked that I come to visit him at his office when next in London. I did, subsequently, and whenever he was in LA he stopped in to see me. We became very friendly and, he, at times, considered me a confidante.

Now that I had received approval to proceed, I would have to negotiate the deal with Cliffie's attorney, Larry Greene, whom I knew from New York. I liked Larry and knew him to be a good Lawyer, but very detailed and fussy. This would be my first challenge as a purchaser of a music publishing company.

With Board approval for the acquisition of Central Songs at the price I recommended, Wesley Rose, dropped out of contention and Cliffie Stone accepted. The next hurdle would be to get by Larry Greene, Cliffie's attorney. I knew that Larry would be tough, and he was. I also knew that there was no room regarding the price, so Larry would have no leverage there, though he tried. He took apart the agreement that was prepared by Capitol's lawyers, and was stubborn to the point of threatening to walk away several times. The negotiations were long and drawn out, and at one point Larry did, in fact, walk out and return to New York. I knew that Cliffie wanted the deal, but had to back his lawyer. After a short period, which allowed Larry to cool off, I went to New York to open a New York office for Beechwood in the same building occupied by Capitol. I met with Larry and smoothed over some points of contention. He came back to the coast shortly thereafter and, after some more drama, completed the deal.

Capitol had, in effect bought a company that should have been owned by them all along. Aside from Cliffie, who on occasion produced sides for Capitol, the co-owners of Central were Capitol's own producers. Had Capitol acknowledged the value of copyright ownership, they would have already owned the songs in Central. Whether they would ever acknowledge the value of copyrights was still yet to be determined.

About two weeks after the sale, I received a call from Cliffie asking me to come over to his office. When I arrived, the office, which was usually boisterous, was dead silent. Cliffie pointed to the front panel of his desk and the furniture around him. All contained orange stickers with code numbers. He advised that someone from accounting had come by using these stickers for inventory control. I was livid. I went by each area peeling off every sticker I could find. I rolled them into a ball and went into the office of the, newly appointed chief accountant Ed

Khoury, introduced myself, and then threw the ball of stickers right at him. Ed ducked and was stunned and asked what that was for? I said, "Check the ball."

He looked at it and said, "those were my inventory control stickers."

I said, "Yes, I know, and if you ever try that again, it will be your clerk who will comes back in tape!" He protested it was necessary, and I said, "I don't give damn, find some other way!" We bought that company because of its success. I don't want it to be corporatized! Leave them alone." He began to understand, and Central was never bothered again, and Ed and I, and our wives, became friends.

In the coming months the positive results of this acquisition would become apparent. Within three months Central had 50% and administration of the new Glen Campbell single, "Try a Little Kindness." At that time Glen Campbell was one of the hottest recording artists in the world. Central had an impressive roster of country writers, both in Nashville and Los Angeles, who produced a constant stream of songs that entered the national country charts. In fact, I cannot remember a week in which Central was not represented on the charts.

My biggest surprise, and unknown asset, was the fact that Cliffie Stone underwrote a Canadian company operated by a country artist named Gary Buck. All songs emanating from that company sold or performed outside of Canada, were to be controlled by Central Songs. I was particularly delighted because of my BMI experience in Canada, where I noted so much creative activity, as a result of the Canadian governments' austerity policy, which required Canadian content in recordings done in that country. I was determined to open a Canadian outlet for Beechwood and Gary Buck's operation, being already up and running, was a natural choice.

CHAPTER 22
O' Canada

Upon discovering Central Songs' link to Gary Buck Music in Canada, I discussed the deal with Cliffie and learned that there had been little or no activity reported. I therefore did some research and found that Buck had not operated in accordance with the agreement. I contacted Gary and discussed my plans for opening an office for Beechwood in Canada. I proposed that since he was already operating, that we buy him out for a reasonable price. He refused. I then dropped the bomb, advising that he was in breach of his agreement, and we could sue. Alternatively, he could accept a reasonable price and be employed as General Manager of Beechwood Music of Canada. He immediately agreed. Beechwood Music of Canada was born, and would become one of the top music publishers in Canada for the next few years.

At the same time I continually searched for ways to expand Beechwood. An opportunity came my way to purchase a small catalog containing many of the compositions of Harry Nilsson, a writer I greatly admired and had met while at BMI. Gil Garfield and Perry Botkin Jr. owned the catalog, Rock Music. At the time of my discussions with Gil and Perry, Herb Alpert's recording of Nilsson's "Without Her" had just entered the charts. I moved quickly and purchased the catalog for $100,000, so that we could receive the accruing royalties. Based on the Central acquisition, I received no problems from management.

After the close of the deal I arranged to meet Harry for lunch at The Brown Derby. I was shocked at the physical change in him. When I met him at BMI, while I was still working there, he was a slender, bright-eyed, ex-bank clerk just beginning to have success with his songs. He was now at least 25 lbs. heavier, with a reddish sagging face, a beard, and slow speaking manner. After we were seated he ordered a "Bull Shot." (Vodka and bullion) As discussions of the catalog ensued, he consumed two more. When we ordered lunch he added a bottle of red wine, most of which he consumed. While it was great to meet with him again, it was sad to see his deterioration. Notwithstanding his appearance, he would go on to have a very successful career as a writer, singer, and personality until his death at the age of 53 in 1994.

In an effort to get exposure on Television, I negotiated a co-publishing deal with Sid and Marty Krofft for their forthcoming TV children's show "H. R. Puffinstuff," as well as their future show "The Bugaloos."

By the end of the year I received news that would make 1970 one of the most exciting and successful years of my entire career in music publishing. The establishment of Beechwood Music of Canada turned out to be the most valuable and perhaps luckiest decision I made while at Capitol's publishing company. Unbeknownst to me, at the time of establishing this company, a writer named Gene Maclellan was signed to Gary Buck Music, now Beechwood Music of Canada. Within 6 months Capitol Records of Canada released a recording of "Snowbird," sung by a largely unknown Canadian singer Ann Murray. Gene Maclellan wrote the song. Ann's album was, in fact, entitled "Snowbird. It did so well in Canada that Dick Asher, vice president of Capitol's

East Coast operation, decided to give it a shot in the U.S. Dick, who I knew from my BMI days, called me to advise that he noticed we had the publishing on the title and said any help we could offer would be appreciated.

To prove that nobody I know of has "golden ears," including me, I listened to the track of the single, thought it was pleasant, but was excited about the B-side of the record which had the song "Just Bidin' My Time," also written by Gene. I loved Ann's voice, but being a publisher, I loved the "hook" line to the B-side "I'm just bidin' my time while the glow of the wine makes a fool of me." At that exact time Dean Martin was one of the hottest artists on the scene, with the top TV show. He capitalized on his purported drinking habits, so I figured if the song got to him and he recorded it, it would be a bonanza for us.

Central Songs had a promotion man named Smiley Monroe who we retained after the acquisition. I knew Capitol had what was then known as a WATS line for record promotion. The number was a well-guarded secret but through some devious means we got it. I gave it to Smiley and told him to come to work at 6:AM and start calling stations on the east coast. He had the line all to himself until nearly 9:AM. Not too much was happening until one morning, he told me had good news. The record was breaking out of Key West Florida. However, it was the other side, "Snowbird." He had checked a number of disk jockeys that told him it was a perfect "going out" record since it was only one minute and 58 seconds in duration. So, if there was no time to play a 3-minute record, "Snowbird" did the job. As we had both sides, I gave up and told him to start riding "Snowbird." Between Smiley and Happy Wilson, another Central employee overseeing our Nashville office, both of whom were strong country promoters, it sailed to the top of the charts. With a "Smiley" and a "Happy," I began to feel like we owned a couple of the seven dwarfs.

Another strange attraction to the song "Snowbird" was that it contained no "release" or "B" section. Most pop songs are based on an AABA structure. "Snowbird" was simply AAAA. That's a reason for it being so short and such a retainable melody. Perhaps the strangest component was its appeal to the "hippie" or should I say the "stoner" community who interpreted the lyric as referring to cocaine. Articles in various music and entertainment magazines noted this possibility, until Gene Maclellan disabused them of this idea. Gene stated it had nothing to do with cocaine. Being a country boy, it just related to a winter bird that he was fond of in Canada.

Simultaneous with the release of "Snowbird," one of the great copyrights of all time, "Bridge Over Troubled Water," was enjoying much deserved great success. The song was written and owned by Paul Simon who was represented by Mike Tannen, his attorney, and my long-time friend. Mike had moved to Los Angeles and we often got together for tennis. As the BMI Award dinner was approaching, Mike announced at the end of one match that he was probably going to have to go to New York to pick up the most performed song of the year trophy.

I responded, "Mike, I wouldn't be so sure if I were you."

He said, "You don't expect to win it with that dumb little song of yours, do you?"

My answer was that I knew the BMI logging system very well, and it was a possibility. He just laughed.

Oddly enough, "Snowbird" did, in fact, take the award, but certainly not on the quality of the song but the most performances. While Snowbird reached only top 5 on the pop charts, it made number 1 on the country charts where "Bridge Over Troubled Water" did not appear. As all station performances were equally rated at BMI, we took it, much to the surprise of many, and the chagrin of Mike.

For the dinner I was seated at the table of Sidney Kaye, chairman of the board and founder of BMI and Thea Zavin, my boss at BMI. So I knew something was up. At the close of the dinner they announced the winner of the most performed song. Thea took the podium rather than the president and explained that as I was one of "her boys," she would like to make the presentation. After her short speech, she added "Sam, I'm kvelling!" (In yiddish, kvelling means overflowing with joy.)

Unfortunately, casting a pall over the dinner, for me, was a dispute I had with the relatively new president of Capitol Records, Bhaskar Menon, who, while replacing Stanley Gortikov, (who had hired me) dissolved Capitol Industries, of which Music Publishing was a division. This placed Beechwood directly under Capitol Records. While Menon was extremely intelligent and well respected, he had no experience regarding Music Publishing. As a result, Menon refused to allow me to have the expense of going to New York covered by Capitol, and insisted the trip was unnecessary. I told him I was going whether Capitol was reimbursing or not, a hint of things to come.

While basking in the joy of "Snowbird" moving up the charts and getting released internationally, I decided to carefully examine the rest of the songs in Ann Murray's album. I listened to a track entitled "Put Your Hand In The Hand," also written by Gene Maclellan, then, I listened again. I called Steve Stone into my office and said, "Am I nuts? This song sounds like a hit to me!" Steve, Cliffie's son, had grown up in the music publishing business, and also studied in Bible School. I had come to rely on Steve's judgment when considering songs. Steve and I listened once more. He said, "You're not nuts, I think it's a monster hit!" We made copies of the track and started introducing it to producers of singing groups. I can honestly say this was the easiest push for any song in which I was ever involved. Virtually every producer jumped on it and recorded it with their group. Within a month there were 14 different recordings, including the "Mike Curb Congregation." It got to be a joke among Hollywood recording musicians and studios--"Not that song again!" However, despite the numerous recordings, the song didn't gain the traction we had expected. Needless to say Steve and I were disappointed. About a month after this flurry of activity, Gary Buck called to advise that a group in Canada called "Ocean" had recorded it, and it was getting some action on the little-known Yorkville label in Canada. This action grew and got the attention of a U.S. label, Kama Sutra, which released it to immediate success. It hit the charts at around 65 and we thought we were once again "off to the races" with another Gene Maclellan hit. However, the day after the chart listing I received a call from Gene requesting I that I take the record off the market because the group changed one of his lines. I said, "Gene, you realize this is a strong entry at 65 with a "Bullet." (a term indicating upward pressure)

He said he didn't care, he wanted it stopped. I replied, "I wasn't about to stop a hit."

He accused me of having no integrity and he would sue me. I was thoroughly aware of the terms of the contract and knew that he couldn't. I told him that I was disappointed with his attitude and we both ended the call. I had a short chat with Cliffie Stone to devise a plan, and then called him back. "Gene, I'd like you come down here, at our expense so we can discuss this situation.

He replied, "I'm not coming down!"

I then said, "Gene that's a shame because Cliffie Stone really wants to meet you, and have you as a guest at his ranch" After a pause he said "THE Cliffie Stone, the producer of "16 tons" and manager of Tennessee Ernie?"

I replied, "That's right. He's part of our organization." He responded, " Well, Okay."

Cliffie picked him up at the airport, put him up at his ranch house, got him on a horse and generally entertained him.

Gene was in awe. When Cliffie asked him about the short lyric change, he just said. "Oh, forget about it. It's alright." The song sped up the charts to #2, where it stayed for 10 weeks. It just couldn't get past "Joy To The World" by Three Dog Night. However, it came to be, perhaps, the most financially successful copyright in the entire Beechwood catalog. Sheet music sales exceeded 800,000 and Shaped Notes (rudimentary printing of notes in various shapes used by mostly Baptist congregations) set a record at 300,000. Cover recordings have easily numbered in the hundreds as well as multiple choral arrangements. Financially, it exceeded Snowbird.

At the time, sales of recordings paid only 2 cents per side to the publisher, half of which was paid to the writer. That rate was in effect since 1908 despite numerous pleas from publishers and the copyright community. The rate was not increased until the passing of the 1976 Copyright Act that increased the rate even marginally. So you can see that the sale of sheet music brought much more revenue to the publishers than the then existing mechanical right. Sheet music sales, at the turn of the 20th century, were the only revenue available to music publishers. As a token, piano rolls were paid at 2 cents that was then applied to recordings as the "mechanical rate." There it stayed until 1976. The print sales for "Put Your Hand...," during that period, were somewhat unique as print income was in a diminishing spiral. That song taught me the value of "inspirational" music publishing, and served well for both me, and Steve Stone in later years.

CHAPTER 23
Beechwood Memories

Having grown up in the late '30's, thru the early 1950's and playing in dance bands in high school and throughout college, my taste in music was obviously slanted toward the great "big band era" and its numerous soloists and vocalists. I was, and still am, an admirer of the well-crafted lyric joined with an interesting melody. When rock and roll began to evolve in the early 1950's I was somewhat distressed. While a bandsman in the Navy, I stopped counting the times we had to play "Rock Around The Clock." I soon realized that this type of music was making huge inroads in the industry. It would also introduce songs that were not predominately love ballads. As rock continued to grow, the natural outlet for performing rights became BMI as opposed to ASCAP, who all but ignored this music as a passing fad.

Unexpectedly, one of the first people to welcome me to Hollywood was Herb Gottlieb who had been ASCAP's west coast representative for many years. We had lunch and he invited me to join him at the next ASCAP West Coast general meeting. That meeting was held in the Grand Ballroom of one of Hollywood's large hotel. Stanley Adams, a longtime successful songwriter of the "old school," was still president, and fierce opponent of what was now becoming the new American music phenomena. A huge crowd of ASCAP members welcomed him as he approached the podium. He smilingly acknowledged, and with a strong voice pronounced, "Roll those pianos back into your parlors! The good songs are coming back!" The audience roared their approval. I simply shook my head and realized why BMI had been such a success. Shortly after Adams' departure as president, ASCAP decided to play "catch up" in a big way. Not only was the door opened to the new music, but these new artist/writers were soon to be heavily pursued.

As a result of the success of "Put Your Hand In The Hand" two new individuals entered into my music life. The very first "cover" recording of that song was by a group called "The People," owned by two agents, Mark Wildey and Wally Amos. Their company had an employee named

Terry Slater. Slater, an English bass guitarist, joined the Everly Brothers as a regular during their tour of Great Britain. A strong bond was formed between Phil Everly and Terry, and Phil sponsored Terry's move to the United States. After his initial arrival, Terry worked recording sessions with some of Hollywood's elite musicians, including the famous "Wrecking Crew," who supplied tracks for many of the popular rock groups of the era. Terry provided the "music chops" needed by Mark and Wally. I met Terry on his many visits to Beechwood. Terry was a happy-go-lucky personality with a "can-do" attitude. At that time he was easily recognized by the ever-present beanie on head. He was, and still is, tall, lean, and seemingly ever cheerful.

Mark and Wally's firm came into hard times and they had to cut staff. They let me know that they would have to let Terry go. I jumped at the chance, interviewed him and put him on as a song plugger. I had enough professional staff at Central Songs and needed someone to help build our pop music catalog.

In the spring of 1970 the annual Music Men's Golf tournament was being held in Palm Springs. I and my senior professional staff made reservations to attend. Terry approached me and asked if he could also attend. I regretfully told him that I couldn't include him for budgetary and seniority reasons. He said, "Oh, that's OK." I arrived at the hotel early on the evening before the tournament. As I was about to check in, I looked into the cocktail lounge and found Terry sitting and enjoying a drink with Glen Campbell, probably the hottest artist in America. I came in and he introduced me to Glen. He later told me he thought it would be a good idea to come down and chat with artists even though he wasn't in the tournament. That's all I needed to know about Terry. From that point on he was my go-to pop music man!

Later Terry told me that Phil Everly was having trouble regarding his BMI royalties, and asked if I would meet with Phil and go over the problem. I met and understood immediately what it was all about. I prevailed on an uneasy Dick Kirk, who was reluctant to acknowledge the problem. With some arm twisting and intimating that it was in his, and BMI's, interest that the matter be resolved, Dick moved ahead with the request and the problem was quickly mended. Phil was grateful and a friendship and long term business relationship was established.

During 1970, through some personal contacts, I was able to negotiate the rights to provide the music and song to a forthcoming Motion Picture entitled "Fools" starring Jason Robards, Jr. and Katharine Ross. As part of the film, which was scored by Shorty Rogers, the song created, by Alex Harvey, at Kenny Roger's and our request entitled

"Someone Who Cares" was performed by Rogers in the film. Steve Stone produced the album recording in place of an indisposed Jimmy Bowen. I was determined to get a major cover recording of the song and asked Terry to try to get it to Andy Williams. Terry stepped right up and got it, and Andy did a great job. It was included in his next album. Meanwhile, I did my best to get the Rogers recording released as a single and prevailed on my friend Joe Smith, co-CEO with Mo Ostin, of Warner Brothers Records. Joe liked the recording, but had other plans for Kenny's next single. That single had not yet been recorded, so I decided to try to force the track from the album to become a single through radio airplay. We bought close to 1,000 albums at the promo rate and retained Tony Richland and Lou Fields to do a concentrated radio promotion. Tony covered the entire West Coast and Lou, the Southwest. It worked, and Warners was forced to release the song as a single, even though Joe was somewhat angry with me. It wasn't a hit, but did fairly well in the pop charts reaching #51 and staying on the charts for seven weeks. I have to believe that it would have done better had Warners really promoted it.

In addition to the Andy Williams record, Perry Como, and Shirley Bassey also recorded the song. The movie was only moderately successful, but the producers were grateful for our efforts.

CHAPTER 24
Beechwood Daze Remembered

While devoting my efforts to building the Beechwood catalog, I was becoming aware of the differences between a non-profit company, such as BMI, and a for profit corporation such as Capitol Records and Beechwood Music.

I had anticipated cooperation between the record company and music publishing, particularly after the acquisition of Central Songs, now proven to be a company that should have been owned by Capitol all along. However, this was simply not to be. Each division had its own profit incentive, or should I say opportunities for individuals, and that was not about to change. I even offered an incentive to record producers to bring the publishing of writers, and especially artist-writers they dealt with into the fold, but to no avail. I did some research on some longtime Capitol producers, and found their writer pseudonyms in ASCAP and BMI files. One producer was very creative by writing under the names, Murray Berlin and Jacques Strappe. This, once again, proved the lack of understanding of the value of music publishing by Capitol. Record companies such as A & M and Motown are examples of those that did understand such value, and went after publishing rights. Those entities became powerhouse-publishing companies, providing a measure of steady revenue.

Stan Gortikov continued to hire, (or raid) other companies of their executives who, for the most part, were proving to be ineffective. After hiring a new President for Capitol Records, he called me to his office to meet him. I was already familiar with this candidate from his former position in New York, and less than impressed with his reputation. This was only confirmed upon meeting him. I mentioned to him that I dealt with another senior executive at his former company. His reply was, "Oh yes, he did a good job for me."

I knew then and there that this man was not right for the job. Afterwards Gortikov asked what I thought of his selection. I told him that I thought he was an ass and totally wrong for the job. I went even further and said, "He will bring this company down and, possibly, you with it." Gortikov was furious with me and told me I was wrong, and excused me from his office.

After a cool-down period, I was invited to attend the Billboard music convention, known as the IMIC, in The Bahamas. Gortikov, Bob Karp, and Glen Wallichs, among other Capitol executives, were also in attendance. My best remembrance from that occasion was Glen Wallich's invitation to have dinner with him and Stan Kenton. I was completely overwhelmed at the opportunity to meet Stan Kenton, the leader of one the greatest and innovative bands of the 20th century. I had collected all the Kenton records I could afford during high school and college. When I arrived, Wallichs and Stan were already seated. Glen introduced me to Stan and I assured him I was well aware and a fan. Stan was most gracious. I told him that I first saw the band in 1950 when they were playing at Kennywood Park, in Pittsburgh. I went on to name every player in the band and their instrument, and mentioned the new trumpeter in the band, Maynard Ferguson, who was hitting stratospheric high notes. Stan was amazed and said that HE couldn't remember all the names of those band members. For years afterwards, Stan and I kept in touch. I'd help out with music business problems and he'd call me "Judge." At one point, as a member of the board of The National Music Publishers Association, I pulled him out of a legal jam. The NMPA, as a class, were about to sue him for not recognizing and accounting to publishers for his company's arrangements, sold at College Jazz seminars. I promised to rectify the situation with Stan, and they withdrew the action. Stan was forever grateful.

Kenton was brought to the convention by Wallichs to help petition for a slice of performing rights for the recording artists (and, of course, the record companies.) At the time performing rights revenues were derived almost solely from radio and TV broadcasting. Therefore, the plea from recording companies was for an implied share of the income earned by publishers and writers. Hence, Kenton's presentation was largely met without enthusiasm from a majority of the attendees. Though the music-publishing element in the audience was respectful of Kenton, they realized what this might mean. I'm sure they also realized that with the entrance of the writer/artist now in the mix in broadcasting they had to be respectful, though not endorsing. After the Kenton statement, Gortikov stood up and made a short speech urging the publishers to share, but now realizing that they were cool to the idea, accused them of being greedy, a big mistake. Sal Chiantia, who was recently elected as the first salaried president of The National Music

Publishers Association and a gifted speaker, answered Gortikov's accusation and literally put him away. It should be kept in mind that the recording industry had blocked any attempt to raise the statutory mechanical rate (the total payment for both publishers and writers) from two cents per recording, the rate at that time. That rate was assigned to piano rolls in 1909 before the release of musical recordings, and remained that way until 1976 when the rate was raised to .0275 by an amendment to the copyright law. Since that time, however, the rate has continually increased based on various living standards.)

As the meeting broke up, Gortikov looked at me and asked why I didn't stand up and support him. I looked at him strangely as Bob Karp chimed in, "Stanley, didn't you realize that you hired a damned music publisher?"

A precursor of events to follow occurred in mid 1969 when Lee Eastman, Linda McCartney's father and one of the most successful, if not wiliest, lawyers in the music business was in town to negotiate an artist deal with Capitol for Paul. I knew Lee quite well from my days at BMI. He was, without doubt, also one of the most savvy acquirers of copyrights and catalogs, not only for his clients but for himself as well. His companies, LLee Music and Cherio Music, among others, were hugely successful. We often met for lunch at Shepherd's restaurant at the old Drake Hotel in New York.

Lee was now managing Paul after successfully terminating the Beatles management agreement with Allen Klein. He was, therefore, able to negotiate a separate artist agreement. He stopped by my office, all smiles, and told me he had great news. He advised me that he was starting a new publishing venture with Paul called McCartney Music (now MPL Communications) and was appointing me CEO.

I said," Whoa, Lee! I just moved my family out here and signed a three-year contract. My kids are in school. I can't just pick up and go back."

He looked at me as if I were crazy and said, "You're going to stay and work here?" I confirmed that I must and he seemed shocked. He said he couldn't believe it and thought for sure I'd take the job. He left saying he wouldn't forget it.

Toward the end of 1970, rumblings of discord were being noticed at Capitol. The newly appointed president of the record company had made some moves through a former associate, now working at Capitol, to try to get me back into the Capitol Records' fold and reporting directly to him. I sidestepped this ploy and insisted on being part of Capitol Industries. Other politically motivated moves obviously were taking place. In early 1971, just prior to my trip to Cannes for the MIDEM convention and meeting the other EMI aligned music publishers, I received a call from Gortikov's secretary requesting I come to his office immediately. As I entered, Stan said, "Sit down, and please don't say I told you so." He had fired the Capitol Records President, changed the lock on his office, and taken away his company car.

He said, "Sam, I'm going to need all the help I can get."

I simply said, "Stan, I don't know of anything I can do."

My trip to Midem was successful, however, on the last day I had an accident, the consequences of which still remain. My wife and I spent a wonderful day in Brighton, in the UK, after the convention, with the recognized dean and grand old man of British music publishers, Jimmy Phillips and his wife. While strolling back to his home after a luncheon, I spotted an antique store that displayed a beautiful five-foot long coach horn. It was Sunday so the store was closed. Jimmy asked if I liked it and, of course, I assured him I did. He said, "Then you shall have it!"

I said, "Jimmy the store is closed," as he started banging on the door. He simply wouldn't stop. A window above the store opened and the owner shouted down, "Stop banging, the store is closed!" Jimmy shouted back "I am James Phillips, a resident here whom you may have heard of, I insist you open your door immediately as my American guest wishes to make a purchase." Amazingly, the storeowner came down, opened the door, and at Jimmy's insistence, I bought the horn. As we left Jimmy demanded, "Give us a blow, Sam!" As we proceeded down the street I performed every up-tempo American bugle call I could think of, to Jimmy's delight.

As we were going to Amsterdam the next day, I had Jimmy keep the horn for me until I returned. I would then pick it up at his Denmark Street office. We returned and checked in at The Grosvenor House hotel for one night, prior to our flight home. The next morning I took a taxi to Jimmy's office at EMI, picked up the horn, thanked him, and hailed a taxi back to the hotel to pack for the flight. The Taxi port was at the back of the hotel. The driver rolled around to a spot near the entrance. However that particular area had a somewhat raised curb. As I tried to exit the cab, balancing the five-foot long horn, and moving almost duck waddle style, I stepped out, missed the curb, and my right leg went straight down to the street. I heard and felt a loud crack in my lower back. I couldn't possibly stand up and lay on my back, holding the horn in front of me. Two porters saw what happened and rushed out to assist me. They literally dragged me to the lobby, laid me down on the carpet, and called Joan. Fortunately, the manager of the hotel was the brother of the head of distribution at PRS (Performing Rights Society of Great Britain) whom I had met during our stay in the UK. So, we had the best of attention.

When I got back to our room, with the assistance of two porters, I suggested to Joan that she go on without me. I had plenty of contacts that could look after me until the next day. She would have none of it. We checked the flight and were advised that it was far from full and there was plenty of room and would allow us to find four adjoining coach seats in the middle of the plane, a 747, so I could stretch out rather than sit upright at no extra cost. So, off we went, unfortunately to the next disaster.

CHAPTER 25
Frightful Flight

We arrived and boarded our return flight near noon. I carefully eased my way across three seats and got comfortable for the flight. We took off and all seemed well.

The stewardesses were soon preparing for our lunch, when Joan said to me, "Sam, we're going in the wrong direction." Almost immediately the stewardesses came hurrying back, picking up the trays they had just set down.

Then came the message from the Captain that we will never forget: "We have just received a message from Heathrow informing us that there is a live bomb aboard this plane that is set to go off in 30 minutes. We are heading to Prestwick airfield for an emergency landing. We believe we can make it there in 25 minutes. However, that field is not built to accept 747 aircraft, but we feel we can land safely. Exiting will be by the emergency slides that will be used on the port side of the plane. Therefore, remove all metal objects and place them in the seat pockets in front of you. These should include glasses, rings, watches, bracelets, pins and cufflinks. Also, remove your shoes and place them under your seats."

Fuel was being ejected from the wingtips and we shortly made what seemed to be a power dive and leveled off. The stewardess sat down in front of us and said nothing. Joan and I went over everything on the way down. The children were with my parents, insurance was paid and our will was in order. Not a word was spoken throughout the plane. The stewardess looked deathly white as the time ticked by. We were aware of the 25-minute deadline but, as our watches were tucked away, we couldn't ascertain time. Finally we hit the landing strip and probably overshot it slightly as we braked in a grassy area and stopped.

The Captain shouted, "Gladys, blow out the doors!" Two of the doors flew open, the air slide shoots filled, and the stewardesses quickly directed passengers to the slides. As the plane was a 747, we were up quite high so the slides were steep. The last word we heard from the pilot was "Jump and run for your lives!" The passengers obeyed quickly, as did I despite my back injury. Unfortunately, one of the early sliders was a very old gentleman, who hit the surface, crumpled and couldn't get up. The passengers following him fell into him at the bottom. I saw what was happening and dug my elbows into the surface of the chute to try to brake so I wouldn't hit him. In the process, I received some extremely painful mat burns. Joan followed and we ran like the wind. I can only assume that I was operating on adrenaline, as I could barely walk before. We found ourselves in the middle of a grassy area as far from the plane as we could get, in our socks shivering with the temperature at 40 degrees. Eventually, some emergency vehicles appeared and took us to the airport's international lounge. When we arrived at the lounge my back was in spasm, and I had to lie flat on the marble surface. A Scottish doctor arrived and administered some heavy-duty pain pills. Pan Am personnel were all around me assuming that my injury occurred as a result of the evacuation. I assured them that it was not, much to their relief. All passengers were moved to a restaurant area where free drinks and snacks were offered. Pan Am was advised that the threat turned out to be a hoax initiated by a person recently fired by the company. The plane was, therefore, now being emptied of luggage, the stored shoes, and other pocketed items. We returned to the international lounge to identify our belongings, a rather tedious endeavor. The one missing item was my horn. They said nothing else was found. I insisted that it was on the plane and demanded they go back. Reluctantly, they did and returned with it sometime later saying it was so awkward that it had been placed in the tail assembly at the back of the plane.

Pan American arranged for a smaller plane to take us back to New York and transfer to another flight to Los Angeles. Joan and I were given first class accommodations and enjoyed a relaxing flight back to New York. Before transferring to our next flight, I telephoned my office only to receive some shocking news that would eventually lead to another crisis in my career.

CHAPTER 26
Capitol Capsize

It seemed that in my absence the apparent rumbles throughout Capitol came to a head. Stanley Gortikov was terminated, and with that move, Capitol Industries dissolved. This meant that music publishing was now part of Capitol Records and Capitol Records had no CEO. Who would take over was anybody's guess.

The suspense ended within a month with the appointment of someone that no one, other than EMI executives, would have known. Bhaskar Menon, native of India and a relative of famed Krishna Menon-- known as the 2nd most powerful minister in that country, (behind Nehru) was appointed Chief Executive Officer of Capitol Records. He had served EMI in India and was a well-respected executive among EMI hierarchy. Glen Wallichs held a gathering of Capitol personnel to introduce Menon and spoke highly of him and his dealings with him. He assured every one of his high qualifications for his position as President of Capitol Records. His understanding and respect for music publishing, as I was soon to learn, was another matter.

It was during this time that our second huge hit, "Put Your Hand In the Hand," was flying up the charts, following the success of "Snowbird." Central Songs was also enjoying country music chart's success as was Beechwood of Canada, the original publisher, of "Put your Hand in the Hand." In addition to that activity, Beechwood controlled the publishing of the Saturday morning children's show, "The Bugaloos." Kenny Roger's single of "Someone Who Cares," from the movie "Fools," had also entered the National charts. As none of these assets involved Capitol Records, they received no interest from Menon.

I requested a meeting with Menon to discuss a matter of importance to Music Publishing. An A&R (Artists and Repertoire) executive, whom I had a hand in recommending to Capitol, had arranged for a share of publishing for himself, from a UK based group that was being released, through his auspices, by Capitol in the U.S. I had known this producer for many years and his background in music publishing affairs. I had warned him about this activity and told him in advance to stay out of it, or I wouldn't recommend him for the position. He pledged that any available publishing would be referred to Beechwood. He, nonetheless, reverted to form by setting up his own publishing with a UK firm to avert my attention. However, I had many contacts and tracked it down.

I brought this to the attention of Menon, who to my shock was unconcerned. It was clear to me that he had little interest in music publishing, and focused his attention solely on the record company. We had little or no contact with each other again until late in May when I advised him that I would be going to New York for the BMI awards dinner. I knew that Beechwood Music was in contention for the most performed song of the year and that I had to be there. Menon routinely denied the trip. I advised him, whether he would allow it or not, I was going even if I had to pay my own way out of my pocket, which I, in fact, did. Before I departed for New York I requested another meeting. At that meeting I again brought up the matter of the producer's conflict of interest. Again he dismissed it and said. "If you controlled all of the music publishing in a record album, you would make, at most, 10 cents. Regardless of who has the publishing in an album we, as the record company will make at least one dollar. Which do you think is the most important to me?"

I replied to him that this was fuzzy thinking. "In the long run, publishing would receive income from performance, print, permissions and, most importantly, cover recordings, none of which would be available to the record company." He would have none of it. He was simply interested in generating income immediately.

I then decided to switch tactics and pointed out the value of Capitol's music publishing holdings. "Mr. Menon, the year before I arrived here I happened to know that Capitol considered selling Beechwood Music for $500,000. When I arrived I was given the mandate to build the company into a force in music publishing. To that end, we purchased a number of companies. The total cost of all these acquisitions amounted to $1.45 million.

"We have also enjoyed numerous chart successes. I would estimate that the company is now worth in the neighborhood of $3.5 million, including the original estimated $500,000. It seems to me that I have enriched Capitol's value by some $1.5millions in my 2 1/2 years." Menon scoffed at the figure and said that it was merely talk. He doubted that anyone would be willing to offer that figure. I said that he was wrong and that it was a fair market value. I further stated I could get that price, and he dared me to prove it.

The person I contacted was Al Bennett, whom I had met early on in Hollywood, and had lunched with several times. Al was originally in the automotive business but broadened his interest to music with his purchase of Liberty Records and their publishing company. He also had recently acquired the popular East/Memphis publishing company containing Otis Redding's most popular song, "Sittin' On The Dock Of The Bay," which was considered a real coup. I told him of my discussions and pitched Beechwood to him at the $3.5 million price. He said it would be tough to come up with that amount. I told him it was just an offer and doubted if they were in a position to move on it. I also told him that I thought it was worth it, considering if he was taken up on it, he would receive virtually all the "Put Your Hand In The Hand" royalties for that song, which was flying up the charts, the residue of "Snowbird" and what looked like the first single by Michael Jackson soon to be released. That single, "Got To Be There," obtained through Terry Slater's great ears and contacts, would be out imminently. Al hesitantly agreed and asked what the next step was.

Before I left for New York I learned, from close associates at Capitol, that Al Bennett had called Walter Rozett, Chief Financial Officer at Capitol. Al explained that he understood that the publishing unit of Capitol was available for an asking price of $3.5 million and that he wanted to be first to bid. Rozett was confused and called Menon relating Bennett's offer. Menon was apparently surprised and called Ed Khoury, Capitol's financial controller, whom he knew was friendly with me, but a trusted ally of Menon. To his shock Khoury said, "If Trust told you the company was worth $3.5 it's probably worth $5.0 million." With this information I departed for New York without Menon's approval and at my expense. I also realized that this must have left Menon in somewhat of a dilemma.

Upon my return from New York, Billboard headlined a story on their cover page...CAP PUTS PUB ON BLOCK; ASKS 5 MIL. To this day I have no idea where they got this information. The story went into detail citing that Beechwood had just won BMI's most performed song of 1970 award, and the impressive growth of the company in recent years. It wasn't long before I received a telephone call from Menon accusing me of planting that story. I advised him that I had nothing to do with it, and reminded him at our last meeting I quoted the value at $3.5 million.

He then remarked sarcastically, "Well, I'm sure if your services were included in the deal, it WOULD be worth $5 million!"

I was miffed and shot back with "That must be a figure you rubbed out of your magic lamp!"

After a short pause he said, "Goodbye, Mr. Trust."

I said "Goodbye, Mr. Menon." Shortly after that conversation I resigned, giving up the remaining six months' salary in my contract. I later regretted my remark, which could be taken as a racial slur, but realized in the heat of the moment I couldn't prevent it. Nevertheless, I received Christmas greetings from him for the following five years at my home address. Further, he made no attempt to retrieve the beautiful cut glass Snowbird award that I simply took home rather than leave it with Beechwood.

While I knew that it would be impossible for me to stay with that company, I also realized the difficult position I now placed on myself and my family. This would become one of the most trying times of my life...and put enormous stress on my already fragile back.

What now? After considerable thought, I knew that I couldn't be idle waiting for another job opportunity. I decided to get into music publishing on my own. Menon wasted no time in downsizing publishing at Capitol. Cliffie Stone and a number of others were terminated. Steve Stone was placed in A & R. (Artists & Repertoire) and the New York office was closed. Beechwood once again became, more or less, a holding company. It seemed that Capitol reverted to its past policy of ignoring music publishing. With that in mind, I contacted Steve who was now producing a number of Capitol artists, and proposed starting up a new publishing company, just as his dad had done with country producer Ken Nelson. Steve was also a good writer on his own. And so, with this idea in mind, Steve and I created Mandina Music/BMI and Rocksmith Music/ASCAP. Mandina was a combination of his daughter's name, Mandy, and his wife's name, Ina. Rocksmith was Rock (for Stone) and Smith. (my little known middle name).

Terry Slater called me to request I administer a catalog of songs created by Phil Everly and Terry called Bowling Green Music, named after the first hit in that catalog. It seemed that I might be administering other catalogs, so I created a corporation called Trust Music Management, Inc. I found office space in Burbank at 3817 West Olive Avenue adjacent to a very popular Taco Bell restaurant. Now that I leased office space, I had to get furnishings, telephones and a telex. (Remember those?) All of these expenses had to be paid for with my meager savings. I knew that I had to find revenue to sustain my family.

My secretary, Gina Kellogg from Beechwood, joined me even though I couldn't pay her what she had been making. The telephones had just been installed, and we were waiting for furniture to be delivered when the telephone on the floor started to ring. We looked at each other in wonder as the telephone had just been installed! Who could possibly have the number?

I answered and a voice with a heavy Australian accent asked, "Is this the office of Mandingo Music?"

I replied, "It's Mandina."

The voice then said, "Is that you Sam? I've had the deuce of a time getting ahold of you!" The caller was Frank Donlevy, general manager of Castle Music of Australia, an EMI affiliate who I dealt with at Beechwood.

I said, "I don't know how you did it; this is the first call we've received. What can I do for you?"

He said where can I send this check for $5,000?"

I said "What for?"

He replied "To make sure you don't go anywhere else in Australia." I was almost speechless. Maybe I could survive on my own.

CHAPTER 27
Seat of The Pants Survival

The office space I rented was actually a small white building with two offices and a secretary/reception area in the middle. An architect occupied the space on the left, Gina was in the middle, and I was in the office to the right. Within three months the architect decided to move. I took that opportunity to invite Cliffie Stone to take over that space. Cliffie had become a close friend and I enjoyed his company. He immediately set up a production company and publishing outlet that Trust Music Management administered.

While at Capitol I discovered a small educational band print company in Lebanon, Indiana, Studio PR, owned by Jim Houston. I helped that company grow by obtaining print rights for them for the very successful TV shows "Danny Thomas," "Dick Van Dyke," "I Spy," "Andy Griffith," and "That Girl." Earl Hagen created all of the music to those shows. Earl was also one of the most sought after instructors of film scoring in the United States. When we later resided in Calabasas Park, he became a close neighbor, just a few houses down from us. Earl was a fine golfer and Captain of the Calabasas Golf club. If an aspiring composer was accepted by Earl, his tuition was one new golf ball per lesson. Studio PR eventually became the publisher of Earl's successful book on film scoring. Jim Houston immediately put my new company on a small monthly retainer for my first year.

While at MIDEM attending EMI Music Publishing meetings for Beechwood, I had made good friends with Alain di Ricou, who represented EMI Music in France. When he visited the U.S., I was able to arrange for him to represent A&M's music publishing firms, Irving/Almo Music for France. Those companies were very hot at the time with Herb Alpert's "Tijuana Brass" as well as A&M's many other acts. I received a telex from him requesting the name of my bank as he was sending an advance of $7,500 to obtain rights for my new company's catalogs for France.

Steve Stone was now producing a number of Country acts for Capitol Records. Fittingly, one of his artists was Tennessee Ernie Ford, an artist discovered by Steve's dad, Cliffie, who not only managed him, and his successful television show, but also produced his most famous recording, "16 Tons."

Steve and Jack Hayford, wrote "Come On Down," a somewhat gospel song that Ernie liked. Steve produced it and it became a hit...the first one in Mandina and Rocksmith Music. The association with Jack Hayford would turn out to be the most important and rewarding for Steve, me, and Jack as well.

Steve had met Hayford at Life Bible College in Los Angeles, where Jack was acting dean of men. Jack told Steve that he was also a songwriter. Steve having been raised in the music business took this information with a "grain of salt," until he listened to what Jack had written and was impressed. Jack went on to become minister of the small Foursquare Church in Van Nuys, Aimee Semple Mcpherson's original church, which had dwindled down to a congregation of 14. Upon a chance meeting some time later, Jack invited Steve to visit the church. Steve, impressed with the church and Jack's stewardship, joined the congregation, as so many hundreds soon did who were attracted to Jack. Jack, and the Foursquare Church, became immensely popular and eventually had to provide four services each Sunday to accommodate the growing congregation. Jack, eventually, turned over all his musical compositions to Rocksmith Music.

Late in 1971 I received a call from Stan Catron at BMI. Stan and I had become great friends while I was at BMI and he was at South Mountain Music, a company owned by Don Costa. Later, as I was leaving BMI, I recommended Stan for a position at BMI in Writer Relations. He had just met with David Clayton Thomas, lead singer of "Blood Sweat & Tears," who was just starting his own music publishing company and needed an administrator. Stan recommended me, and suggested I call David. I met with him and signed his company to an administration agreement with Trust Music Management.

While building a clientele was encouraging, the need for steady funds was also essential to get me to the point where income earned by these clients materialized. To that end, I am forever grateful to Morty and Iris Manus, owners of Alfred Music Publishing, one of the most successful educational music print publishers in the world. They arranged a monthly retainer for my company based on obtaining print rights for future copyrights that might come under my control. My old tennis pal, Mike Tannen, Paul Simon's attorney and administrator who I had also used for some legal work, came through with a small retainer for me to supposedly exploit Paul Simon copyrights on the West Coast. I knew that I couldn't possibly justify these retainers during the time they were given, and was well aware that they were given to me more out of goodwill and fellowship than any other motive.

As 1972 approached I felt it necessary to once again attend MIDEM, the international music industry convention in Cannes, to let everyone know that I was "still alive (barely) and kickin." At the convention I firmed up alliances with independently owned publishing companies that I had been restricted from dealing with when I was part of the EMI publishing group while I was at Capitol. This was an eye opener for me. Some of these companies developed into long-term relationships. Again I was able to enjoy the company and humor of Frank Donlevy of Australia, who was one of my closest friends for many years. I also enjoyed Alain di Ricou's meetings, which developed into Franco/American golf contests both in France and during his visits to the United States. A number of good-humored insulting letters were exchanged between us through the years. But in terms of business, we always came to each other's aid.

On my way back I stopped in London to call on Jimmy Phillips, the legendary dean of British music publishing who had insisted on me buying the, now infamous, coach-horn. Jimmy noticed I was carrying a small pillow and asked what it was for. I told him of my back injury after I left his office the previous year. I was forced to carry it to insure I had lower back support when I traveled, otherwise, I'd be in trouble.

He said, "We'll fix that right away!" He went on to explain that he knew the osteopath of the Saddler-Wells Ballet Company and would arrange for an appointment immediately. He picked up his telephone and called a Dr. Naidoo to schedule an appointment, and was told that the doctor was not available. He chastised the party who had answered, advised who he was, and demanded an appointment for his friend who was in great pain. "He must see Dr. Naidoo this very day!" After a short pause an appointment was made for that afternoon. Jimmy assured me that this doctor would resolve my back problem, and wished me good luck as I left. I couldn't believe that this doctor could really relieve me of the pain, since I had been to a number of physical therapists and chiropractors in Los Angeles.

I arrived at the doctor's office, which was somewhat dark and decorated in an ornate Indian style. The doctor, a short native of India, welcomed me and asked the nature of my problem. After I explained, he asked me to undress completely. He then asked that I walk directly to him from a fireplace that was in his office, then turn around and walk back towards it.

As I was approaching the fireplace he exclaimed, "Aha, I see it." He put me on a strange upholstered table with part of the middle section lowered, placed me in a weird position then pounced on me... I heard and felt a loud crack.

He announced, "Mr. Trust, you are fixed." He said, "Sit up!" This was something I hadn't been able to do in a year and responded that I doubted I could. I tried and was shocked how easy it was. He then threw a cricket ball at me, which caused me to reach out below to catch it. No pain. I was in a state of awe and asked if he knew of anyone in the Los Angeles area who could help me if my back went out again. Regretfully, he knew of no one. Some time, much later, my back did go out and a chiropractor had to come to our house. I told him of Dr. Naidoo's magic and he was impressed. He couldn't believe that this famous and well-respected orthopedic doctor, who was apparently an idol to chiropractors, actually administered to me.

During the rest of 1972 the Mandina/Rocksmith catalog managed to have record releases of songs written by Johnny Cunningham, Bob Duncan and Steve Stone. A song written by Kelly Gordon, (co-writer of Sinatra's hit "That's Life") that we published was featured in the successful motion picture "Tender Mercies," starring Robert Duvall. In addition, David Clayton Thomas had a few of his songs released in his "Blood Sweat and Tears," album. The beginnings of usage of Jack Hayford's music from his "Majestic Praise" creation began to show up, principally, "Majesty," which was to become the most significant copyright in Rocksmith Music in later years.

It was essential that I attend all music activities during this period in order to "network" with as many music business personnel as possible. At a meeting of the California Copyright Conference I came into contact with a lawyer having a problem that I was sure I could solve. This led me to a deal that relieved most of my financial burden for the remainder of the year, and early 1973.

CHAPTER 28
Wheelin' and Dealin'

Bruce Ramer was an attorney from the prestigious law firm Gang, Tyre, and Brown that represented Capitol Records. I met Bruce while I was at Capitol and was impressed with his handling of clients. We would be in touch with each other from time to time.

I happened to be sitting next to him at this particular Copyright meeting and noticed how glum he appeared, which was unusual for Bruce who was usually very cheerful. I asked him "why the long face?" He told me he had spent most of the day with a very stubborn and difficult lawyer who was driving him crazy. I knew the lawyer as I had dealings with him and could understand. Bruce was representing the publishing interests of Johnny Rivers who was offering his catalog for sale with an asking price of one million dollars. The catalog contained some of Jimmy Webb's most important early songs, including "Up, Up And Away," and "By The Time I Get to Phoenix." At that time Webb was one of the most sought after songwriters in the world, which more than justified the asking price. Bruce explained the conditions the lawyer was demanding were ridiculous, and now he was also fishing for a lower price that was bringing the deal to a standstill.

I gave it some thought and came up with an idea. "Bruce, would you give me until Monday morning to come up with a viable candidate who would be willing to pay the million dollars?" He readily agreed. Now I had to do some scampering to deliver.

I had known Jay Morgenstern and Frank Military from my days in New York at BMI where both were employed at Tommy Valando's Sunbeam Music, a music publisher of several Broadway Musical successes. These two were practically a team. You could not talk about one without mentioning the other. Valando eventually sold his company and Morgenstern found employment on the west coast, while Military remained in New York having accepted a job at Chappell Music.

After both were employed with large companies for some time, they decided to team-up and found their own firm, Music Maximus, in association with Broadway Production Company, Lansbury/Duncan. From time to time Jay and I and our wives met socially. I was aware of Jay and Frank's start-up firm and their backing from Lansbury/Duncan. I called Jay and told him of this opportunity to put their company in the limelight with this acquisition and he agreed, but advised that he'd have to run it by Lansbury/Duncan. He called back with tentative approval, but was hesitant regarding earnings to justify the purchase to his partners. I had recently returned from MIDEM, where I had firmed up my international publishing contacts and told him that I believed I could get him close to $300,000 in foreign publisher advances which would offset the investment and act to more quickly amortize the deal. With that assurance, Jay Ok'd my setting up a meeting for them with Bruce Ramer. We agreed on a 3% finder's fee to Trust Music Management for implementing the deal, a percentage more than reasonable in such transactions.

The deal went through quickly and Bruce Ramer was grateful. However, my payment took somewhat longer to receive, due to the lack of cash flow in this new firm at the time. Eventually, as foreign advances were received, my full payment was received in increments. Those payments helped keep my company afloat while recording and performance income slowly accrued.

In early 1973 I received a telephone call from a lawyer in New York that would, once again, re-direct my career in most un-expected ways.

CHAPTER 29
Who, Me?

The call I received was from Alan Arrow, partner in a successful Music/Entertainment law firm that represented a British entertainment conglomerate's interests in the United States: ATV. (Associated Television) I had known and dealt with Alan, and representatives of his firm, both while at BMI in New York and Beechwood Music on the west coast. He called to advise me that I was on a short list of candidates to run ATV's music interests in the U.S. This was all news to me.

I was only vaguely aware of ATV, as I heard of their acquisition of the Lennon/McCartney, Northern Songs catalog off the London Stock exchange. I also remembered that Don Kirshner was representing the catalog in the U.S. in a joint venture known as ATV/Kirshner. So I was somewhat mystified by the call. Apparently, ATV did not intend to continue the joint venture and decided to set up on their own. Alan advised that two representatives of ATV, Jack Gill, Deputy Managing Director and Louis Benjamin, Chairman of Moss Empire Theaters and Pye Records, were going to be in Beverly Hills soon to interview candidates. He said he'd like to schedule a date for my interview, which we did.

When I arrived at the Beverly Hills hotel suite, both gentlemen greeted me. Louis Benjamin was somewhat short and muscular with a deep tan and nattily dressed. He spoke with the accent of a UK working man. Jack Gill was soft-spoken and smiling with, what could only be interpreted as, a gentle touch. We discussed my background in the industry and my present business, which was developing nicely. They asked what I would require as a salary. I had thought about this and suggested slightly more than double of what my contract at Capitol called for. They made no comment*. They were interested in how I would plan to grow the business and I proposed a rough outline. The meeting was pleasant and they promised to get back to me soon.

About 10 days later I received a call from London requesting I meet Sir Lew Grade, founder and CEO of ATV in London, on a designated date. ATV provided a first-class, round-trip air ticket and all expenses.

When I arrived in London, a Daimler limousine picked me up at Heathrow and delivered me to the Grosvenor House hotel facing Hyde Park. Shortly after my arrival I received a call from Louis Benjamin letting me know that he would pick me up for dinner, and afterwards a tour of some of the theaters owned by ATV (which he oversaw.)

It was a whirlwind tour, hopping from one show to another, going backstage, and meeting theater managers. The final theatre, saved for last, was the world famous London Palladium. As we exited, Louis turned me around and asked me to notice all the shining brass at the entrance. I remarked how impressive it was. He responded in a sincere tone, "As a lad it was my job to polish that brass daily. Today I manage the theater."

The next morning I was given a tour of ATV House on Great Cumberland Street, and finally met "Sir Lew." (He was soon to become Lord Grade.) He came out of his office in a white shirt with sleeves slightly rolled up and his ever-present Dunhill/Churchill cigar. He was bald, of medium height, and a package of energy. He greeted me and welcomed me to the company and asked if I had met Tony Lucas, their chief lawyer, which I had during the office tour.

He said, "Good, Good, we'll have him work up a contract." I had to advise him that I already had a publishing company and a number of administrative clients. He quickly answered, "No problem, we'll buy them."

I simply said, "They're not for sale."

He replied " Now Sam, there's always a price."

I said, "I didn't acquire these clients to deposit at your doorstep."

He thought for a second and said, "Never mind, we want you here, so figure out a way to keep them while you work here." With that he departed.

After some thought, I contacted Tony Lucas and offered what I hoped would be a solution. I proposed that I not be hired, but Trust Music Management, Inc. be retained on a three year basis to provide the services of Sam Trust as President of ATV Music for North America using the agreed upon salary as the retainer. TMM would pay me my salary. All of my existing clients would be administered through ATV Music affiliates throughout the world, though I would retain ownership. Tony submitted the proposal to Sir Lew, and he agreed. Though it took a while to finalize, (some 6 months.) I knew that Sir Lew's handshake could be taken to the bank. That formula obviously worked, as it lasted for 12 years.

The emotional highlight of my trip was yet to come. Unbeknownst to me, my trip was scheduled at the time of the annual "Tin Pan Alley Ball," celebrated by the British music publishing community and the year's top songwriters. Louis Benjamin had already purchased tickets. The banquet was held in the ballroom of a large hotel. As is the custom at such affairs, as each person or persons enters, he is announced by a spokesman in a red tuxedo, just prior to entering down a few steps to the room. The announcement blared out, "Mr. Louis Benjamin and Mr. Sam Trust."

My dear friend, Jimmy Phillips from EMI, immediately turned around and walked to the steps, came up and hugged me with, "Sam my darling, I'm so happy for you!" He then turned to Benjamin and said "Louie, you devil, you've just hired the best!"

*Some years later both Jack Gill and Louis Benjamin laughingly told me that they had expected me to ask for more.

CHAPTER 30
Setting a Foundation

Returning from the UK with the mandate to build a respectable music publishing company in North America for ATV, I had a huge project before me. It was a relief not to have to worry about supporting my family and myself, but on the other hand came the pressure to deliver success for a company that had placed such confidence in me.

My initial project was to find office space for this new company, keeping in mind the growth that I projected. The perfect candidate was 6255 Sunset Boulevard, a newly constructed many-storied building that was just completed and looking for residents. We picked out a reasonably large space at an attractive price and designed a floor plan. The location was perfectly situated for the music business. Within a short time more music companies took occupancy. These included, BMI, Motown, Screen Gems Music, Interworld Music, MetroMedia Music, The Jackson Five, and Radio & Records Magazine, to name a few. Nearby were RCA Records and Studio, Columbia Broadcasting Studios, Capitol Records, Paramount Studios, and ASCAP.

ATV had acquired in late 1969,the Beatles music publishing company Northern Songs, which included its U.S. sub-publisher Maclen Music, via intense negotiations, and somewhat circuitous deals, from the London Stock Exchange in late 1969. ATV Music Ltd. was established in London the following year to administer the rights to this catalog in the UK and throughout Europe and Africa. It was the intent to build music publishing on this foundation.

In 1970 Lew Grade had established a foothold in the U.S. by appointing Don Kirshner, a very successful music publisher and subsequent TV music host, to head the company by creating ATV-Kirshner Music. The association of these two entertainment giants did not last long and the need to establish a wholly owned U.S. subsidiary brought me into the picture.

Prior to ATV's acquisition of Northern/Maclen, Dick James, the original owner of these catalogs arranged for administration, with the exception of several songs assigned to Gil Music, an independent, and MCA Music, (which subsequently became Universal) to The Copyright Service Bureau, owned and run by Walter Hofer, a New York attorney. Hofer was assisted by his wife Sandy and another attorney, Bob Casper. While at BMI I had dealt with both Hofer and Casper. It seemed that Dick James was well served by this company. I had visited Hofer's facilities while at BMI and was impressed with the systems they had in place. Naturally, when Kirshner took over, all files were transferred to his offices. With the Kirshner termination at the end of 1972, ATV moved the files to a small interim office set up in New York, prior to my hiring. (April 1, 1973) Once again, they would now be transferred to our new west coast facilities, which would not be ready until late in May of 1973. When they finally arrived I made it a priority to check these files closely to determine all was in order, as they would be the initial backbone of this new company.

Before our move to 6255 Sunset, I was forced to interview candidates for employment at my small building in Burbank. I was fortunate to find Laurie Holland, a legal secretary, who had worked at Orenstein and Arrow's legal offices in New York before moving to Los Angeles. She was, therefore, familiar with the music business and a whirlwind typist with the ability to prioritize messages and letters that were now inundating me. Based on my experience at Beechwood, the selection for the head of our professional department was a foregone conclusion, - Steve Stone. Eventually, I would also bring in his dad, Cliffie, as I had planned for ATV to become a force in Country Music, and he would be of great influence. (In later years, Cliffie would be elected to the Country Music Hall of Fame.) I was able to find an expert on copyright licensing, and a few clerks, so that by our move-in date, we could start rolling.

When the Maclen files finally arrived we started sorting them so that some order could be established prior to coding them for easy reference, a system that had never before existed. During this process one of the clerks, Bob Sisto, who had some experience in the music business brought to my attention, something peculiar to each license. This finding turned out to be the first success for our fledgling company but would cause anger, frustration, and dismay to my former employer, Capitol Records.

CHAPTER 31
Capitol Punishment

The files that were shipped to the new ATV Music Corp. office in Hollywood contained all contracts, correspondence, and license agreements. By far the largest amount of paper in the files was mechanical licenses. At that time, 1973, the chief sources of income were mechanicals, (recorded songs), performance rights, (ASCAP & BMI), and printed editions. Mechanicals, absorbed most of the files, and probably accounted for the most income, followed closely by performance. It's useful to acknowledge that at the turn of the 20th century, the only publisher/writer income was print. In 1909, copyright law recognizing the advent of the player piano roll, included a fee of two cents per roll as the mechanical rate, and there it stood until Copyright Revision in 1976 raised it to two and three quarter cents, (effective 1/1/78) with a provision for timely review. Performing rights were meaningless until ASCAP was created in 1914, but did not pay royalties until 1920. With the invention of radio and the increase in recording technology, performing income became meaningful. The vast majority of mechanical licenses were issued by the "Harry Fox Agency", which became the convenient "one stop" source for users requiring a license to record. That agency represented virtually all music publishers at the time. The licenses issued by the Fox Agency provided usage of the recording "in perpetuity."

When Dick James authorized Walter Hofer's Copyright Service Bureau to administer Northern Songs' U.S. sub-publishers, Maclen Music and Comet Music, he either, knowingly or unknowingly, allowed that agency to issue mechanical licenses directly. (not using the Fox Agency) It was during our examination of the files that Bob Sisto brought a Copyright Service Bureau mechanical license to my attention. He said it looked different from the licenses he was used to seeing. As I examined it, I could hardly believe what I was reading. Each license provided for a term of 5 years, not the usual "perpetuity." This meant that virtually every license issued on behalf of the BEATLES from as late as 1967 and subject to sales thereafter had expired. Capitol Records was, therefore, distributing un-licensed recordings. I knew the penalty for distributed un-licensed recordings was severe, so to be absolutely sure of our findings I called the Orenstein/Arrow law firm, who represented us at the time, for verification. I even couriered copies of licenses to them as a validation.

After receiving confirmation I telephoned Charles Tillinghast, an attorney I had worked with at Capitol, to advise him of the situation and the action that I intended to take. He was dumbfounded and advised that I back off. I told him that we were serious and to get ready. I did a rough total of the back income that I expected, including invalidating Capitol's policy of "controlled composition" rates.

Recording companies were now insisting on paying a maximum of 20 cents for mechanicals in albums, meaning if there were more than ten selections in an album, each composition was pro-rated so that the maximum payment was held to twenty cents. That caper was called "controlled compositions." On counsel's advice, I added six percent imputed interest, as well. I then gave them a deadline, which they missed, and demanded that the six percent be added for the lateness. Needless to say, they were furious but had no recourse but to pay. After about five months, Tillinghast called to inform me that a courier was on the way to my office. The package included a final statement and a check for $1.4 million. I forwarded the payment on to a delighted Sir Lew Grade.

It was never my intention to seek vengeance from Capitol Records for my unhappy experience at that company. I was merely doing my best for my new company. However, afterwards it did seem to me that the old saying, "Whatever goes around, comes around" was true. I had warned Bob Karp that his licensing department was a mess. AND, I tried to impress upon Mr. Menon the importance of music publishing. I freely admit to some afterglow.

CHAPTER 32
Ready, Set...?

Starting a company from scratch, and being looked upon only as the U.S. outlet for The Beatles, was an un-anticipated challenge. It was far different from starting out with an existing American company and a recently acquired hot country catalog, which allowed me to get chart activity shortly out of the gate at Beechwood Music. While it was my mission to build a new U.S. company, we had no writers as yet, only the Lennon/McCartney catalog, and the promise of McCartney's and Lennon's new single artist status at one half the royalty rate enjoyed by Northern and Maclen's publishing companies when they were Beatles.

Some explanation is needed to understand the differences in the music industry between Europe and the U.S. In European territories there is only one performing rights organization in each country. For examples, GEMA for Germany, SACEM for France and PRS for Great Britain. Mostly, as a result of anti-trust regulations, there are two dominant performing rights in the U.S, ASCAP and BMI. To a lesser degree, particularly at that time, there also existed SESAC. (a much smaller independently owned organization) Publishers in foreign performing rights societies have the right to choose which U.S. organization to represent their sub-publishing company. Dick James, owner of Lennon/McCartney songs at the time, acknowledging BMI's double payment for foreign copyrights, chose that organization for his Maclen sub-publisher. As a result of ASCAP urging, he decided to test the ASCAP royalty system by acquiring an ASCAP publisher, rather than assigning sub-publishing to an American ASCAP publisher. The songs for the test would be in the Beatles next release in November of 1967, "Magical Mystery Tour." The ASCAP Company he acquired was Comet Music, (their BMI affiliate was Sweco Music) from Cookie Gale, a diminutive, longtime New York music publisher, not to be confused with Juggy Gayle, also a veteran New York music publisher. All songs for that release were placed in that company.

After comparing the results of the ASCAP credits, James was

dissatisfied, and returned his further publishing to Maclen Music at BMI. However, as a result of Comet acquisition, several important U.S. copyrights were acquired, that had been successes for Nat King Cole, "Ramblin' Rose," in Comet's BMI affiliated company, Sweco, and "Those Lazy, Hazy, Crazy, Days of Summer," in Comet. These two songs were to become ATV's initial efforts in the U.S. market, as well as exploitation of Beatle copyrights for the now defunct foursome. Time would be needed to develop U.S. writers.

Pye Records, in the UK, was owned by ATV well before there were any thoughts of acquiring a music publishing company, and enjoyed periods of great success. When publishing of songs they recorded became available, they were placed in their own publishing outlet, Welbeck Music, and as there was no ATV owned music company in the United States during that time, sub-publishing, for the most part, was assigned by Welbeck, to MCA Music for the U.S., chaired by Sal Chiantia. We therefore acquired no benefit, other than the use of the name Welbeck for our new ASCAP affiliation.

Louis Benjamin was the CEO of Pye, as well as the Stoll/Moss Empire Theaters, and took great pride in his Record Division. He was very select in his choices of Record companies designated to release Pye's recordings in the U. S., but seemed never really satisfied with the job that any of them did on behalf of Pye. Unbeknownst to me, he had the idea of making our new ATV Company a "stalking horse," for a fully owned record releasing company in the U.S. Entering the Record Business was the last thing I had in mind and knew I was nowhere qualified to run one. I declined this idea to Louis, but he was insistent and promised to support the proposed company.

ATV Music Ltd. was the initial music publishing company established in London in 1970, shortly after the Northern Songs acquisition. By the time we were setting up in the U.S., they were well established and looking to us for exploitation of their own artist/writers, at the time, principally Lynsey DePaul and Barry Blue.

In retrospect, it seems inevitable that it would take more time than I was anticipating to develop a successful American music publishing entity under these conditions. Nevertheless, I suffered frustration from what I considered to be too long a period of being "cold" in the market.

As 1974 began for our fledgling company, I could look back on the short first year as only getting organized. As yet, other than Cliffie Stone and a young Steve Love in our New York office, we had not put together a professional staff. Steve Stone would not join ATV until later in the year. Before my arrival, Alan Arrow, the lawyer who had contacted me regarding the job at ATV, employed Love in the New York office. It was only then that I realized Alan had been representing ATV's interests, particularly Pye Records, for a number of years. Alan, had, in fact, pretty much set up the New York office well before my arrival. Through a settlement deal with John Lennon, ATV Music provided a space within their offices for Lennon.

When I first visited the New York office to meet my already existing staff, I was surprised to also meet a lovely, smiling Asian girl working in the office as well, May (Mae) Pang. It was explained to me that she was looking after John Lennon's material. I was later to learn that Yoko Ono, who was at that time, separated from John, had placed May there. Even more surprising was the fact that John and Maywere a romantic item, seemingly with Yoko's blessings. Sometime later I was to meet John and be in contact with him regarding ideas for the placement of some of his songs.

Meanwhile, back in Hollywood my main focus, in addition to seeking songwriters, would be establishing a record company, at Louis Benjamin's semi-command.

While I knew I had to come up with recording artists, I felt that this could be turned into an opportunity to release music for which we also controlled the publishing. I wasn't about to challenge the major record companies so my plan was to carve out a niche segment in the market. With an asset like Cliffie Stone as part of our company, I decided to play on his proven record as a producer, and release Country records as a starter. Production costs for Country music were far less than for pop, or Rock and Roll, and as yet we had not received funding from Benjamin.

Almost simultaneously, I heard a writer in Cliffie's office singing one of his songs entitled, "I'm Gonna Sing My Song." As his office was adjacent to mine, it was quite distinct. I went over to his office and met the writer, Ron Fraser. I was so impressed that I offered to sign him immediately. At that time one of the hottest writer/artists in the industry was John Denver, who was managed and produced by my close friend, Milt Okun. This song and several others I listened to were perfect for Denver. I arranged for Milt to listen to some of the songs for John. While he was polite and recognized Ron's talent, nothing really materialized. I don't doubt the fact that Milt controlled all the publishing for Denver, and wouldn't for Ron, also played into his thinking. So, with that in mind, Cliffie and I decided to produce Ron Fraser as the first artist on our new label, Granite Records. The album title was "I'm Gonna Sing My Song." While the album only touched the bottom of the charts, a single, "San Susanna Lullaby," written by Ron,

Curtis Stone, and Joe Henry did fairly well in the country charts. Interestingly, Joe Henry, a fine poet and literary writer, who became a good friend while I was working out of Burbank, also became a very close friend of John Denver and co-wrote some thirty songs with him.

Knowing I lacked record experience, I shopped for knowledgeable executives from that industry. With some help from my buddy, Eddie Ray, who I met at Capitol, we retained Sol Greenberg from MGM Records to oversee the operation, Frank Leffel who had loads of experience at Mercury Records in Country music promotion and distribution, and an independent promotion man, Del Roy. The major problem for us, of course, was that we were new to the industry that had a built-in "show me" attitude. If you didn't come in with an immediate hit or a name act, getting paid was a problem. To add to the problem, Mickey Goldsen, a longtime respected West Coast music publisher, notified me that he owned the name "Granite," which he used from time to time for recordings. Mickey was the original music publisher for Capitol Records. When he left that label, Glen Wallichs gave him "Dream" and a number of other hit songs he was associated with to start his company, Criterion Music. Knowing the jam I was in, Mickey simply allowed us to continue, another example of courtesy among fellow music publishers.

At the same time, with the lack of our own writers, we continued pushing Lennon/McCartney material and were lucky enough to come up with a top ten recording of "You Won't See Me" by Anne Murray, and a follow-up with "Daytripper."

With one Granite release under our belt, I decided to stay with Country Music. Tex Williams was available for Cliffie to produce with a minimum budget. Tex was a relatively known commodity with a past hit record of "Smoke, Smoke, Smoke That Cigarette" to his credit. We produced a somewhat upbeat album titled "Those Lazy, Hazy, Crazy Days of Summer." In the album was also "Ramblin' Rose." Both of these songs were part of the Comet/Sweco catalog that Dick James had purchased for his experiment with ASCAP. The album had modest success and "Ramblin' Rose" did fairly well in the country charts. As I now had three full-time employees for Granite Records for which I hadn't budgeted, I once again sought financial support from Louis Benjamin, and received no response. It became evident what my next move must be.

CHAPTER 33
Introspection

1974, my first full year heading the new ATV Music Corp ended with a thud. To say I was disappointed is an understatement. My forced entry into record production thus far, brought no joy and took away time and energy from finding quality writers. To make matters worse, it became clear that no financial support would be forthcoming from Benjamin unless we produced record hits, which was unlikely without some funding.

Adding to my misery was the apparent success being enjoyed by ATV Music Ltd. in the UK. I say apparent, since I knew most of the widespread PR regarding them was the result of their sub-publishing representation of successful U.S. writers: Neil Diamond, John Denver and others. I was later to learn that the deals they offered were a great attraction to these successful artists and publishers. Nevertheless they were getting the notoriety, and as far as we were concerned, we were "dead in the water." I also had the distinct impression that we were thought of by them, and others, as merely an extension of ATV Music Ltd., the lead company.

In December we were finally able to bring aboard Steve Stone, whose song savvy I respected, and a young Steve Love from, the New York office, to the West Coast. Love would serve as our youthful ears as he had just turned 20. We also opened a small Nashville office and an outlet in Canada, as I was determined to diversify our song publishing to many areas. So far, though, other than straightening out our administration, we had nothing to point to.

Joan and I had invited her parents, who had moved to the West Coast, to visit us for the Christmas holidays. I was not in the merriest of moods and it showed. So, after Christmas we decided to get away for a short stay at our favorite location, Carmel. Joan's parents volunteered to stay with our children. They knew that I needed a change of scenery.

We booked the best room at The Pine Inn, oddly enough called the Tennessee Ernie Suite, and arrived early in the afternoon of New Year's

Eve. I had only recently taken up golf so I brought my clubs. We heard of a great course in Pacific Grove, which purported to be the closest thing to a Scottish links course in America. So, despite a chilly and windy afternoon we decided to try it. Joan, not yet a golfer, decided to tag along. Steve Stone's wife, Ina (remember Mandina Music) knew I was into golf, and knitted a funny, woolen putter head-cover that had ears on it that I kept in my bag. Before leaving for golf we booked our New Years Eve dinner at a wonderful restaurant so we were all set. I was sure to break out of my funk.

Joan had also begun taking golf lessons and was wearing a windbreaker with her golf glove in one of its pockets though she wasn't actually playing. I was using a pull cart and from time to time would ask her to bring me a club, such as a putter when I reached a green. It was getting cold, so Joan reached into her pocket and found her glove, for her left hand. In order for her to put on the glove she had to remove her engagement ring.

At times when she got me my putter, she'd put the fuzzy head-cover in her pocket. After a pleasant nine holes we drove back to the hotel to get ready for our New Year's Eve Dinner. While getting ready, Joan noticed that she wasn't wearing her ring, and remembered that she had put it in the pocket of her windbreaker, so she went out to the car to retrieve it. She returned empty handed and confused. We went over everything we had done when she suddenly remembered that she had put the fuzzy putter head-cover in the same pocket. When she would return the cover to the putter...along went the ring somewhere on that golf course. We immediately called the course and advised them. No luck. We had no time to go back because of our reservations, so we proceeded to the restaurant where we were seated by the bay window. We were both downcast by our situation and not in the mood for chitchat, when a smiling waiter came by, poured us a glass of champagne and wished us a Happy New Year. What a year we had gone through, and now the loss of her ring! We lifted our glasses, and I don't know what happened, but I started laughing and couldn't stop, which caused Joan to start laughing, as well.

I said, "Forget the ring. I'll get you a bigger and better one. Next year things are going to turn around! I'm determined."

That was a pivotal point in my career, as it turned out. Success slowly, but regularly followed.

CHAPTER 34
Gaining Traction

Early in 1975, a song by one of our new ATV writers, Harry Shannon, hit the top 100 charts. "The Other Woman" recorded by Vicki Lawrence, who played "Mama" on the Carol Burnett TV show, broke the ice for us. Though it only reached 81, it was a start.

The following year Harry Shannon also scored a number one single in the country charts with a song entitled "Cowboy" co-written with Ron Fraser and recorded by Eddy Arnold. Our confidence in Fraser, though not fulfilled on Granite Records, started to payoff.

Late in 1974, with the help of Charlie Williams of our Nashville office, we purchased Bobby Bare's Return Music catalog for a very reasonable price. Contained in that catalog was an exclusive writer's contract for Billy Joe Shaver, who was just then coming to the attention of country music fans. He was soon to be recognized as a leader in the "outlaw" movement in country music along with Willy Nelson, Waylon Jennings and Kris Kristofferson. Recordings of Shaver's songs were becoming more frequent and he was, himself, beginning to enjoy a recording career. His songs were and are unique. I can probably recite the lyrics to his songs more readily than from other writers.

I can never forget an experience I had while sitting with Billy and Charlie Williams, a successful writer who was running our Nashville office at the time. Charlie was holding his guitar while writing a song about a rodeo rider's wife entitled, "When He's Got Time." The hook to the song was, "but he loves me, when he's got time."

In frustration, Charlie yelled out, "Damn, Billy, I just can't get a line to describe the rodeo rider!"

Billy was sitting in a chair leaning against the wall, wearing his cowboy hat and chewing on a long piece of straw-grass.

After a few moments he said, "How 'bout... eight seconds wrapped 'round four-legged thunder?"

I stopped everything I was doing, and gasped in awe. This was pure poetic genius, from a writer who never got past the eighth grade in public school.

His song titles, alone, tempted you to listen: "Black Rose," "Jesus Was Our Savior And Cotton Was Our King," "I Been To Georgia On A Fast Train," and "Old Five And Dimers Like Me."

Income from that catalog began to appear and increase.

Three more recordings were scheduled to be released by Granite, but I was determined to trim the costs and try to benefit from a publishing perspective.

Earlier in the year we signed Edwin Starr to a writer's contract. Starr had a successful career at Motown Records topped off by his huge hit "War," featuring him with "The Temptations." It had been a few years since his last hit, so he was available as a writer.

When we signed him he became the first black writer/artist in ATV Music. It was a much-needed diversification. I decided, as he was a successful artist on Motown and other labels, to release an Edwin Starr album with his songs on Granite. Though the album, "Free To Be Myself," was well reviewed, it didn't achieve the success we had hoped for. It did, however, bring attention to Edwin who ultimately produced a new and very successful album a few years later on 20th Century Records. Two hits came out of that album. "Contact," which was a disco and R & B hit worldwide, and "H.A.P.P.Y RADIO," almost its equal. Those records recouped our writer advance payments, costs of the Granite recording, and returned a sizable profit to us.

Granite's second release was an album by Lowell Fulson, a longtime blues singer with hit records to his credit such as "Every Day I Have The Blues," "Three O'clock Blues," and "Reconsider Baby." It's interesting to note that Ray Charles got his start with Fulson's band. Lowell was considered somewhat of a "blues," legend in the music industry. Our Granite release was entitled "The Ol' Blues Singer," and did moderately well. We had a modest hit in the R & B charts with "Do You Love Me." This was an inexpensive album and we sub-licensed it to a U.K. company for release, thereby recovering most of our expense. I got to know Lowell quite well, attended several of his play dates and got to meet his family. It was a great personal experience for me.

Our final Granite release was a result of Cliffie's association with the famous Western group "The Sons Of The Pioneers." I grew up listening to their fine harmonies with the "standards" they created such as "Cool Water," and "Tumbling Tumbleweeds." Cliffie was a neighbor of Roy and Dale Rogers. Roy had created the "Sons Of The Pioneers" in 1933. I had met and dealt with Tim Spencer, one of the originals of the group and long-time member, when I was at BMI. Tim owned the publishing rights to the inspirational standard "How Great Thou Art." Each year Tim would arrive in New York and we'd negotiate an advance for that song as well as his catalog, Manna Music. Rapport between slow talking Tim in his high boots and cowboy hat, and me with my quick patter and "Manhattan" appearance should not have existed, but we got along famously. Roy Rogers and Tim comprised two of the original trio of the "Sons," which subsequently expanded. Later, as a music publisher, I would deal with Tim's son, Hal, who took over the company, Manna Music. Hal was very helpful in educating me in that market. While I had great hopes for "The Sons Of The Pioneers" album, the demand was simply not there. Nashville had done a great job of eliminating "Western" from what was formerly known as "Country and Western" music. Thus ended my ill-fated experience in the Record Industry. From here on it was going to be nothing but Music Publishing.

CHAPTER 35
Arigato

As 1975 ended and the following year commenced, my confidence in the progress of ATV Music Corp. grew. Recordings were underway and I had convinced the powers in the UK that operating under a 15% management fee of Maclen revenue could not meet our financial needs for growth. While we were successful in obtaining charted cover recordings of Maclen songs with Anne Murray, and Blood Sweat and Tears, as well as other groups, they could not replace the sales of the now non-existent Beatles. I kept my eyes open for acquisitions that would be accretive to ATV.

During that time a number of interesting incidents took place that made a lasting impression on me. While flying to Cannes for the 1976 MIDEM convention, Ivan Mogull, a well-known independent music publisher whom I knew for many years, approached me to advise that Shooichi (Shoo) Kusano, the popular owner of Shinko Music, the Japanese sub-publisher of Northern Songs was on the same plane. As Ivan knew Shoo quite well, he offered to introduce me. Shoo was pleased to meet with me, and it was evident that we were to get along fine. Shoo asked if I was ever in Japan. My response brought out a story going back to my student days at Cincinnati Conservatory of Music, and my time in the Navy.

While at the conservatory, it was necessary for me to have a number of jobs, including working full-time during holidays and vacations, to help pay my way. During Christmas holidays I played church services and carols then proceeded to the Post office to sort holiday mail from midnight until 8:AM. Few students remained at the dormitory during the holidays. However, a Japanese student named Yoshi Ogawa, a short, stocky, somewhat introverted violinist was always there. I befriended him, as I realized he was a loner. We'd have dinner together, sometimes at a Japanese restaurant, where I'd observe how he handled his food, particularly with his chopsticks.

During my senior year Doctor Naylor, Dean of the Conservatory,

107

surprisingly, granted me a tuition free scholarship. Naylor had become aware that I had put together a "touch" football team of Conservatory students and also organized a basketball team. We'd play University of Cincinnati students, as well games between dorm and non-dorm students. The touch football games became very intense and we'd play regardless of the weather. Unbeknownst to me, Dr. Naylor was aware and thought this to be a healthy diversion for students, hence the scholarship.

When the vacation was over I invited Yoshi to join us for a football game. Yoshi knew little of the game but could run like the wind. We taught him the basics and put him in the backfield for a few games. To our delight he ran for a touchdown in a game. From then on he was known as "Crazy Legs Ogawa."

Yoshi came to think of me as a close friend. At the end of my senior year, knowing that I soon would be drafted into the army, Yoshi said, that if I were ever to have duty in Japan to let him know so that he could advise his parents, who would be happy to host me.

As it turned out, I was drafted into the Navy, and in 1956 found myself on the way to Japan aboard the U.S.S. Yorktown aircraft carrier. I remembered Yoshi's offer and wrote him while at sea giving him an estimate of the time we would dock. His reply came in plenty of time, complete with traveling instructions and a map of where to go after exiting the train at his home in Motoyowata, a small village in the Ishakawa prefecture. I departed the Yorktown early on a Friday with a weekend liberty pass. I had packed a small bag with some civies (a Hawaiian shirt and slacks that I picked up at Pearl Harbor) but traveled in my dress white uniform. I received some strange stares from the Japanese travelers on the train. When I arrived I followed Yoshi's map to my first designated stop, a Shell gas station, where the owner was to give me more specific instructions to Yoshi's home. I arrived at the station and announced who I was and that I wished for instructions to Ichiro Ogawa's residence. Ichiro was Yoshi's father's name. The attendant looked at me strangely, so I repeated the request with no response other than a questioned look. I was getting desperate, so I stretched out my left arm and pretended to be bowing with my right slowly pronouncing I-chir-o. The light finally came on with an "Ah, so!" He hurriedly brought out a motor scooter, tapped the backseat pad for me to get on, and we were away! It was a fast, circuitous ride through dirt streets, which I could never have figured for myself. Now I knew why Yoshi sent me to the station.

I arrived at the house and knocked on the door, which was opened by a lovely small woman dressed in a beautiful kimono. She was all smiles, but held up her hand for me to wait. She rushed back with a letter in her hand pointing to it saying "Yoshi, Yoshi," obviously expressing that she was expecting me. She spoke no English but gestured for me to come in and led me to a parlor where six little girls, also dressed in kimonos sat in a row. The room was a piano studio where she was giving lessons. Mrs. Ogawa introduced each girl to me in Japanese after which each came to the piano and played a short piece and bowed. After the little girls departed, she motioned to me to follow her to a beautiful garden in front of the house, which had a small pond with colorful koi fish. I made gestures showing my admiration as we walked about the garden. At one point she repeated "Dozo, Dozo," (Please, Please) pointing to some small divots in the garden. She made some golf-like swinging motions saying "Mr. Ogawa!" I later saw some pictures on the wall of Mr. Ogawa swinging a golf club, and trophies indicating his prowess.

She then excused herself to make some telephone calls after serving me some tea.

The calls shortly brought Mr. Ogawa and another gentleman who spoke very articulate English with a British accent. It turned out that he was Oxford educated. He was brought to the house to interpret our conversations as Mr. Ogawa spoke no English. He subsequently advised me that a young lady from Tokyo Christian College, who spoke English, would soon arrive and stay for the weekend to assist us. She was Miss Ono, a tall slender girl unlike most Japanese women. I later learned that she was from Okinawa, which seemed to produce taller women than in Japan. Miss Ono was very helpful, not only to me and Mr. Ogawa, but to Mrs. Ogawa by helping her prepare our evening dinner, which was served in traditional Japanese style, sitting on the floor with our feet resting in a square opening beneath us. The home was a model of traditional Japanese. There was almost no furniture on the matted floor, with sliding paneled doors between rooms. The simplicity was beautiful.

After dinner Mr. Ogawa and I adjourned to another area. I learned that not only was he a violinist, but also a busy music editor. He then brought out an invention of his that he hoped to patent and have manufactured. It appeared to be only a baby rattle, but as you turned your hand to the right, the bell inside would produce a music note one step higher, to the left a note lower. In time you could figure out intervals by the length you turned your hand. I thought it fantastic. I handed it back to him, and he played a musical passage and looked at me inquiringly. I identified it as Beethoven's theme to his symphony number three, "The Eroica." He handed it back to me with a motion for me to play one. I played Brahms' "Academic Festival" overture, which he identified immediately and the game was on!

After a traditional bath it was off to bed. A rice mattress was placed on the floor and I was given a quilted kimono plus a blanket. It was a wonderful sleep and I awoke to a hot breakfast served again in Japanese style, but with ham and eggs. Mrs. Ogawa and Miss Ono presided.

Mr. Ogawa planned a tour of Tokyo for the afternoon, which included a meal in a restaurant in the famous Ginza district. Somehow, despite the language problem, we managed to speak to each other. The tour was a treat and I learned so much about Japan. I felt a bond had grown between Mr. Ogawa and me. That proved to be evident the next morning when I departed.

Before leaving for the train station the next morning Mrs. Ogawa presented me with a kimono, which I have to this day. Before I put it on, Mr. Ogawa motioned to me to wait and watch Mrs. Ogawa, who was intensely working on what looked like a tiny black ball. Suddenly, she hurled it out with one hand while holding a spool of thread in the other. I picked it up and saw that it was a meticulously threaded black sash to be used for the Kimono. I was amazed.

Mr. Ogawa then drove me to the train station. In Japanese train stations friends can accompany passengers to their train and stand outside their compartments to chat with them before departure. Mr. Ogawa stood next to my open window as I expressed my thanks and he nodded acknowledgement. There was a brief moment before departure when nothing was said as we looked at each other. I saw tears come to his eyes as I became too choked to speak. We both smiled as the train pulled away.

When I finished relating this story to Shoo Kusano, he was silent for a while. He turned to me and said: "Sam, Ichiro Ogawa and my father founded my company, Shinko Music. Mr. Ogawa passed away, but we still send a share of our profits to Mrs. Ogawa and Yoshi." We were both amazed that the one person I knew in Japan tied us together. We were not, at that time, to realize how close the friendship between our families would come to be.

CHAPTER 36
Not Easy Getting Green

In July of 1976 we decided to take a summer family vacation, at what was becoming our refuge from Hollywood, the Monterey Peninsula. This time we booked rooms in Pacific Grove near the beach. Not long after we arrived, I received a telephone call from New York from a woman with a soft, wispy voice, who introduced herself as Yoko Ono, asking if she was speaking to Sam Trust. I assured her she was, and she explained that John Lennon asked her to call me to request some assistance. She explained that John's final trial regarding his request for a "green card" was being held on the following Monday morning and he wanted me to be his witness from the music business. I asked why me, since he could have chosen any luminary from the industry? She said she didn't know, and had questioned him as well. He was insistent on me. I received the call on a Saturday and was expected to be present at the hearing in New York on Monday at 9:AM. We hurriedly packed and headed back to Los Angeles.

Not long after we arrived home I received a telephone call from John's attorney, Leon Wildes, expressing the importance of my appearance. He insisted on meeting on me as soon as possible when I got to New York so he could brief me. I gave him my flight schedule and arranged to meet him upon my arrival. Unfortunately, not long after takeoff, actually over Palm Springs, an engine blew out and we were forced to return to Los Angeles. After several hours delay, we boarded another plane and finally landed in New York after midnight.

When I arrived at my hotel there were messages from Leon Wildes asking me to call him back regardless of the hour. I returned the call and found that he was very upset. He insisted on meeting me at 7:30 the next morning. When I arrived at the lobby that morning I found a man nervously pacing. I approached him and asked if he was Wildes. He looked at me shocked, and asked if I was Sam Trust. I assured him I was. He seemed surprised and said he expected a short, bald man smoking a cigar. I asked if that was his impression of a music publisher,

111

and he was somewhat embarrassed. We went to the restaurant for some coffee where he stated how important my testimony would be. He said Yoko had selected all the witnesses but me, who John had chosen. He gave me the impression that he had no confidence in her selections as they had no idea of the music industry and he wasn't sure who even knew, or had met John. After some questioning and advice he left. Shortly afterwards I headed downtown to the courthouse.

This trial had been going on for some four years, originating from Richard Nixon's demand to have Lennon deported back to Great Britain. It had now been remanded back to the immigration department from the Court of Appeals the previous October. This was to be the final trial to determine, once and for all, John's green card status.

The witnesses chosen by Yoko were Gloria Swanson, Norman Mailer, Geraldo Rivera and the noted sculptor Noguchi. Mailer sat next to me grumbling about the situation before anyone of us testified.

Gloria Swanson was the first. She and her husband had met Yoko and John in a health food store and was happy that he was eating healthy foods and could be an example for good eating to New York's youth. Attorney Wildes looked my way and rolled his eyes. The sculptor Noguchi said he had never met John, but had sculpted a table for Yoko and was happy that she had such a good artistic influence on John. Next came Mailer who called John a great artist and complained about the treatment of creative people by the United States government causing great artists such as T.S. Elliot to leave. I was the last to be called. The state's attorney asked how I knew John. I explained our business relationship. He then asked if it was a good relationship. I responded that it was, giving a recent example of John calling me to discuss possible artists who could "cover" songs from his latest album.

He then asked, "Why should we grant John a green card?" I looked at him with a smile and said for one great reason. "The music industry at this time is in the doldrums. A writer/artist such as John has the ability to turn it around with a hit record. Would you rather have the worldwide revenue from a hit recording sent to London or New York?" I can swear I saw Wildes hint at throwing me a kiss. The judge then dismissed me, paused and gave a short summation ending with: he "saw no reason to not grant John Lennon a green card."

The packed courtroom broke into immediate applause as John, dressed in a black suit and tie, hurried over to me thanking me over and over, saying "I owe you, I owe you, what can I get you? Maybe a car?"

I told him he owed me nothing. "As his publisher it was my pleasure." He said he must give me something. To end it, I said, "Okay, when you finish your next album, write a note on it to my daughter Jenny and one for my son, Ben. He said, "That's it?" I replied that's more than enough. Yoko stood by saying nothing. Unfortunately, that was the last conversation I ever had with John. Every subsequent effort I made to talk to John was intercepted by Yoko, explaining that she spoke for John."

Several months later I received two copies of John's next album, "Shaved Fish," with greetings and a drawing by John of himself for Jenny and Ben. Below his signature, in green ink, was a flower and Yoko Ono's autograph.

CHAPTER 37
Steppin' Up To The Plate

Toward the end of 1976 an opportunity presented itself, which I simply could not pass up. I was approached by Bobby Roberts, who was acting as an agent for the writing team of Barry Mann and Cynthia Weill, two of America's top songwriters. I had known Roberts from his various jobs in the entertainment industry and, of course, Barry and Cynthia from the time I sat at their table for my first BMI awards dinner in 1962. At that time they were exclusive writers to Aldon Music, a successful publishing company owned by Don Kirshner and Al Nevins. Not long afterwards the company was sold to Columbia Pictures forming the hugely successful Screen-Gems/Columbia Music Corp. Shortly after the formation of that company Lester Sill became CEO and steered it to become one of the top music publishers in the world, with writers such as Mann and Weill, Carole King, Ellie Greenwich, Gerry Goffin, and many others.

Mann and Weill's contract was to expire as of September 30th of that year. The amount Roberts was asking was quite substantial, $750,000 to be paid over five years.

As these writers were having a recent "cold" period, some may have thought their best years were behind them. As Lester and I were close friends, I told Roberts that I wouldn't consider the deal without Lester's having the final word.

I called him and asked why he wasn't renewing them. He said that he wasn't going to be put in the position of having to pay such a huge advance. I said, "Lester, you're being foolish. You have all of their past songs which, alone, would earn the advance back." Barry and Cynthia wrote "You Lost That Loving Feeling," " Soul And Inspiration," had co-written "On Broadway" plus so many past rock and roll hits, I thought it a "no brainer" to renew the deal despite the advance. I told him if he wasn't going to sign them, I would.

He said, "Go ahead, Sammy." I told him he was nuts and hung up.

As time went by, we hammered out the deal. (which raised doubts of the many "experts" in the industry) On September 30th, with the deal ready to be signed the next day, I telephoned Lester and told him it was his last chance, and chastised him again. He wouldn't budge. We signed the deal the next day.

This was to be the biggest deal I had thus far engineered for ATV, putting my reputation on the line. I had two reasons for pursuing this deal. The first was to offset ATV being looked upon as a Lennon/McCartney company. We would now have bona-fide U. S. and worldwide respected writers. The second, after spending some time with Barry, I knew that he was obsessed with getting back to being a hit writer, and I was willing to bet on it.

While Barry and Cynthia didn't start firing out of the box, eventually the hits began to evolve. The biggest success was, within the following year when Barry teamed up with recording artist Dan Hill to co-write Dan's biggest worldwide hit, "Sometimes When We Touch." A few years later Barry and Cynthia came up with "Just Once," recorded by James Ingram. Both of these songs became major hit records and have similar interesting stories behind them.

Dan Hill is a Canadian writer/artist whose rights we acquired from our fledgling Canadian company, ATV Music, Canada. I had appointed a lawyer, Bernard Solomon, to represent the company in its early days. Solomon negotiated the worldwide publishing rights to Dan's songs on a co-publishing basis. Twentieth Century Records released his product in the U.S. Though Dan was quite popular in Canada, his poetic lyrics didn't relate to the U. S. market. Sales in the U.S., in fact, were abysmal.

Twentieth Century Records' CEO at that time was Russ Regan, who I knew to be a "song man." We, in fact had similar tastes, but I knew that Russ was about to give up on Dan. While Dan's lyrics were quite poetic, he simply couldn't come up with a memorable melody, let alone a "hook." I decided that it was time for me to take a trip to Canada to meet with Dan and his "three Bernies."

Bernie Solomon, our representative in Canada, had negotiated our original deal with Dan's representatives, Bernie Fiedler, his agent, and Bernie Finkelstein, his manager. Both of these two "Bernies" insisted that Dan wait outside our meeting, in the lobby, until an agreement on further action regarding Dan's future was agreed upon. My unrelenting position was that Dan needed a co-writer to achieve success outside of Canada. Both Fiedler and Finkelstein strenuously objected. They stressed that Dan was a true artist and poet, who might well be considered as poet laureate of Canada. My feeling was they simply didn't want to water down his share of income.

The discussion became so heated that I shouted, "Let's see what Dan thinks." I stood up, went out the door and dragged Dan into our meeting room.

The Bernies were somewhat in shock, while I immediately asked Dan how he would like to work with Barry Mann and/or Cynthia Weill. Dan's eyes opened wide, and he said, "Do you really mean the famous Barry and Cynthia?" I assured him I did. He was overwhelmed by the offer and quickly consented, much to the dismay of the Bernies. I advised him that we'd arrange for a trip the very next week. He was overjoyed. When he left the room the Bernies were furious, but had no alternative. I had contacted Barry and asked him to be at our offices when Dan was scheduled to arrive. When Dan did arrive, he showed me a piece of paper with some lyrics on it that he had been working on. The lyrics implied an ambivalent love affair. I called Barry into the office, introduced him to Dan, and asked him to take a crack at it with Dan in our demo studio. I could only hope for the best and went back to my work.

In what seemed to be less than an hour later, Steve Stone, our most studio adept executive, came into my office and said, "Sam you'd better come to the studio and listen to this." Lindsey Davidson, our studio engineer set up the tape to the demo and, to my surprise, listened to the performance of "Sometimes When We Touch" sung by Barry, not Dan. I was blown away and asked Steve to roundup every female in the office and bring them to the studio for another playback. We packed the control room. When the demo was over, almost every girl had tears in her eyes, or were close to it.

I called Russ Regan at Twentieth Century Records and told him we had just finished demoing, what should be Dan's next single, and I was couriering it over right away. I asked him to call me as soon as he heard it. He called me after he listened to it and was just as impressed. "You got it, Sam! I think it's a smash!"

As they say, the rest is history, but with one side note I must acknowledge. As the song rose up the charts, Dan went on tour and Barry accompanied him. When the tour reached Edmonton in Canada, I was persuaded to attend, (with the Bernies) despite the weather at 28 degrees below zero. It was a packed house that cheered Dan's every performance. The highlight of the evening came when he announced "Sometimes When We Touch." He said, however "I want you to hear the original" and introduced Barry Mann, who performed it brilliantly. Then came the surprise. Dan pointed up to the balcony and said "There's a man up there who is responsible for my success with this song, my publisher, Sam Trust." I was flustered but managed to stand up and acknowledge the applause.

A similar situation occurred a few years later, with Barry and Cynthia's smash hit, "Just Once," performed by James Ingram. Ingram had regularly worked with us as a "demo" singer. The demo of this song was pitched to Quincy Jones, who was interested in the song and was complimentary about the quality of the recording and the singer. It was suggested that the singer ought to be considered as the artist for this recording. Quincy thought about it and decided to sign him. James' recording was terrific and reached the top of the national charts.

At the Grammy ceremonies for that year, James Ingram was awarded as "best new artist" of the year. At his acceptance, James said, to the effect, that none of this would have happened without the opportunity provided to him by ATV Music.

I mention these two situations as they are quite unique in the music business, where music publishers are rarely recognized for their efforts.

During their association with ATV Music, Barry and Cynthia easily earned out what had been considered an outrageous advance payment. In addition to the above songs they had top ten, or number one hits with "He's So Shy" by the Pointer Sisters, "Never Gonna Let You Go" by Brazil 66, "Don't Know Much" by Aaron Neville, "Somewhere Down The Road," by Barry Manilow" and even a country hit with "Another Goodbye," by Donna Fargo. Most importantly, these works became part of the ATV Music catalog.

CHAPTER 38
"Lucille"

1977 was becoming one of the most interesting and successful years for ATV Music. Three important events took place, which enhanced the company, not the least of which was the acquisition of the song "Lucille," and the writers who created it, as well as the company that published it.

While driving to work I first heard the recording of "Lucille," performed by Kenny Rogers. I was struck by the story and the great hook. When I got to the office I checked Billboard and found it on the "Bubbling Under" chart category. I checked all the information I could find, then, met with Cliffie Stone. The publisher was listed as Brougham-Hall. The owner was George Richey, a sometimes writer and current producer, whom I was aware of. Cliffie knew him well, as he once wrote for his company Central Songs. I was determined to get that song before it broke wide open, so I had Cliffie call George that day and arrange for a meeting in two days in Nashville. I contacted our legal representative in New York and told him to meet us in Nashville and be prepared to draw a purchase agreement.

Our meeting with George dragged on for the entire day. I was aware that a representative of CBS' April-Blackwood Publishing was also in town and interested. Food was sent up to our hotel suite and we labored on into the night with George until he finally said: "I think I'd rather just sell my publishing company than one copyright, since I'm so busy producing." That really appealed to me since I already knew that the writers of the song were under long-term exclusive agreements.

We hammered away at the price and finally settled on $425,000. However, I convinced George that as we had no time for "due diligence", we could withhold $50,000 for a period of three years. Payments of $125,000 would be made each year for three years. If at the end of that period no claims were made against Brougham-Hall, the $50,000 would be released.

The next morning I stopped in at BMI to visit my old colleague and friend Frances Preston. Just as I sat down in her office to talk, her phone rang. She answered, "Oh, hello George." Then after a pause she said "George, you say you're lighting a 10 dollar cigar with a 5 dollar bill? Sam Trust just bought your company for one million dollars? Well, congratulations!" She put down the phone, then looked at me and said: "You didn't pay him a million dollars did you? I know you too well!"

I just smiled and replied," I can't comment."

Soon it spread all over the music community that I paid George a million dollars. I received calls at my hotel from a number of small publishers who wanted to meet with me. At later dates, I was able to capitalize on the deal with the parties I had met. It seems that fans still have the impression that Kenny Rogers actually wrote this song. While he may have heard the story on which the song was based and relayed it to some writers, the song was actually written by Hal Bynum and Roger Bowling. Naturally, after the completion of the sale I spent time with these writers and became particularly close with Roger Bowling. There can be no question that this song was the making of Kenny's career as a country artist.

I attended the NBC Country Music Awards the following year with Roger Bowling. It could easily have been called The Kenny Rogers Show. He received awards as "best new artist," "best single," "best album" "best artist" on and on. After each award he thanked his record company, his manager, his brother, his producer, his family, everyone except the writers of the song that put him there. After each acknowledgment, I could see Roger starting to boil. When the show was over Kenny spotted Roger with me as we were fairly close to the stage.

Kenny greeted him with a hug and said: "Thanks for the song, man!"

Roger stepped back and said: "That's OK Kenny; a monkey could have taken it to Number one!" Obviously, Roger later cooled down since Kenny, subsequently, recorded other songs by Roger.

Needless to say, the acquisition was a grand slam financially. At the end of the three-year period, George got the additional $50,000 and was happy. ATV netted $1,200,000 during that time. The song charted high in virtually every major territory. In Germany it hit number 1 and 2 simultaneously. Kenny's version was #1 and the German cover #2. In the U.S. it barely missed BMI's "most performed song of the year." That acquisition provided a new dimension to ATV Music and, of course, attendant problems.

As part of the purchase agreement George insisted that his brother Paul be given a position at our Nashville office. I agreed, thinking he would be useful, as he knew the Brougham-Hall catalog. Unfortunately, from his first day at the office Paul assumed a rather haughty and arrogant attitude, showing little respect for our Nashville manager Gerry Teifer, a well-respected veteran in the industry, with a wonderful reputation as a publisher. Gerry called me in despair and in need of advice. I suggested he send Paul to visit our Canadian office to meet Frank Davies and his staff, who were performing quite well. As part of his visit Frank put together a small reception. That reception proved to be the end of Paul's short tenure at ATV. Frank called advising that Paul behaved badly and worst of all, was passing out illegal substances. When he returned, I called Gerry and told him to fire him. When he was told, he immediately called me and stated that he had a contract so I couldn't fire him. I advised him to check his contract, and realize that we had the right to terminate the agreement for cause, and we had cause. He was furious and stormed out. Later that day I received a telephone call from Al Gallico, a legendary New York publisher who had tremendous success in Nashville. Al was one of the most colorful people in the music industry and we were good friends. He was in Nashville at the time. He said: "Paul Richey sounds crazy. He says he's leaving for Los Angeles to see you and he's packing a 45." I asked Al how he was going to get here. Al said he was driving his car. I had seen that car, an old Cadillac "Brougham," apparently the inspiration for the name of their company. I told Al "If he's driving that car, he won't get past Kansas." Fortunately, he never arrived. Instead, some time shortly after, I was served with a lawsuit claiming un-lawful dismissal and a payment claim in the amount of $100,000. Later in the day he telephoned me to gloat over the subpoena. I told him that we had no intention of paying him anything. He laughed and said, "We're going to sue you in the state of Tennessee."

I replied "Fine."

He then loudly said, "Well there's justice, and Southern justice, and I'm connected!"

A deposition was ordered for a month later. I called my longtime friend Wesley Rose, owner of the legendary Acuff-Rose catalog, created by his father, Fred Rose, and the famous country entertainer Roy Acuff. Wesley had vied with me for the purchase of the Central Songs catalog that Capitol Records ultimately purchased. He dropped out of the bidding with no hard feelings, and, in fact, we became even closer friends, and often played golf. I explained our situation to him and requested the best Southern "country lawyer" he could recommend. He immediately gave me the name of Bill Carpenter, though I'm now not at this time quite sure of that name.

The day of the deposition arrived, and to my delight and surprise Paul walks in with Ralph Gordon as his lawyer. I had used Ralph a few times in Nashville and enjoyed working with him. We had even lunched together at one time. Bill Carpenter was everything Wesley had promised; upper middle age, tall with graying sideburns, silver rimmed glasses, wearing a string tie and long southern style jacket, with a slow and easy manner of speaking.

Ralph opened with Paul's claim. Bill then responded with a number of questions that started to produce Paul sweating. Then came the killer from Bill: "Now, son, I have before me several affidavits from persons who were at the reception you attended in Toronto, Canada. They say that in addition to your strange behavior you were in possession of, and passed out illegal substances."

At that point Paul was shaking and leaned over to whisper something to Ralph. Ralph requested a 20-minute recess. Forty-minutes later Ralph came back and requested an adjournment. He had just taken Paul to a hospital. He said he was afraid that Paul had a nervous breakdown.

About a month later I received a call from Jerry Margolis, an L.A. lawyer who had also represented us in litigation. He, too, was now representing Paul, but obviously realized that he didn't have much of a case. "Sam, we're willing to settle this matter for $25,000." I told him that he must be kidding; had no intention of paying him anything. He called back and suggested $20,000 and again I refused. The next day he called again asking, or rather pleading to close it out for $10,000 to be done with the matter. I relented and insisted that this would be the end of the matter, which both he and Paul accepted.

Several years later I was in Nashville walking up 16th Avenue towards the Country Music Hall of Fame and who do I see walking towards me but Paul.

I looked up too late to avoid him. He yelled "Sam, Sam," and was smiling. He then came and hugged me saying "I can't thank you enough!"

I said, "What?"

He stated, "What you did to me changed my life. I've been 'born again.' I don't drink anymore, I don't do dope. You changed my life. I can't thank you enough!" I proceeded up the avenue in a state of pleasant shock, and haven't seen Paul since.

Notwithstanding the fiasco with Paul, his brother George and I continued to correspond. During this period George had confided in me of his love for Tammy Wynette. (while he was still married) I had even visited him at his home during that time with this knowledge.

When I later came back to Nashville for a BMI awards dinner, George contacted me and requested that I "beard" for him by taking Tammy to the dinner as my guest. He would arrive separately. As destiny would have it, a picture of Tammy and me entering the dinner appeared on the front page of The Nashville Tennessean, with the caption "Tammy escorted by unidentified gentleman." At the close of the dinner I brought her over to George. It was less than a year later when George divorced and married Tammy, his 3rd and Tammy's 5th.

A short time later Tammy let it be known that she was interested in selling her office building on 17th Avenue South. As we had been renting in the old Metromedia headquarters, we jumped at the chance and immediately closed a deal for the acquisition. It became ATV/Nashville.

Naturally George and Tammy became good friends of mine. I visited Tammy and George's home and was fascinated to find the weave in the wall-to-wall carpet had the word LOVE all through it. Some years later Tammy died, of what some claimed to be suspicious circumstances, causing an investigation. A few years later George married again, for the fourth time before his death.

Tammy, aside from being a wonderful singer, was one of the sweetest persons I've ever met.

CHAPTER 39
Beatles Redux

In early 1977 unlicensed recordings of The Beatles started turning up with great frequency. A compilation, listing recordings from 1964 to 1968 and 1968 to 1972, was doing a brisk business to the detriment of Capitol Records, as well as our Maclen Music. I expressed my discontent to Capitol. I'm sure they also must have heard from Apple, the Beatles management company that oversaw all merchandising of the group. It was decided that the best way to fight fire was with fire. Capitol finally released a similar compilation using the same years. This official set, as well as warnings to the illegal purveyors, produced great sales, despite Capitol's late wake-up call.

With little likelihood of a Beatles reunion, stage shows featuring Beatles look alike characters performing their songs began appearing. Not only was the song usage unauthorized but the use of the trademark "Beatles," owned by Apple, was also unauthorized. We immediately retained a lawyer to sue and close down these performances. Jonathan Zavin, son of Theodora Zavin, (BMI) was our attorney. He always seemed to be traveling, as one show closed down, another opened. We eventually tagged Jonathan, as "Paladin--Have Brief, Will Travel." We, of course, were building up substantial expense, so I contacted Apple requesting they contribute to this effort, to no avail.

At about the same time, I was approached by rock 'n roll managers Steve Leber and David Krebs. They had been aware of these unlicensed performances and decided to create a legitimate stage production to be called *Beatlemania*. Though cautioned by our New York attorneys not to proceed, I decided to give them permission, provided that I had final approval. I realized that Leber/ Krebs had some previous falling out with our New York legal firm. When this law firm suggested that they could refer me to a much better management team, I told them it was Leber/Krebs' idea, and I would not stand for their interference. That ended the discussion and we proceeded. As part of the deal, I granted

123

their much-desired exclusivity for the show, provided that they assume legal costs for shutting down the unauthorized productions, which they accepted. Further, they were advised that we could not grant them usage of the term *Beatlemania*, as it was the property of Apple. Our grant of permission was only for usage of the songs owned by Maclen Music and Northern Songs throughout the world.

When the first *Beatlemania* show previewed in Boston, I sent our New York office representative, Jerry Simon, to review it for me. Jerry had experience in the entertainment industry, so I trusted his opinion. He gave it a good review, so permission was given to Leber/Krebs, with my blessings. The show opened at Broadway's huge Winter Garden theatre with great success.

At the time of *Beatlemania's* New York run we had the services of a British accountant named Tony Curbishley, sent by the UK offices to observe our operation. While we were both in New York, I decided to take him to the show. Tony was from Northern England and therefore well acquainted with the Liverpool accent, which the original performers had "nailed." I advised him beforehand that they were Americans, so he was skeptical that they could pull it off. By mid-show he leaned over to me and said, "You're having me on! Those lads are from Liverpool!" After the show, we went backstage to meet the actors. The first one he met was the "Paul" character. Tony respectfully asked him which section of Liverpool he was from. The actor smiled and said, "Flatbush." Tony got red as a beet while the actor continued smiling and conversing with his Brooklyn accent.

With the success of this show, a renewed interest in the Beatles was sparked. Dick Clark, a well-known producer, who gained national fame early in his career with his TV show *American Bandstand*, announced that he planned to produce an ABC-TV Special dedicated to the Beatles and their music. When this story broke, I received several calls from long-time music publishers I knew, wishing to be a "fly on the wall" during my negotiations with Dick. Back in the early days of *Bandstand*, Clark made it a habit of demanding a piece of the publishing for any song performed on his show. It didn't take long before he developed a valuable catalog of copyrights at the expense of these music publishers. Notwithstanding Clark's tremendous contribution to the establishment of numerous artists, and particularly opening the door to black performers, this stigma was still in the memories of those publishers. It didn't take long, at that time, before the government stepped in for an investigation of "payola" involved in these programs, particularly at the urging of critics in high government offices who detested this new and "degenerative" form of music.

While Dick could have easily been indicted, he was given a "pass" at the urging of political figures who knew that he had become somewhat of an idol to millions of his young fans. He was, however, forced to dispose of his music publishing interests, citing it to be a definite conflict of interest.

Dick called me at my office and asked if I could meet him at his offices. I declined, to his surprise, and requested that he come to my offices, and set a date and time. When he arrived, our receptionist excitedly called to tell me he was in the lobby and might she show him to my office. Remembering my music publishing buddies, I said, "Let him wait and, perhaps, offer him some coffee. I'll call you when I'm ready."

After a decent interval, I invited him to my office. He arrived all smiles. After some introductory chit chat, we got down to business. He read off a list of songs to be performed in the show and I came up with a ballpark figure that would be firmed up shortly with a letter of confirmation. I also suggested to him that it might have been better to check with us earlier in order to avoid this last minute negotiation. With that, the meeting ended. The program was scheduled to be broadcast two weeks later.

The following week I left for meetings in New York, which included a *Beatlemania* show with my wife. When we arrived at the theater, to our surprise, in walks Dick with his wife and sits down directly in front of us. He turns to me immediately and exclaims, "Sam, is that really you? I've been trying to get in touch with you for days, and you couldn't be located. In fact, yesterday was my wedding day and I was up all last night with worry! I had to add another song to the show and I know what a stickler you are about clearance. The show is the day after tomorrow and I need to clear it now." I asked him the title of the song and he replied, "I Saw Her Standing There."

I said, "Dick, that's one of the songs we don't own, sorry you were kept up all night. The song is owned by George Pincus at Gil Music, here in New York. Call him tomorrow and mention that you've been working with me. Now, enjoy the show." In some small way I think my publisher buddies enjoyed this story when they asked about my dealing with Dick.

125

The deal that our lawyers struck for *Beatlemania* was history making in terms of what a music publisher could earn from the theatrical performances of its music. So much so, that prominent Broadway attorney, Edward Colton, representing the theatre called Lord Grade directly to complain. We had, in fact, been sending approximately $30,000 per week back to London to Lew Grade's delight. Grade tried to act understanding, but explained there was nothing he could do about it, as that "SOB Trust" had full control by virtue of his contract. He suggested to Colton that he invite me to lunch to work on me. He then called me to advise of his conversation with Colton, and to certainly not give in. He said he had to blame me because he had to protect HIS reputation. I laughingly said, "Thanks a lot Lew!" and hung up.

Colton called me and set a luncheon date at Twenty One, perhaps the top celebrity-dining establishment in Manhattan, at the time. We both arrived at the same time and Ed was welcomed by the maître'd as if he were royalty. We were given a table that provided a measure of privacy. After some introductions and small talk Ed ordered cocktails. When they arrived, he got right into his request.

The conversation went something like this: "Sam, I've been practicing entertainment law, particularly regarding Broadway, for a long time. I even go back to Al Jolson's appearances. But I have never encountered a contract whereby a music publisher demanded as high percentage of ticket sales as *Beatlemania*!"

I paused and then said. "Ed, in all those years, were you ever involved in a Broadway musical where each song performed had sold a million records before the show even opened?" There was a moment of silence after which I said, "Ed, we could finish our drinks and leave at this point since you now know my position." He looked up and said, "No, no, Sam, let's have lunch." We enjoyed a fine lunch, and nothing further was discussed regarding our deal.

Ed Colton was a legendary Broadway figure, and a true gentleman. I was pleased to see him given a "lifetime achievement" award some years later at a nationally televised Tony award celebration.

During one of my frequent trips to New York, I received a call from Lee Eastman. (Linda McCartney's father) I hadn't seen or talked to Lee since I turned down his offer to run McCartney's music publishing company, now called MPL Communications. He suggested lunch at Shepherd's in the Drake Hotel, a restaurant where we often met when I was working at BMI in New York. Lee showed up in good humor and seemed to have forgotten his past disappointment. We had an enjoyable luncheon and he finally got around to his purpose in calling me.

"Sam, I have to talk to you about *Beatlemania* at Paul's request." I asked what the problem was, as it was still playing to packed houses. He said, "Paul objects to the show itself and would like to see it gone."

I replied, "I'm sure he hasn't had a problem cashing his royalty checks." Lee said, "No, that wasn't the problem, he just doesn't like the idea of the show." I looked at Lee as though he had "lost his marbles." After a pause, he smiled and said, "Look Sam, he's my son-in-law, I had to state his position. Personally, I hope the show runs another ten years."

A short time later when I was in London, I received a call from Paul McCartney who claimed he was personally distraught with the show. I acknowledged to him that Lee had complained but couldn't point to a specific reason, and asked if he could tell me why?" I was shocked by his answer. He said that he had been planning a similar type show, but much better. (though I'm sure he had never seen it) I simply said, "It seems you were beaten to it. That's showbiz." He hung up and that was an end to it.

The show had a long run on Broadway then traveled to major cities in the US and around the world. Strangely enough, it even had a cast album of the show.

I was invited by Steve Leber to travel to Japan with the cast for their grand opening in Tokyo. I was happy to accept, as I also looked forward not only to the show, but returning to a country, which as a much younger man, I had so enjoyed.

CHAPTER 40
Back To Japan

As soon as I knew the date for my trip to Japan I contacted Shoo Kusano of Shinko Music, who confirmed that he would pick me up at the airport upon my arrival. When I arrived both he and his right hand assistant, Joe Miyasaki welcomed me. Joe spent quite a bit of time in the U. S. courting publishers for sub-publishing rights to their works for Shinko in Japan. He was very successful since he spoke perfect English, as well he should, as he was in fact an American living in Japan as an important employee of Shinko. Joe had spent his early career working for a pop music radio station in Cleveland, Ohio where Shoo met him. He persuaded Joe to come to Japan, even though he couldn't speak a word of Japanese. Joe explained that he learned the language watching Japanese TV shows which were originally in English.

Rather than drive straight to my hotel, they took me to their offices where several reporters were waiting to interview me. I was photographed and, to my surprise the picture of a very jet-lagged and tired me appeared on the cover of Japan's largest music trade magazine. I was questioned on my views of the music business and apparently a long article appeared in that magazine and others. I really couldn't tell what they said, since it was all in Japanese. However, I did learn that my statement regarding the mechanical rate in Japan was widely quoted among the Japanese music industry. When asked what I thought of the then current "mechanical rate" of 4% being paid to Japanese music publishers, I said I thought it was too low. When I was asked what I thought it should be, I replied "at least 7%." Apparently that was a shock. I believe the rate in Japan eventually reached and possibly exceeded that rate in time.

I was then taken to my hotel, The New Otani. It was a beautiful hotel and I was given a wonderful room near the top. The room was filled with flowers and a large basket of luscious fruit. After I unpacked and was just sitting down to relax, there was an un-expected knock on my door. When I answered it, there stood Yoshi Ogawa with a big smile welcoming me to Japan.

This was a wonderful reunion, obviously set up by Shoo Kusano. We later all had dinner together, but there was even more to come. After meeting with Steve Leber and attending the opening of *Beatlemania* at the Budokan, one of the largest arenas in Japan, Shoo scheduled a golf date for the four of us (Shoo, Joe, Yoshi and me) at one of the many golf clubs in which he was a member. Yoshi was easily the best player among us. I remembered seeing pictures of his father's swing when I visited as a sailor more than twenty years before. I realized that his dad had trained him well. By that time the music magazine with my picture on the cover was appearing on newsstands.

A few days later, after a luncheon with Yoshi, I told him of my desire to return to his home in Motoyawata. I knew that his father had passed away, but that his mother was still alive and I had remembered how beautiful and welcoming his home had been. Yoshi was very quiet, and then said, "I don't think so, Sam." I pressed on and told him how much it would mean to me to see it again. I said, it would just be a quick visit by train, but he again said it would be too much trouble. I assured him it wasn't. He finally gave in and said that he would drive us rather than take the train. I realized his village was much closer to Tokyo than it was from Yokusuke, the naval base where our ship had been moored.

When we arrived at the village, I could not recognize it. Tall buildings were everywhere. The dirt roads were now paved. When Yoshi pulled up to the house I had difficulty remembering it. I looked forward to once again seeing Mrs. Ogawa, who had been so gracious and dressed so beautifully when we last met. Yoshi knocked on the door and Mrs. Ogawa appeared again in a traditional kimono, but so stooped over that her face looked toward the ground. She painfully raised her head to look up, and once again welcomed me. We entered the house but it did not resemble the neat, uncluttered home I had remembered. In the living room there now was a sofa and side table. In a bedroom was a huge, mahogany bed and dresser. I must have shown a questioned or somewhat surprised look on my face, which, of course, was hard to disguise as nothing appeared as I remembered. Mrs. Ogawa motioned for us to go outside to the garden. Again I was disappointed to find it quite barren of the plants and flowers I had seen before. Mrs. Ogawa tried to raise her head to smile at me and pointed to the koi pond. She kept repeating something in Japanese that I couldn't understand. I asked Yoshi what she was saying. He slowly responded, "She say, same-a fish."

After tea, we departed. On the way back to my hotel, Yoshi

unburdened his disappointment concerning his return to Japan. He was unable to attain a position in any professional orchestra, his marriage had failed, and the only work he was able to secure was teaching music and violin in an elementary school.

My departure was to be two days later. Shoo and Joe planned to take me to the airport. Yoshi insisted that he see me off as well, though I told him that it was not necessary.

Yoshi arrived at the airport and hung onto me, much to the chagrin of Shoo and Joe. He pulled me aside and tearfully told me what a failure he thought he had been, and what a disappointment he must be to me, who had been so successful. I assured him that he was not a disappointment to me and that I valued him as a friend and always would. Nevertheless, the tears continued until I departed.

About a week after I arrived home I received a long, tear-stained letter from Yoshi, which was apparently written while he was still at the airport. Again he wrote about his failure in light of my success, and how he had hoped that our relationship would have served as a "bridge" model of Japanese and American friendship. I answered his letter, but have never again heard from him.

The saying, "You can't go home again" is generally attributed the famous writer Thomas Wolfe. To that I would add, nor can you return to the past.

CHAPTER 41
A Steeler's Steal

At the very end of 1977, I decided to go for a deal that literally put my job on the line. If it could work, it would be a great "end run." If it didn't, I'd be looking for another job.

A music publishing catalog called Venice Music was made available in mid-year. This catalog was the publishing outlet for a recording company known as Specialty Records, containing early rock 'n' roll and R&B hits. The company was referred to as a "race record" outlet, since the majority of their artists were black. Probably the best known of these artists was "Little Richard." Other top black artists who got their start with Specialty were Sam Cooke, Percy Mayfield, and Lloyd Price.

I had known about the availability of this catalog and even mentioned it to Lee Eastman at our last luncheon meeting in New York. I had great respect for Lee's judgment in buying catalogs over the years and asked for his thoughts. He said that he wouldn't go near it since that company was known for buying out the writer's share of income, which to him was unholy. He felt that any publisher who would do such a thing could not convey rights with "clean hands." I also knew that the asking price of three million dollars was considered rather high at that time. Word on the street was that it contained some great songs, but could be a risk to buy.

In late December I learned through the grapevine that both Trudy Meisl, a very successful German publisher and Stig Anderson, perhaps the most successful Scandinavian publisher in history, were quietly in town. (Stig was the successful creator, producer, and publisher of ABBA.)

At the time, they were not our representatives for their territories though they were very sociable with us. I noticed and found it odd that no one in the Hollywood music business had been socializing with either of them. So, I decided to do some checking to determine just what they were up to. I found out that they were in town to acquire Venice Music

131

for, what I assumed to be, a jointly owned company. They left town just before Christmas for a holiday in the Bahamas.

In the period between Christmas and New Years, I called Specialty Records and spoke to the wife of Art Rupe, the owner, to arrange an appointment. She asked the reason for the appointment, and I advised her that I was interested in purchasing the Venice Music catalog for ATV Music. She told me that it was unlikely as they had already reached a deal with another party. I told her that, regardless of that deal, I would still like to talk to them. She reluctantly agreed to speak to her husband and get back to me as that period of time was really downtime, in the music industry. Art Rupe called back and agreed to meet me on Wednesday of the same week. To show that I really was serious, I brought along our company controller, Tony Curbishley. Art Rupe repeated his wife's statement that a temporary agreement had been reached with Trudy and Stig, and they were, in fact, in Jamaica celebrating the deal. I asked if the three million dollar price had been agreed upon, and he admitted it was, "in principle."

After some further discussion, I said, "Wait a second! You're from Western Pennsylvania."

He said, "Well, Yeah...."

I interrupted and went on, You're from either Clairton, Mckeesport, or Duquesne."

He yelled back, "What are you, some kind of "gumshoe?"

I smiled and said, "No, just a Pittsburgher with a good memory." He told me he was from McKeesport, but hadn't been back to Pittsburgh in 30 years. He couldn't understand how I could identify an accent that he was sure was long gone. I told him that the first four years of my life were spent in Clairton, and I could remember my dad taking me to my first football game between Clairton and McKeesport.

He said, "Are you a Steelers fan?"

I replied ----"Are you kidding? As a kid I used to work at Forbes Field hawking ice cream on bitter cold days, and peanuts on hot days just to see the Steelers and Pirates."

"Then you worked for that slave-driver O'Brisky."

I said, "Yes, I worked for that SOB".

"So did I." He then looked over to Tony Curbishley and said, "Do you mind, Sam and I have a lot to talk about. Perhaps I'll see you later." Tony bowed out, and Art and I went over Steeler history, which I was up on. As Art was older than me, we talked about "Bullet Bill" Dudley, Johnny "Zero" Clement, Elbie Nickel and players of his era.

After our recollections, he said, "Sam, I'd love for you to get this catalog, but I'm so far along with Trudy and Stig." I asked if anything was signed, and he told me nothing was drawn as yet.

I asked him about his buy-out of Little Richard's writer's share. He told me that he had refused to do it. Richard was desperate for money and kept pursuing it. Finally Art told him he would not do it unless Richard had benefit of counsel. Richard hired a respected lawyer and brought him along to witness and approve the deal, so Art reluctantly agreed. Art even brought out the document with the lawyer's signature for me to see. That was the only time he ever did this, mainly because Richard was so desperate. (So much for Lee Eastman's conclusion)

I decided that I had to make a dramatic move and said, "Art if I can put a certified check for three million dollars on your desk next Monday, do I get the deal?"

He said, "You can do that?" I replied, "Yes, but with one provision: Hold the check for two weeks while I send in accountants for due diligence. If we find nothing alarming, you cash the check."

"Sam, if you can pull that off, it's a deal."

Then came the challenge...calling Lord Grade. I decided to wait until midnight to call him since I knew that he was always the first one to open the office in London and would be undisturbed. I had already studied the songs and artists in the catalog in anticipation of my pitch. When I told him that I needed the check by Monday, he thought I was insane. I then told him that the early songs recorded by The Beatles before their own writing began, such as "Long Tall Sally," "Rip It Up" and others that were part of the catalog, as well as the "Little Richard" hits including "Tutti Frutti."

He responded, "But three million!"

I said "Lew it's worth it."

He then said, "Do you really think it's the best usage of ATV's money?"

I responded that it was. The last thing he said was "Alright, but if it isn't, it's your ass!" I assured him it would work out, and the conversation ended. The check arrived as scheduled, to Art Rupe's delight.

I decided to keep the deal quiet until the MIDEM convention, which would occur only two weeks later. To gain maximum impact, I called Irv Lichtman, an editor and reporter at Billboard magazine, whom I respected. I told him I had a scoop of a story that I would give his magazine exclusive coverage, if they would headline it in the MIDEM edition. That edition was usually given out to every passenger arriving at the Nice airport for the convention. He said, "We'll give it great coverage. I told him it had to be the magazine cover story, and he agreed.

Irv delivered, so we had the cover, and featured story of that edition which was handed to everybody who deplaned in Nice. When we arrived at our hotel, there were 12 messages waiting for us, several of which were from Trudy and Stig, as well as other European publishers.

I immediately called Trudy, who still seemed to be shocked. She was sure that she and Stig had the deal and had already made plans for exploitation. I assured her that she could still enact those plans since I would offer her and Stig the first crack at the deal for their territories, but I would be looking for a significant advance. By the time we left MIDEM, I'd obtained over $600,000 in advance payments from Trudy and Stig along with representatives from other territories. This meant that ATV had already recovered 20% of its payment in its first week of ownership. The remainder of that payment would be easily earned within the seven-year period I always used for amortization purposes. This acquisition added a new dimension to our catalog.

Within two weeks of my return another surprise regarding this acquisition was waiting for me.

It was a Friday afternoon and a loud racket was taking place in front of our building. A group of protesters were marching with signs saying "ATV – Unfair to Little Richard." Little Richard, was now aware that the songs he had assigned to Venice Music were now owned by ATV Music. He must have viewed us as a "deep pocket" and set up the protest. His claim, of course, was that we had stolen his songs from him. This, of course, referred to the deal he entered into, or rather begged Art Rupe to give him. The picketers, undoubtedly, knew nothing of this. They were merely marching on behalf of a poor, mistreated, black artist.

I chose to ignore this protest but they returned the following Friday and again a third time. By this time, Little Richard was getting attention from newspapers and local TV stations. Up until our acquisition, his career was dead in the water. Now he was making the best of this situation.

As our offices on Sunset Boulevard were between CBS studios to the east and RCA to the west, we were obviously drawing great attention, and sympathy was building up for Richard, even though no one thought to contact us at any time. To everyone's surprise he even appeared on the "Johnny Carson Tonight Show." During his interview he complained about us and singled out "Mr. Trust, who wouldn't give me my BMI's." He was, at last, getting the exposure he craved after being cold for so many years.

I decided that this was enough and sought out his telephone number. After a long search, I got it and called him.

When he answered I said that I was the Mr. Trust that he was bitching about and said, "Why didn't you come and complain to me?" I invited him to my office and he shyly accepted.

After getting to know Richard Penniman, who was roughly the same age as me, I made a proposal to him. I would insure that we would pay him his writer's royalties if he would sign an exclusive three-year writer's contract with us. As far as his claim that BMI was not paying him, I doubted very much that was the case but said that we, as his publisher, would notify BMI that we held no claim to his performing royalties. Richard was blown away by the proposal, and couldn't stop thanking me. The writer's deal turned out to be merely a gesture since his writing days seemed to be over. However all the publicity he received from this fiasco did re-awaken interest in this past "R n B" and "Rock" music legend. He started to get parts in some popular motion pictures and appeared on numerous TV shows and interviews. As a result, performances of some of his great "Rock" standards, which we now owned, were showing up with great frequency. In the end, it was a "win, win" situation.

Some years later I was attending a "Grammy" show celebration at the New York Hilton. I had just gone up an escalator, and turned to look down. There was Richard coming up so I waited. When he saw me, he rushed over, gave me big hug, and a joyful greeting.

CHAPTER 42
Famous Amos

Walking up Vine Street one day on my way to Capitol Records, I saw Wally Amos slowly walking in my direction. I hadn't seen Wally in some time and was somewhat shocked at his appearance as he came closer. Wally had always been cheerful and even effervescent, but not this time.

While running Capitol Record's music publishing division, I had met Wally who was operating a management, production, and music publishing company with Mark Wildey. I made a deal with his company for the publishing rights for a group he was managing called "People." That group was, in fact, the first to come up with a recording of "Put Your Hand In The Hand."' Unfortunately, their recording wasn't the one that hit. When Wally's company folded I picked up his exploitation man, Terry Slater, who turned out to be one of the best song pluggers ever. Terry went on to great success heading EMI in the UK, and was responsible for some of EMI's biggest hit recordings.

Wally seemed disheveled, not the Wally I knew. He explained that he'd gone through some personal and financial problems and was generally feeling down, which was evident. I suggested we stop into the nearby Brown Derby coffee shop and have a talk.

Wally felt that his West Coast endeavors had just not worked out, and that perhaps he should have stayed in personal management, a position he held previously at the William Morris office in New York.

After a short discussion I decided to offer him a job as a song-plugger at ATV. I knew he had the personality for that type of work and was willing to give him a shot. He thanked me but declined the offer, again stating his desire to go back with William Morris. Unfortunately, he didn't have the funds to get back to New York, so I made him a proposition. I told him that I had a trip to New York scheduled soon and, as a senior executive, was entitled to travel first class. I suggested that I would cash in my first class ticket for two in coach and "comp" him to a night's stay at a hotel. If he worked out a deal at William Morris, fine. However, if not, he would come to work at ATV. Wally agreed and we took the trip.

The result of the trip was that nothing was available at William Morris, so Wally started work at ATV Music shortly thereafter. I knew that Wally's heart was still into personal management and decided to let him continue that activity while working for us. He fit in with office personnel immediately, and started pitching songs to producers and contacts that he already knew in the music industry.

Every so often he would bring in chocolate chip cookies that he'd made at his apartment for our staff that loved them. Apparently, Wally had been baking these delicious morsels for a long time. He learned the recipe as a youngster, from his Aunt Della. I admit, having enjoyed the toll house cookies made by my aunt Helen, where I went for lunch while at elementary school. Wally's compared favorably. Wally decided that he would take small boxes of these cookies to the producers he would visit to plug songs. I agreed it was a good idea. Occasionally he would bring in a variation of the recipe for my appraisal, such as butterscotch, peanut butter, etc. However, my taste was always to his original.

While we were as optimistic regarding the success we might have by combining our demo records with Wally's cookies, our hopes came crashing down when several producers called and asked to speak with Wally. Unfortunately, they were not planning to record any of our songs; they were requesting more cookies.

Several weeks later I received a telephone call at home from Wally. He was calling from the "Little Club" in Beverly Hills where a client from his days at William Morris was performing, a comedienne named Joan Rivers. He insisted that I come down to see her. As it was already past 8 PM, I reluctantly accepted his invitation and drove down to the club. It seemed that Wally had more on his mind than entertaining me with the show.

After watching some of the show, he pulled me aside for a serious conversation. "Sam, I've been doing a lot of thinking and decided I want to get into the cookie business. I've received so many compliments that I feel that it's my calling. And get this, I've got the greatest name for my company— "Famous Amos."

He said that he already was promised some backing from Jeff Wald, Helen Reddy's husband and manager, who I knew quite well, and Helen. He asked me for an investment of five thousand dollars, which would get me a 20% interest in the company. At the time I had just invested in a real estate venture and had no disposable cash. He asked me what I thought and I explained my financial situation.

I also noted, "Famous Amos? Wasn't that the name of Amos' taxi in the "Amos and Andy" radio series?

He replied, "for God's sake, keep that to yourself!" I laughed and assured him I would. I knew that this was, in effect, his resignation from ATV Music and wished him well. From time to time Wally and I got in touch. Once he called me at my office and was in need of $120 as a loan until his business started, which I gladly gave him.

He debuted his cookie store on Sunset Boulevard with resounding success. (though somewhat short-lived.) I would continue to see Wally and gently remind him of the loan. About a year went by and Wally was generating great publicity for his company but much more for his personality and dress. He came bursting into our offices to the delight of all, carrying 40 bags of his cookies. He came directly into my office and dumped them all on my desk, saying, "Sam, here's the 120 bucks I owe you, enjoy!" Needless to say, the cookies lasted less than a week as our staff devoured them.

Famous Amos cookies and Wally became the entertainment rage for some time. Wally started showing up on television for interviews and taking parts in TV series. He generously lent his name to some wonderful causes. He was featured on the cover of Time magazine and was even given a medal from the president of the United States for his entrepreneurial achievement.

For several years Wally's operation did quite well. He opened additional stores in Los Angeles and Arizona. His national breakout occurred when Bloomingdale's in New York offered to distribute his cookies in their store. After his one year at Bloomingdale's (who chose not to extend their agreement) he moved his product to Macy's. This resulted in huge exposure for Wally as "Famous Amos." He was even asked to participate in the famous Macy's Thanksgiving Day Parade. The fact that Wally, admittedly, had no experience in marketing and distribution, having hired mostly friends from the entertainment industry with no experience, prevented Wally from enjoying the financial rewards everyone anticipated. It also became apparent that the taste of Wally's original cookies could not be mass-produced at the national level. As a result, within 10 years his company was in trouble and forced to sell, which resulted in additional legal problems for Wally since he was prevented from using his monicker "Famous Amos" on any further products. After sales from the original purchaser to other companies, Keebler finally picked up the company and continues to operate the line.

As a personality Wally had become a household name and a force in many excellent childhood improvement projects. Wally retired to

Hawaii with his wife Christine, but continues experimenting with some baking projects sold in that state.

From time to time, prior to my retirement I'd run into Wally. Once, while visiting a production company, I saw him giving a presentation in their conference room, when he noticed me through the glass partition. He literally stopped in mid-sentence, rushed out to greet me, and make me promise to visit him in Hawaii. He later sent me a signed copy of his biography, "The Face That Launched A Thousand Chips" pointing out the tribute he paid to me in that book.

CHAPTER 43
The Saturday Night Putt

When I was appointed worldwide CEO for ATV Music I did a lot of traveling, and made many friends, particularly in England. One was a former Scottish soccer player named Bill Martin, a successful songwriter. He and his co-writer Phil Coulter created a number of huge hits, and decided to open their own music publishing company, Martin-Coulter Music, which also became quite successful. Bill and I became good friends. During his frequent trips to the U. S. we'd play golf at my course in Calabasas. He promised when I was in the UK that I'd be his guest at his course, The Royal Auto Club, outside of London, where he was Captain.

At the time of my visit, Martin-Coulter Music had the number one record in the UK, "Saturday Night," by The Bay City Rollers. I'd heard the record and knew it was to be released in the U.S. on Clive Davis' Arista Records, a company that was red hot at that time. So, before we teed off I said, "Bill, I'll give you an advance of $10,000 for that song for the U.S. and Canada."

Bill scoffed and said, "Forget it! I can get $50,000 from any number of U.S. publishers."

I replied, "I don't have that kind of money, but I'll commit to $10,000 right now."

He replied. "No way, forget it!"

I had a quick thought and made a proposal, "I tell you what, if I beat you today, let me have it for the ten grand."

He took the challenge immediately and said, "Sure!" This is my course, you haven't a prayer of beating me. Besides, I play better than you anyway." It was a beautiful course, one of the best courses I ever played in the UK. It was more like American courses I was used to, with beautifully kept grass, and trees. At the time I was a 15 handicap, Bill was about a 13, but we agreed to play even. We played dead even until the last hole. He hit his ball up on the green to about four feet from the hole. My shot landed at the top of the green at the high point, about 60 feet from the hole.

He then yells, "No worries now," bows to me and smiles, "Your shot, Sam." I knelt down to align the putt, not that it would do me any good as I was looking at downhill, undulating effort. I tap the ball and, as if in slow motion, it winds its way down to the center of the hole.

Bill just stands there aghast, dropping his putter as I shout, "Your shot Bill." He is four feet away. He lines up his putt, and misses.

I walked down to Bill and yelled "The song is mine for $10,000."

He looks at me in disbelief, and yells back, "You son of a bitch!"

I laughed and said, "Now Bill, you can hire me a car to take me back to London so I can make out a check for you."

Again, "you son of a bitch!" We went back the clubhouse for a drink, but Bill seemed to never get over it. The car arrived, and I bid him farewell as he muttered "You son of a bitch!" When I arrived back at my hotel, I telexed my office to submit the payment to Bill's company and clear the song through Welbeck Music, our ASCAP affiliate. I also telexed Clive Davis, at Arista Records to clear the song through that company. There is, however, a bit more to the story.

About a month later I received a call from Lance Freed, the head of A&M's Music Publishing. He was calling from New York, where he was about to attend an ASCAP board of directors meeting. He informed me that he put my name up for nomination, saying that I "must" be on the ASCAP board. Lance had served with me on the board of the National Music Publishers Association.

I thanked him for his effort, but told him that it would never happen. "I'm still considered a BMI guy, even though I haven't worked there for so many years."

He said, "But we need you." Again, I told him it won't happen, and, of course, it didn't.

Sometime later I was in New York and arranged a meeting with the late Paul Marks, a highly placed ASCAP executive who had been Director of Distribution at the time I was Director of Logging at BMI, a similar position. During that time we figuratively bumped heads vying for clients by comparing each company's financial benefits based on their method of royalties accounting.

When I left BMI I had called on Paul to propose an idea that would save both companies money, and end the bickering. It was simply a method to combine both methods of song identification, ASCAP and BMI, to be handled by a mutually approved independent source. Each company would receive the same performance information and choose how they would pay their members. The savings would be in the millions, which could be passed on to the writers and publishers. Paul would simply have none of it, reciting the old ASCAP adage that they "would have nothing to do with BMI." I happened to mention that I learned that my nomination for ASCAP board membership was brought up at a recent meeting, not that I would have accepted, but was blocked I assumed by Paul, as well. He responded, "Sam, you've been a BMI guy all your life."

I said, "Paul, do you have a copy of this week's Billboard?"

"Yes, I do." I suggested that he open to the National Chart section and check to see who was number one. He did and answered "Saturday Night, by the Bay City Rollers."

I asked, "Who's the publisher?"

"Welbeck Music."

I responded, "And who is Welbeck Music?"

"Oh that's you, isn't it?"

"Now Paul, I could have put that song into our BMI outlet, ATV Music, but I didn't. I knew that particular song would earn more at ASCAP than BMI. My obligation is to the company I presently work for, not for one in the past. Now, does that make me the bad guy for ASCAP that I'm presumed to be, or just an honest business man?" Paul had no comeback, and I believe I made my point, though I knew nothing would really come of it.

About three years later, Joan and I were at MIDEM one late evening walking the croisette back to our hotel. Bill Martin, who was known to down a few, was coming our way, weaving and obviously slightly tanked. As we meet, he looks up to me as if seeing a ghost, and with his Scottish burr mumbles "that fookin' putt, that fookin' putt," and proceeds right past us.

Many years after that, as I'm boarding a 747 plane to Portugal, via London, for a BMG convention and proceeding to the upper area, I see looking down on me, Bill Martin chanting, "That fookin' putt, that fookin' putt!" We spent the rest of the trip catching up, and talking about---what else, the music business.

CHAPTER 44
Vienna

In 1981, Johann Michel, owner of the very successful German music publishing company Melodie Der Welt, invited Joan and me to attend the 50th anniversary of his career in music publishing in Vienna. Vienna was where Johann's music career began with the firm Joseph W. Weinberger. That company, along with Melodie der Welt, were the hosts of the event. All expenses, including travel and hotel were taken care of by the hosts.

Johann had enjoyed a run of very successful years and acknowledged his gratitude to me for assigning rights to Northern Songs to his company, when I became chief executive. He also enjoyed the huge success of "Lucille," which reached Number 1 and Number 2 simultaneously in the German charts. (The original and the German version.) I had assigned publishing rights to Trust Music Management clients to his company long before my career at ATV Music, so we had a long association.

This event has to be considered the most spectacular we ever attended. It was held in a world famous palace. All guests were in formal dress, and as we entered in a line proceeding up the stairs to the ballroom, at each level were gentlemen dressed in formal 18th century clothing, complete with powdered wig to welcome us. Each couple was received by Johann and his wife, and formally announced to all before entrance.

An orchestra was on hand in the ballroom. As it was May wine season, each course of dinner was preceded by a fanfare and announcement of the type of wine, as lovely girls dressed in traditional Austrian costumes danced their trays of wines to the tables, accompanied by the orchestra.

Seating was meticulously arranged. We were seated with Lee Eastman, the powerful music business attorney, who was now Paul McCartney's father-in-law, and his wife Monique, a gracious woman who became Lee's second wife. Tragically, Lee had witnessed the crash of the airplane that his first wife had just boarded during take off at La Guardia, some years earlier. It turned out that Monique was, in fact, a European Countess, who in years past had experienced some of this type of splendid dining and entertainment.

She leaned over to Joan and me and said, "Remember this night, you may never see the likes of it again in your lifetime." It no doubt was, and is a memorable night, not only for the gala, but for an event that occurred which would have a profound effect on the remainder of my career.

Between the main course and dessert, Lee excused himself to take a telephone call that was waiting for him. When he returned, he leaned over to me and said, "You'll be interested to know that Northern Songs and ATV Music have now been placed for sale."

I looked at him disbelieving, as I knew Lee had a flare for the dramatic, and said "I'm sure that can't be so." He smilingly assured that it was.

By the time we returned to New York, word had already spread confirming Lee's message to me. I also learned that Lew Grade was in town staying at the ATV penthouse in the Galleria on East 57th. I called to set up a meeting the next morning at his lodgings.

When I arrived he greeted me in his beautiful bathrobe at the door saying, "I think I know why you're here."

I was furious and grabbed the edges of his robe, pushed him back and said, "You damn well know why I'm here!" He was shocked, to say the least, as I said, "You promised me that you would never offer the company for sale without first discussing it with me!" He somehow burbled his apology and confessed that his company was in major financial difficulty, which forced him into this action. He said he thought the most "moral" thing to do was to offer it to the "boys" (meaning Paul and John) first, hence the call to Lee Eastman. I asked him what price had he quoted and he replied $30,000,000. I told him that it was worth double that amount.

As it turned out, Eastman, on behalf of Paul, turned him down saying the price was too high. When offered to Yoko, on behalf of John, she countered with $5,000,000, confirming her total ignorance of the value. As an aside, shortly after this offering, I had lunch with Thea Zavin who confided that Lee had met with her discussing the deal and his refusal because of the price.

Much to her surprise, Lee said, "After all, Thea, there's not a "Stardust" in the whole catalog." Hence, Lee's refusal on behalf of Paul, even at this early bargain price, refutes Paul's argument that he was never offered his songs. Obviously, in Lee's more elderly taste, he could not reckon the value of the songs of The Beatles with the "chestnuts" he usually bargained for. Though Eastman was greatly respected for his savvy acquisitions of catalogs, it should be realized that the basis of the now McCartney owned (MPL) copyrights originated in Lee's earlier purchase of his client E. H. "Buddy" Morris' publishing company, a catalog containing the music to some of the now legendary Broadway shows. The Ardmore catalog, (now part of MPL) containing such hits as "Autumn Leaves," "Witchcraft," and other such gems was given to Eastman by Capitol Records as an enticement for McCartney to re-sign as an individual artist with that label. Eastman also finessed Columbia Records into an even larger gift by that company, handing him the Frank Loesser catalog with all the music to the hit musicals "Guys and Dolls," and "Most Happy Fella," among others, when he subsequently moved to that label. This gives credibility to the belief by most music publishers, that record executives had no idea of the value of music publishing.

The reason that I considered this offer of sale by Grade to be a "fire sale" dates back to an edict of the UK controlled television bureau, IBA (Independent Broadcasting Authority) made regarding producers of television programming. That edict prevented anyone over the age of 70 to be director of a contracting company. As Grade turned 70 late in 1976, he had to resign his chairmanship of ATV as of January 1977, and elect a successor. He did so, but he had no intention of leaving the field of entertainment. Having the experience of producing numerous television specials, series, and movies for television that were successful not only in the UK but worldwide, he turned his attention to the production of feature motion pictures. His early success with Blake Edward's "Pink Panther" films only whetted his appetite for more challenging and costly productions.

Grade was smitten by this media and contracted numerous star actors to perform in these films. While some of these productions were quite good artistically, his lack of distribution "know-how," as well his general unfamiliarity with this medium cost him dearly. As an example, his early film "Voyage Of The Damned," was, in fact, the real story of the plight of some 900 Jews aboard the ship "The St. Louis," sailing in 1939 from Hamburg Germany to Havana, Cuba and the United States. The voyage was set up by Hitler's propaganda minister Josef Goebbels to prove that no one was prepared to take the Jews. Unfortunately, he was proven correct as the ship was turned away from both Cuba and the United States. Many of the passengers aboard ended their lives in Nazi concentration camps after disembarking in the Netherlands, the only country that would allow them to dock.

Just prior to the release of the film, Grade was awarded peerage at the recommendation of then Prime Minister Harold Wilson. His "Sir" status became elevated to "Lord." He was proud of his connections with top motion picture stars and used these big names in all of his productions. In "Voyage Of The Damned" he cast Faye Dunaway, Oskar Werner, Lee Grant, Orson Welles, Max Von Sydow, James Mason, and Maria Schell, plus less notable names. The film, basically a sad and pathetic story was released at the worst possible time, during the Christmas holidays. The plethora of star actors and a 2 ½ hour film bothered several critics. Consequently, the audience, instead of attending in droves, stayed away.

Subsequent releases such as "The Cassandra Crossing," "Farewell My Lovely," "Capricorn One," "The Eagle Has Landed," "Movie, Movie" and "Legend of The Lone Ranger," did well to break even. Convinced that the lack of success was due to improper distribution, Grade decided to form his own distribution company, which was another hugely expensive and disastrous move. The final and most costly financial blow was the production of Clive Cussler's novel "Raise The Titanic." Anything that could possibly go wrong, did. During an interview with NBC's Jane Pauley, Grade admitted "Frankly, it would have been cheaper to lower the Atlantic."

So after five financially disastrous years, Grade was looking for money, hence the sacrifice of what many considered his "Jewel in the Crown,"----music publishing.

Shortly after both parties turned down the offer, Grade became aware that someone in Australia was gathering up ACC (ATV changed their name to ACC, Associated Communications Corp.) stock, which was at historic lows due to the failure of the film ventures, which was well-known. The offer to sell the catalogs was put on hold as Grade researched the party, one Robert Holmes a'Court, an Australian entrepreneur. Believing Holmes a'Court was buying the stock as a vote of confidence in his leadership, he decided to go to meet this young man. Holmes a'Court played on Grades misconception and ingratiated himself to him. In a short time he invited Lew and his wife Kathy to visit his operation in Perth, Australia, where they were treated as royalty. One can now only view that journey as Grade's "Voyage Of The Doomed."

146

CHAPTER 45
Aussie-shock

Upon Lord Grade's return from Australia, and convinced of Robert Holmes a'Court's brilliance and dedication to him, he informed the Board of Directors of ACC that it was his intention to sell his voting shares to Holmes a'Court. Though the directors fervently tried to dissuade him, Grade stated that he had given Robert his word and would never go back on it. Those voting shares allowed Robert to virtually take over the company as he had already captured the majority of the non-voting shares at bargain basement prices. Grade was perfectly aware, and gave him his blessings as Chairman and CEO, stating to the Board that Robert was the future of the company. Holmes a'Court had assured Grade that he would always be the creative force of the company. Grade naively went along inhaling the smoke that Robert was blowing his way. It didn't take long before Robert showed his true self by denying Grade his budgets for films, and dismissing longtime employees who Grade had initially employed. It became increasingly clear to Grade, in a rather short time, that he had been "taken." The final insult was when Robert, in a boardroom coup, removed Grade as a director of the company he had founded. In early 1982 Grade resigned leaving Holmes a'Court to control all aspects of ACC.

One of the first moves taken by the new "Chairman" was to announce that ATV Music and Northern Songs were no longer for sale. To smooth over frayed feelings, he then announced the appointments of Abe Mandell of ITC, ACC's television distributing company in the U. S. and me, to the Board of the new company. In retrospect it seems this buttering up was part of his overall plan to green mail* the company, a practice he was already known for in Australia.

Paradoxically, just prior to Lord Grade's departure his film "On Golden Pond" was released to a huge reception in the U. S. After attending the screening of the film with my wife at Universal Studios prior to its release, I immediately telexed Lew Grade predicting that it would receive multiple Academy Award nominations and would surely

147

collect a few Oscars. I'm told he ran around the offices in the UK reading my telex.

We attended the Academy Awards that year as Dave Grusin's score to the film was nominated. "On Golden Pond," was, in fact, nominated for "Oscars" in nine categories and awarded in three. At the reception afterwards I spotted Lew sitting at the Marble Arch Production table with Marty Starger, the co-producer with Grade. I stood there pointing my finger at him smiling. He looked up in surprise, and then grabbed Marty shouting, "There's Sam! He's the only one that told me this was going to happen!" As I knew that he had already resigned, and Holmes a' Court confirmed it, I replied, "If only it would have happened sooner." He shook his head in sad agreement.

Notwithstanding his shortcomings I was always on good terms with Lew Grade and remember the many wonderful times I had in his presence. One, in particular, stands out.

It was early on during my employment while I was staying at a hotel in London. I simply couldn't get over my jet lag. So, I decided to get up at 4:AM and jog through Green Park and Hyde Park in my hotel supplied sweat-suit. It was approaching 6:AM and I decided to find out if the legend, that Lew Grade was always the first in his office at that time, was true. I jogged over to Marble Arch and approached ATV House at about 6:10 AM, banging on the glass door entrance. A small one-armed, elderly man dressed in a smart uniform came to the door to see what the racket was. I advised him that I wanted to see Sir Lew.

He asked, "Is his Lordship expecting you?" I told him to just call and tell him Sam is here to see him. He returned, unlocked the door and accompanied me to the elevator, which, though automatic, he presided over. I found Grade standing outside his office, cigar in hand, waiting for me. I immediately said, "So it's really true, you get here at 6:AM."

He replied, "Look at my cigar." Half of it was already smoked. He invited me in and asked if I'd like some breakfast. He phoned his dining room upstairs and a delightful breakfast was sent down. During our dining I asked, "Who was that doorman who let me in and why did he serve as an elevator operator for one that was self operating?"

He explained that Joe had been with him for many years. He had lost his arm in World War 1. No further explanation was necessary. Lew was a people person, unlike his eventual successor.

*The practice of taking over a financially distressed company at a price lower than its book value, and disposing its individual entities for sums which, in total, bring far more revenue than the price "valued" for the whole entity.

CHAPTER 46
Imagine

On Monday evening, December 8, 1980 John Lennon was shot and killed by Mark Chapman in front of his residence at The Dakota on West 72nd Street in Manhattan. It was an event that shocked and horrified the world. The music world, and ATV/ Northern Songs Music Publishing in particular, most acutely felt its impact. The next day my office in Hollywood was filled with newspaper, radio, and television reporters asking for my thoughts. One television interviewer asked what I thought was his most defining song. Without hesitation, I replied "Imagine." Some further discussion of the song ensued and I pointed out that, of all the songs created by Paul and John individually after the breakup of the Beatles, this song stands out as the best. Little did I know, at the time, the importance this song would play in my future stormy relationship with Robert Holmes a'Court.

In 1981 Yoko Ono called requesting a meeting to discuss the administration of John's music publishing catalogs including their joint company Lenono Music. I hadn't seen Yoko since the green card hearings and really had no interaction with her at that time. She requested a luncheon meeting at a restaurant where few, if any, other people would be present. I spoke to the owner of "Le Crepe" on 55th street, across from our New York offices, who agreed to close the restaurant at 2:30 PM and let us in when we arrived. She arrived in a Lincoln limousine, which parked in front of the restaurant, with the driver waiting.

Yoko was interested in my background and was pleased to learn that I had been a musician. We found that we were the same age, and she was delighted to learn that my daughter was born on my birthday, as was Sean on John's birthday. When I told her my birth date, she was thrilled and announced that those dates were "master numbers." So far, everything was going just great. She then asked the birth date of our managing director in the UK. I looked at her in surprise, and asked if she expected me to give her the birthdates of all our worldwide managing directors. She appeared shocked, and said that I displayed hostility and that the meeting was over. She got up and returned to her limousine. I was speechless. I paid the bill for the un-eaten lunch and returned to my office.

Several months later she called again while I was in New York to request another meeting, which I arranged for at our offices. Jerry Simon was the head of our New York office, so I used his office for the meeting. She arrived, most demurely, and sat across the desk from me. Just as I was about to start the conversation, she pointed to something on the desk, stood up, and announced that she could no longer meet with me as I had "war-like" tendencies. I asked what she was talking about, and she pointed to the paperclip holder on Jerry's desk that I hadn't even noticed. It was in the shape of an open grenade with the clips spraying out of it.

I said, "That's it? That's your proof?" I walked to her side of the desk, grabbed under her shoulder, lifting her up saying, "Let me accompany you to the elevator!" That would be the last time I would meet with her until 1984, a meeting that would eventually result in great embarrassment to Robert Holmes a'Court.

CHAPTER 47
a'Courtin' Disaster

In re-reading "Northern Songs: The True Story Of The Beatles Song Publishing Empire" by Southall and Perry, I note that Simon Carrell, Holmes a'Court's trusted financial assistant, states "Robert actually liked Sam, but they were never really on the same wavelength." Upon reflection, I believe that statement is true. I was, in fact, Robert's only guest for the premier of the London Palladium's staging of "Singin' In The Rain," starring Tommy Steele. The opening was actually delayed by Robert's telephone call from his car notifying the theatre's managing director to hold the curtain. When we arrived at the royal box, all stared up at our entrance, including Mike Stewart in the first row, in shock, at seeing me (whom he knew so well) enter the box. Mike was then chief executive of the music publishing company that owned the music rights to the show.

Then, there was the visit to Perth where I was treated to a round of golf with a golf pro. Jerry Leider, who had just finished producing "The Jazz Singer" remake with Neil Diamond, accompanied me on this trip. I also remember visiting Robert's stud farm for a meeting. Prior to the meeting as I was walking the grounds I noticed a short, stocky, elderly woman leaning on a fence railing staring at some horses. I came by and said hello. She introduced herself as Robert's mother and asked who I was. I told her I was Robert's guest. Then to my surprise she asked me if I knew her other son, to which I replied I didn't. After a short pause she said, "Too bad, he was the good one."

It was during that trip that Robert invited me to a private luncheon in his conference room. It was obviously done as a rejoinder to a previous dinner at the flat of Bert Reuter and his new wife in London. At that time, Bert occupied the position as Robert's deputy, eventually taken over by Alan Newman. The occasion was Robert's and my simultaneous arrival in London —he from Perth, and me from LA. We were both somewhat jet-lagged.

After a wonderful meal prepared by Bert's wife, Robert pulled out one of his small, cheap Dutch cigars that he regularly smoked and was about to light it, when I reached over and pulled it out of his mouth. He looked at me in shock as I said, "Robert you've just had a wonderful meal prepared by Mrs. Reuter and now you're going to insult her with that cheap cigar? Here, have a fine Cuban Monte Cristo." Bewildered, he reached for it and I pulled it away. "You're not about to bite off the end are you?" I pulled out a cigar cutter and asked if he preferred a straight or V-cut. I cut it for him then proceeded to light it with a long match and twirl it until it produced an even ash. I handed it to him and said, "There, you now have a gentlemen's cigar." Though, somewhat abashed, he thanked me, as Bert witnessed in astonishment. At the end of our private luncheon in Perth, Robert said "I have a surprise for you" and handed me a Monte Cristo with a rare smile.

On another occasion my wife and I had dinner with Robert and his wife Jan at his apartment at ATV House where we were also staying. Notwithstanding, this seemingly warm and friendly treatment, I had the feeling that all was not sincere. I was aware of his past activities with companies he controlled and parlayed, and found that he was not at all interested in the workings of music publishing. At the same time, he showed his hand with the quick disposal of ACC's Central Television Network and the highly respected Berman and Nathans costumer company. Beneath his exterior, I also sensed disrespect for the American entertainment industry, which he felt was financially excessive. At no time did I find him creative at ACC*, other than in ways to save revenue. Also, his boardroom dismissal of Lord Grade weighed heavily on me.

Bert Reuter, his original deputy who oversaw our publishing activities with interest, and I got along very well. For some unknown reason, he was peremptorily dismissed and reassigned back to Australia. His replacement, Alan Newman, was a completely different character. Alan was definitely a cool, no nonsense, whip-cracker. His only interest was the bottom line. Though we tolerated each other, there was always a feeling of distrust. He seemed in awe of Robert at all times, and suspected (correctly) that I wasn't.

*ATV changed its name to ACC, --Associated Communications Corp in 1981. While Lew Grade insisted we accommodate, and change our name as well, I refused telling him it took so much time to convince the public that we weren't a TV repair company, that I wasn't about to change it. He finally gave in and we remained ATV Music.

In 1983 the famous "America's Cup Yacht Race" was held. Alan Bond, a business associate of Holmes a'Court, backed the Australian entrant, which ultimately won, upsetting the American team, which was trying to keep a 132-year consecutive winning streak intact. I was about as knowledgeable of that sport as I was about curling, with an equal amount of interest. I was in London at the time and totally unaware of the race, when I received a call from Robert to come to his office. When I entered the office he was on the telephone and motioned me to sit down. He was talking to Alan Bond, getting a "knot by knot" description of the Australian position during the race and, in his exhilaration, calling him "Bondy." He would relate to me the Australian lead in great delight, up until their final victory. I don't even remember why he called me, except to gloat over his victory over the Americans.

Bond, with Robert's blessings, eventually held a majority interest in Robert's largest holding, Bell Resources, and siphoned off $1.2 billion to his own financially bereft company, the Bond Corporation, thereby nearly bankrupting Bell. In 1992 he was convicted and spent four years in jail. It was speculated by Simon Carrel, Robert's financial adviser while at ACC that, had Robert not died unexpectedly in 1990, he too might have faced the same fate.

At the end of 1983 ATV Music in the U.S. and Canada was enjoying great success with charted songs of Mann and Weill, Billy Joe Shaver, and other writers as well as chart activity in Canada. I was very pleased with the work of our Canadian manager, Frank Davies, and wrote a request to Alan Newman for an employment contract. He passed it on to Robert. While in the UK, Robert saw me in the hall at ATV House and asked me to meet him that evening at 7 PM in his office. When I arrived he said that he'd like to discuss his business philosophy with me. He proceeded to sight examples of successful companies that did not offer contracts, stating that the employees had confidence in management. Then he brought up my request for a contract for Frank. He asked if I thought Frank would leave if he was denied a contract, and I had to admit I didn't think he would, but he would feel better if he had one. We talked further and I finally agreed I would talk with Frank and advise him that a contract was not available. Robert then leaned across his desk toward me and said, "Now Sam, how about yours?" I had two more years on my contract, and leaned toward him, almost nose to nose, and said, "No fucking way!"

He eased back in his chair, turned and stared out the window for a good ten seconds then replied, "Do you like curry?"I said I did and he advised that he knew a wonderful place nearby on Seymour St. We dined at the curry restaurant and not another word was spoken about our meeting. When the bill arrived it totaled 2.5 lbs., which he gleefully showed me stating it was a great bargain that he had found.

Our association bumped along until the end of 1984, when it became apparent to me Robert was not in our business for the long run. He had already dismissed Louis Benjamin, a corporate board member who oversaw the Stoll/Moss Group of theatres and Pye Records. Walter Woyda, who had been managing director for Pye Records, resigned early, warning others of Holmes a Court's tactics. Pye, from day one of the takeover, had been told that they were not to sign any new artists, the life-blood of any record company.

1984 was proving to be a pivotal year. In mid-year I received a telephone call from Allen Klein, the controversial short time Beatles manager, who was largely responsible for the split between Lennon and McCartney and the eventual break-up of the Beatles. In a heated battle he succeeded in convincing John and Yoko, as well as George and Ringo, to retain him as the group's manager. However, Paul and Linda were determined to have Lee Eastman, (Paul's soon to be father-in-law) and his son John Eastman awarded that responsibility. I knew Allen prior to his fame with the Rolling Stones and the Beatles, and couldn't believe his request. As he was still representing Yoko, he requested that I consider gifting back "Imagine" to Yoko. After telling him he was out of his mind, and offering an unmentionable suggestion, I hung up on him. About three weeks later I received a call from John Mason, the former law partner of Owen Sloane, who continued to represent ATV Music. Mason had a different approach. He had been retained by Yoko as her attorney.

His request was, "Sam, as you may know, I'm now representing Yoko. She feels so badly about the way things turned out between you and her, particularly as John thought so highly of you, and would love to have you get in touch with her."

I replied, "I assume you are either at the Dakota or have been there. If so, you probably noticed that she has a telephone. She can use it to call me."

John's immediate reply was, "Now Sam don't be like that." I simply said, "When she decides to call me, I'll consider meeting with her" and hung up.

About 10 days later Yoko did call relating the same message as

Mason and hoped for a meeting. As I planned to be in New York the following week, we set a meeting to be held at her apartment at the Dakota. I was unaware that Robert and Jan Holmes a'Court would be visiting New York at the same time. Plans were for me to meet at her apartment for dinner. Unfortunately, that evening a terrific thunderstorm occurred shorting out the electricity in all of Manhattan. I called Yoko to try to re-schedule but she was determined to have the meeting, so I agreed to meet. I was able to find a taxi, and arrived at a darkened Dakota using only candlelight. I checked in at reception and was told that the elevators were not in operation, so I would have to use the stairs. I trudged up what I believe was five flights of stairs and upon reaching the Lennon apartment was grabbed by a stocky man who shoved a 45 into my ribs. I tried to explain that I was an invited guest of Yoko and finally convinced him to knock on the door. Yoko arrived and confirmed that I was her guest. She apparently forgot to advise her bodyguard that she was expecting me.

As I entered the apartment she introduced me to her friend, another Sam, who seemed to be interested in everything she did. She apologized that since her stove was not working as a result of the storm, she had prepared (or purchased) a large selection of cold cuts. The meeting was quite cordial and no business was really discussed. The administration agreements had been extended in London, as a result of some bargaining done by the new owners. She simply wanted me to listen to her new album, which largely contained the material of other writers such as Nilsson, whom I respected. She also discussed some of her experiences with John. While I certainly was not excited about her album, and particularly her as an artist, I listened politely and did not offer any negative comments. Our past confrontations seemed to have been covered over, and after about three hours I departed.

The next morning I received a telephone call from Jan Holmes a'Court. She said, "Sam, I know you are friendly with Yoko and I do so want to meet her. Could you arrange for Robert and me to visit her?" I assured her that it would be no problem and gave her Yoko's telephone number. I immediately called Yoko and advised her to expect Jan's call. She was more than delighted.

They met at Yoko's apartment that afternoon. Yoko called me early that evening and said it was a wonderful meeting. She further stated that, at Jan's request of Robert, she was "gifted" the song "Imagine" in remembrance of John, and their wonderful new acquaintance. I was floored and could only imagine the emotional presentation by Yoko that must have persuaded both of them. Here was a man that scrutinized every little expenditure, but gives away a major asset of the company, without consultation.

Later in that year, when it became obvious to me that Robert was preparing to sell our company, I was asked to come to London to discuss publishing matters. Presiding over the meeting was Alan Newman, with Simon Carrell in attendance. We discussed the value of various Northern Songs copyrights. When it came to "Imagine" I advised them we no longer owned the song. They couldn't understand what I was saying. I told them what Yoko had stated to me, which they totally disputed. I suggested they check with Robert. They telephoned him, but he put them off. I then suggested perhaps that they should call Yoko and offered them the number but they refused. To this day Simon Carrell cannot believe that Robert could have done this, yet before the end of that year Yoko was assigned the copyright. Carrell claims that the song was about to revert to her from a past agreement. If that were so, Yoko and Allen Klein would have known it, and had no need to pursue it.

While Robert tried to hide the fact that he was considering a sale, it was suspected. He would continue to tell employees that it was not true, until he enlisted me to pursue possible candidates.

CHAPTER 48
Some Good Times, Too

While the reign of Robert Holmes a'Court dissolved ACC,* as well as ATV Music and Northern Songs with the consequential grief to me, those times were not without some wonderful and satisfying events. Two such events will long remain with me.

In early 1982, I received a call from a British producer informing me that his company would be producing the annual fundraising event for the Prince's (Philip) Trust, to be held later in the year, at the Royal Albert Hall. The program would honor the music of The Beatles, which would be performed by the top recording artists of the world. As the music would be practically all Northern Songs, he wanted to discuss an overall synchronization fee, in the event the show was to be syndicated. The Prince's Trust helped maintain what we in the United States would refer to as our National Parks. We scheduled a time, well in advance of the performance, when I would be in the UK for our discussion and negotiation.

Considering the type of event to be held, negotiations were friendly and a deal was easily achieved. The producers invited me to attend as their guest in a reserved balcony box. They suggested formal wear, if possible. Fortunately, I had my tuxedo available. I arrived at Albert Hall early to find an enormous crowd. The huge auditorium was filling up as I proceeded up the steps to my designated box. The producers had already arrived, and they showed me to my seat at the left, front corner of the box. I viewed the large audience arriving while exchanging small talk with my hosts. As the time for the concert approached, all seats including the boxes appeared to be filled, except the box on my immediate left. Suddenly the auditorium went black and a wide spotlight covered the box to my left spilling over to ours. The Queen entered on the arm of the velvet-caped Lord Mayor of London, as the orchestra majestically played "God Save The Queen." To the right of the Queen entering simultaneously, accompanied by two lovely young ladies, was Prince Philip. When the ceremony concluded Prince Philip reached across the common barrier between boxes to shake my hand and announce that he was looking forward to this concert. As we chatted, the Queen interested to see whom the prince was talking to, leaned over, smiled at me and waved. I won't ever forget it. Frequently, the prince would lean over to comment on a particular performance with, "That was really a good one!"

In a state of euphoria, I called home immediately after the concert. That night I stayed at the home of Terry and Penny Slater. He had been made head of EMI's Music publishing companies in the UK, and responsible for the hits of many European groups. We had, and have always remained friends. Terry, in fact, was a central figure in my other memorable experience at the same Royal Albert Hall a year later.

It was through Terry Slater's close friendship with Phil Everly that I became acquainted with Phil. I was able to help him straighten out a problem he was having regarding his BMI royalty statements, and assisted him with various other music business matters. Phil and I kept in touch on a frequent basis. Terry had played bass for the Everly Brothers and became quite close to Phil. One could easily judge that Terry was closer to being Phil's brother than Don, after the early years of their fame. They were in constant contact even after Terry moved back to the UK. Needless to say, Terry, at the time, was not a favorite of Don's, primarily due to his closeness to Phil.

The Everly Brothers Reunion Concert was the result of an unexpected telephone call from Don to Phil, one day in early 1983, suggesting that they should perhaps try to get together, which sparked the idea of a "reunion." They had not performed together for almost ten years. At their last concert in 1973 at Knott's Berry Farm, south of Los Angeles, Phil threw down his guitar in disgust and stormed off the stage, a result of Don showing up drunk for the performance. They had not played together, let alone talked to each other since. With Terry's encouragement, he and Phil immediately went to Nashville to meet with Don and their mother. During that meeting and, somewhat of a celebration that followed, they decided that the Royal Albert Hall in London would be the best venue for a "reunion." The UK was always the most dedicated market for the Everlys. In fact, one of the first references used to describe The Beatles was "The English Everlys."

Terry returned to England and prevailed upon his good friend Mel Bush, perhaps the hottest promoter in the UK, to work on the project. His previous promotions were Santana, McCartney & Wings, Queen, and Zeppelin. Terry oversaw production, retaining outstanding guitarist Albert Lee, and pianist Pete Wingfield. To fill out the band Terry called Cliff Richards to request the use of some of the musicians from his band, to which Richards agreed. During that time Terry contacted me to discuss the recording and taping of the concert.

In 1981 I retained Delilah Communications, a contemporary book publisher, headed by Stephanie Bennett, to produce a definitive book containing all of the songs of The Beatles, as well as interviews with many personalities associated with the group. Milt Okun meticulously completed the music editing. The boxed two-volume publication was entitled "The Compleat Beatles" and sold quite well. As a result Stephanie Bennett requested the rights to produce a companion VHS documentary. That production also turned out well. So, when Terry called to discuss the project, I recommended Delilah Communications to tape and record the concert.

As both Phil and Don wanted approval for the producer, Phil, Stephanie, and I went down to Nashville, where we met Don and his mother. All went well and while Don was somewhat standoffish to me, knowing that I was a close friend of Terry's, everyone was okay with Stephanie's company as the VHS producer.

News of the reunion attracted a great deal of publicity in the UK, and the hall quickly sold out. The audience was treated to everything they had come to expect, and more. The opening was quite memorable. Two relatively tall sets of stairs were placed on each side of the stage. On the top of one side stood Don, on the other, Phil, both in spotlights. As they descended downward towards each other, the crowd roared. They met at center stage, embraced, and the concert began. The audience was thrilled and showed their approval throughout.

At the end of the concert I went backstage to congratulate the boys. Unexpectedly Don came forward to me, reached out for my hand and, to my surprise said, "I want to thank you, and let you know I don't think all of this would have happened without your support." I was both surprised and, of course, pleased.

Sadly, in January of 2014 Phil died of COPD complications. His wife, Patti called me to assist her during and after the funeral. So many flowers were sent to the church by his fellow entertainers that it took several trips in Patti's station wagon to get them to her house. I had never seen such huge containers of flowers which covered virtually every room in the house. I read with interest particularly those sent by Paul Simon, who said that no matter how he and Art Garfunkel sang, they could never equal the quality of sound of the Everly Brothers, and especially Phil's. Paul McCartney expressed much the same sentiment.

CHAPTER 49
Beginning Of The End

While Holmes a'Court asked me to research who could be candidates for the acquisition of ATV Music, no firm price was established, nor any discussion of my participation, if a bonafide offer was made through my efforts. The "ballpark" figure I assumed was in the neighborhood of $50,000 000.

My first candidate was EMI. I had maintained friendly relations with EMI executives in the UK, despite my departure from their US outlet, Capitol Records. I knew that Ron White, who oversaw music publishing, had expressed interest in the acquisition when Lord Grade put the company up for sale in 1981. From time to time I'd met Ron at various music industry functions, and even had dinner or cocktails with him at such occasions. After a number of discussions with White, it became apparent that they felt the asking price was too high to get approval from Thorne, their recent, new owners.

My next candidate was Stig Andersson, successful writer/producer and owner of Polaris Music who controlled all rights of the multimillion selling group ABBA. I met with Stig and his potential fellow investors in St. Petersburg, Florida to discuss the deal. Unfortunately, when they returned to Sweden they also decided that it was just too expensive for the group. My next candidate was my good friend Shoo Kusano, owner of Shinko Music in Japan who expressed interest. Soon after I reached Shoo I contacted Alan Newman to inquire just what kind of deal was being considered for my efforts in finding a buyer, and suggested a number of industry standards for such acquisition services. He relayed my request to Holmes a' Court, who was shocked that I would make such a request, and simply terminated my services in finding a buyer. He further demanded that I make no further inquiries, and keep confidential the fact that he was planning to sell the company. This situation put an even greater strain on my relationship with him, not to mention my increased lack of respect.

In 1982 my dear Australian friend Frank Donlevy, who had

grubstaked me in my Trust Music Management launch when I left Capitol Records, was dismissed as managing director of Castle Music, EMI's music publishing outlet in Australia after more than thirty years with that company. The entire music community was shocked. As soon as I heard the news I called him to advise that he was the new managing director of ATV Music, Australia, effective the following week.

Frank was wise enough to realize what was happening at this time, and was as I, hoping a legitimate buyer would be found. He kept in touch with me by telex. In the same office area as Frank was Bert Reuter, who was sent back to Australia when Alan Newman arrived in the UK. I'm quite sure that Bert was told to keep an eye on our operations as well. The telex machine was just outside his office, so I'm sure that he read each one before Frank received them. He knew that I was not allowed to discuss the possible sale under any circumstances.

Shoo Kusano, Frank, and I were great friends and we were hoping that Shoo would make an offer. Shoo had telexed me that he would be in the UK to discuss the situation, but I couldn't let Frank know. So, I devised a telex that got the news to him without Reuter suspecting anything. The telex discussed efforts at placing various songs, and ended innocently with a mention of our weather. "The weather so far has been quite pleasant; however there is a definite nip in the air." Frank "got it" immediately. Unfortunately, Shoo couldn't meet Holmes a'Court's demands.

Early in 1985, meetings with various interested parties continued to take place in the UK directly with Holmes a' Court, attended by Simon Carrell. Some of the meetings resulted in parties leaving in disgust, due to Robert's changing the terms already agreed upon. He continued to instruct his lieutenants to assure employees that the company was not for sale.

As my employment agreement would end as of March 31st of that year, I notified Newman and Robert that I did not intend to renew. As a result, they sent Julian Appleson, an accountant who had spent some time working in our offices, to preside over our operations. They gave him the title of CEO, with instructions to keep the employees calm and assure them that it was "business as usual." I spent the short remainder of my lame duck term quietly out of the way.

Shortly after my departure from ATV, I received a call from Bobby Roberts, the agent who represented Barry Mann and Cynthia Weill. He advised that he had an investor willing to buy the catalogs and have me back in charge, with a percentage of ownership. The investor was Charles Knapp, a Los Angeles industrialist. I met with him at his office in Westwood and told him everything he needed to know as well as answering all of his questions. He said that he would leave shortly, for the UK and offer Holmes a'Court $50,000,000, the figure I suggested. Before he left I told him that, under no circumstances should he let Robert know that I was involved. I emphasized that point strongly.

Knapp met with Robert, who, was apparently agreeable with the price, but asked who he intended to preside over the company. Knapp said that it was confidential for the present. Robert continued to insist, much to Knapp's annoyance. Finally Robert declared without this knowledge the deal could not move forward.

Knapp later reported to me, in disgust, that he finally replied: "Who the hell do you think I'm going to get to run it? Sam Trust, of course." With that reply, Robert said, "This meeting is over."

Several months later, during the Michael Jackson negotiations, I received a call from John Branca, Jackson's attorney, asking if I would meet with him. I agreed to a meeting at his office that turned out to be very pleasant. He simply wanted my thoughts on the acquisition. I told him to not overlook the value of the ATV and Welbeck catalogs, which actually out-earned Maclen (Northern Songs) in the last several years. Having no understanding or interest in music publishing, Holmes a'Court took no notice of this fact. As to the Lennon/McCartney works I simply said to Branca, "Consider them as rare paintings. Once you take them off the wall they can never be replaced, and should only increase in value."

In August of that year, after months of haggling, the company was sold to Michael Jackson for $47,500,000. The loyal employees of ATV had been "led down the garden path," and released with little or no severance pay.

CHAPTER 50
What Now? Again

After presiding over ATV Music for 12 years, and choosing not to continue through its ultimate demise, (resulting from Robert Holmes a' Court's defrauding the employees, and "green mailing"* the company) I was now unemployed with no idea of my future.

My attempt to purchase the company was quashed by a vindictive Holmes a' Court. The company was subsequently sold, fairly quickly thereafter, to Michael Jackson for a price two and one half million dollars less than my representative was willing to pay. Robert removed "Penny Lane," which he gifted to his daughter. Other assets were also held back from the Jackson sale. Oddly enough, and less publicized, Michael was very much attracted by the Venice Music catalog of hit songs by various black artists, such as Little Richard, Sam Cook, and Percy Mayfield.

All administration rights to Trust Music Management now reverted back to me, and my wife Joan who capably managed licensing. Activity in Rocksmith, our ASCAP Company, was in fact, picking up with the spread in popularity of Jack Hayford's composition, "Majesty." So many licenses were requested, worldwide, for this song that our friendly German affiliate started calling Joan "Mrs. Majesty." This was, of course, fine but it certainly wasn't enough to support a family and keep me busy.

Later in the summer of that year I received a telephone call from Bob Summers, president of RCA Records. I knew of Bob, but never met him, so the call was somewhat of a surprise. He obviously knew of me, and asked if I would be interested in coming to New York to discuss the possibility of heading RCA's music publishing operation. I, of course, accepted the invitation and we set a date. Joan was thrilled at the possibility of returning to New York, as she had never mentally unpacked her bags for the West Coast. We talked about reuniting with the Magruders, our long time dear friends and God-Parents to our children. In fact, during our trip to New York, before my meeting, we had actually looked at possible homes in Smoke Rise, New Jersey, where they resided.

I arrived for my meeting with Bob Summers who welcomed me, but had a concerned look on his face. He asked if I was aware of the new executive RCA had recently employed, Jose Menendez. I told him I was, and also aware of the terror he immediately brought to RCA employees. He said, "Sam, if it were up to me, you would be hired immediately, but as I now have to report to him, you'll have to meet with him," pointing to the adjoining office. Bob called him to advise that I would be coming to see him.

As I arrived in his office, Menendez immediately stood up and greeted me sarcastically, "Aha, Sam Trust, a legend in his own time!" I replied in the same manner, "and I understand that you are also creating a legend of sorts!" That set the tone of the meeting, which deteriorated from there. It was apparent that he had no interest or use for music publishing. He was a native of Cuba, who had overseen RCA's acquisition of Hertz Car Rentals and was placed in this high position by RCA management, for which he was totally unqualified. This was only one of the many poor decisions made by that organization, which eventually was sold, much to the dismay of the whole music world. I walked back to Bob Summers office shaking my head as I arrived. Bob looked back and said, "I understand. Sam, --- I don't think I am long for my job, either." By the end of the year he was gone. He accepted a similar position at CBS. We returned to our home somewhat dejected, after spending some wonderful time with our New York friends.

RCA's Records and Music Publishing were sold to BMG of Germany, shortly thereafter. Eventually all of RCA was sold to General Electric. Previous to that final sale, Menendez left to enter television production on the west coast. His reputation as a ruthless executive followed him. The mention of his name, alone, elicited scorn from all who had ever dealt with him.

The widely spread notice of his murder brought no surprise to the Hollywood community, as it was assumed that he had probably crossed the wrong party. The fact that his own children murdered him was a shock.

*The practice of getting control of a large public company whose stock value has dropped to a price possibly below "book" value, then ballyhooing "new management" but deviously selling off divisions which in total bring in far more revenue than the company as a whole body. This was done by Holmes a'Court to ACC (formerly known as ATV) of which ATV Music was a division.

CHAPTER 51
Lorimar

Near the end of 1985 I received a call from Owen Sloane, the lawyer I had retained for many years at ATV and a wonderful friend. He was well aware of my situation and had obviously kept himself apprised of the changing personnel situations in the music industry. While we had been friends from the first meeting that he and I attended at a California Copyright Conference in 1969, I had not retained his services until 1976. When I did so, I challenged him to prepare a difficult contract. If I were satisfied with it, he would be retained.

The contract was for a Canadian group called "Klaatu," which had broken out in Canada, based mainly on the rumor that they were actually The Beatles under a different name. This, of course, was nonsense. However, the sales were huge for Canada. They were looking to release the album in the U.S. and looking for a large advance. As I knew my way around the Canadian music industry, I located the representative of the group who was looking for the advance. I told him that I would give him no advance and suggested he take my offer of sub-publishing. What better deal could he have than be represented by the company that owned, virtually, all of the Lennon/McCartney songs? He realized rather quickly that it would be better than any advance payment he could negotiate. The contract for sub-publishing, therefore, had to be complex. Owen worked hard on the phrasing of the agreement that by necessity became quite lengthy but covered the situation and protected us completely. Hence, his hiring and continuing with ATV until the acquisition by Jackson.

While Klaatu did only modestly well in the U.S., our wonderful song plugger, the legendary Happy Goday, landed a single from the album, *Calling Occupants* (From *Interplanetary Space*) with Karen Carpenter, who took it to top 40.

Owen had met with Jerry Gottlieb, an executive with the very popular Lorimar Productions, who at the time were riding high in television with *Dallas*, *Falcon Crest*, *Knots Landing* and *Perfect Strangers*.

Apparently, they were not happy with the head of their music and publishing division, and were looking for a replacement. Owen had recommended me and asked me to call Gottlieb for an interview.

I met with Gottlieb, who apparently knew of me, and was, of course, probably prepped by Owen. The interview went very well. Gottlieb decided to introduce me to Lee Rich and Merv Adelson, the co-chairmen of Lorimar. As the year was ending, we decided to start my employment in January of the following year, 1986. Owen had already suggested the terms of my contract, which were fine with me, as they were somewhat better than ATV's, to start with. Negotiations hardly took place and my contract was executed rather quickly.

When I arrived, there was no space set apart for a music publishing operation, so I drifted from site to site until a large enough one was made available. My position was all encompassing. I oversaw the Director of Music, who hired musicians and produced the music for films. I was also to create a music publishing operation, in addition to overseeing the music contained in their past and future film productions.

I was surprised to learn that I had replaced Bobby Roberts, the agent for Barry Mann and Cynthia Weill and the one who set me up with Charles Knapp for the ill-fated attempt to purchase ATV Music. I can only assume that Roberts placement in that position was political or done as a favor, since he had no experience in music publishing, or overall administration. To my surprise, Bobby called me to congratulate me on my appointment. He admitted that he was not qualified for the job, and said that he thought that I was perfect to handle it.

Although Lorimar had taken over the original MGM studio's lot, space was not yet made available. I, therefore, concentrated on the existing music publishing assets, i.e., music from the various TV shows of Lorimar, and the production of the music for these and future films.

It was not long before I heard from some of the composers with complaints about both. Carl Fortina, the music contractor for many of these productions, also approached me. The common complaints centered on the current head of music production. Fortina's complaints had to do with the hiring, firing and scheduling practices. The composers' complaints were about the crediting, or lack thereof, for their music.

The music director finally acknowledged my position by inviting me to a recording session that he'd scheduled. I attended, keeping Fortina's problems in mind. The director, unaware of my music background, put on a show, trying to impress me with his studio directorial experience. He would do a take, and then ask that the chairs be rearranged for better acoustics, as well as other useless criticisms and tricks to impress. I left with a better understanding of Fortina's problems.

The major problem for composers with this music director was brought to my attention by Jerry Immel, the composer of the music to "Dallas", a TV series that must be ranked as one of the most successful of all time, having played on Network Television for 13 consecutive years. Jerry felt that he was being underpaid performing royalties, considering the amount of music he was creating for the show.

I requested music cue-sheets for the show for the most recent years. The director's employees, who were also responsible for clearing all music, prepared these cue sheets. Throughout the cue-sheets, at various intervals, appeared the name of one composer with whom I was not familiar. I studied the name and realized it was an anagram of the Music Director's. I called Jerry Immel with my findings and asked him to meet with me to go over the cues listed. We met, and Jerry confirmed that they were all his compositions.

I contacted the head of Lorimar's Legal staff and presented him with the situation. Without hesitation, he declared the director must be fired. Soon after his termination the director notified Lorimar threatening to sue for unwarranted dismissal. Lorimar's Legal department immediately advised him that if he did so, they intended to turn him over to the Los Angeles Police's criminal division, with proof of his theft. He was never heard from again.

Jerry and I quickly became quite friendly. After a short time he asked, "Sam you really don't remember me, do you?" I confessed that I didn't.

He said, "I was the spotter for Shorty Rogers' scoring of "Fools." I then recalled Shorty introducing me to him. That was my very first involvement with film scoring, for the movie "Fools," while I was at Capitol's Beechwood Music. I offered to go over Jerry's performing royalties statements, which led to an incredible find for both Jerry and Lorimar.

With the huge success of "Dallas" domestically, the series then also caught fire internationally. The distributor for this series for France and surrounding countries was Canal Plus. What I discovered was, while Jerry as a writer and Lorimar as publisher were paid performance royalties for their background music, no crediting appeared for the theme music. I contacted my friend, Alain di Ricou, who had long represented my companies in France, and had become a director on the board of SACEM, the French performing rights society. Alain had been one of the music publishers who had provided me with an advance payment in my launch of Trust Music Management. Needless to say, I worked closely with him and formed a strong friendship.

Alain researched this situation with SACEM and discovered that Canal Plus, realizing the value of the theme music, replaced it with a new one which they published. He further stated that this procedure was illegal. I authorized him to notify Canal Plus of our intention to sue to transfer representation unless the original theme was reinstated, and past royalties accounted for. Alain came down hard on them, and the problem was solved including past payments well into six figures for both Jerry and Lorimar.

Jerry was overwhelmed and could not thank me enough. The royalties he received allowed him to retire to Sea Ranch in Northern California some three months later. He said that he'd had enough composing under deadline pressure. He offered me a standing invitation to be his guest at Sea Ranch, which Joan and I eventually took up several years later. Jerry had a lovely home with a woodworking shop in his basement where he turned out some beautiful furniture.

CHAPTER 52
Lorimar, "Moish" and Merv

With the dismissal of Lorimar's Director of Music Production, I was in immediate need of a replacement. Fortunately, I was made aware of the retirement of Columbia Picture's longtime Music Director, Dick Berres. Dick was with Columbia for 25 years and was respected by the top film scorers in the industry. Lester Sill, my longtime buddy, suggested that I contact him. Lester felt that Dick might just be getting a little bored, being out of the action. I called Dick, and found that Lester was right. Dick came in for an interview and I, of course, immediately hired him and was lucky to get him. He was the consummate professional.

Space was now found for our entire music operations in the original music area used by MGM. There was plenty of room for everybody. I was assigned the former office of longtime MGM Music Director, Henry Lojeski. We could not possibly fill out the entire area, since in the golden days of MGM; there was space for composers, arrangers, copyists, and storage of music manuscripts. MGM's music publishing had been acquired a year earlier by EMI Music, which, at that time had been purchased by SBK Communications, (Swid, Bandier, Koppelman,) basically successful rock and roll music entrepeneurs. As a result, no importance was assigned to the film score libraries of one the greatest music studios in the world.

The space had not really been cleaned since EMI cleared out all of the music in an obvious haphazard manner. I was disgusted to see scores and parts still strewn on the floor. I couldn't believe my eyes when I picked up the conductor's score of "Bad Day at Black Rock," the first music for a major film composed by Andre Previn, with footprints all over it. It was a marvelous score for a very successful film, exhibiting Previn's great talent.

With space now available, I was able to start hiring music publishing personnel. My first choice for "professional manager," was my long time associate Steve Stone, who fortunately was still available, due to the closing of ATV Music the previous August. Rita Zak, who had extensive copyright experience, was hired as Copyright Manager and Diane Craig, who also had some experience in the music industry, became my assistant and secretary.

As Lorimar had no publishing company in place, other than as a depository for songs that were written for their films, as well as the scores thereto, new outlets were created. No time was wasted in developing these entities. One of our first steps taken was the acquisition of a solid country catalog. The publishing catalogs of "The Oak Ridge Boys," a popular Nashville group became available. I was quick to pick them up along with their experienced publisher Noel Fox, who was well established in Nashville. Almost immediately songs from the companies began appearing on the Country charts. Through the efforts of Noel Fox and Steve Stone, Lorimar hit with a number one recording on the country charts in less than a year.

I had been following the career of Jazz pianist David Benoit, and after attending a concert in Hermosa Beach featuring him and his compositions, I decided to sign him as a writer. That decision proved fruitful as within the year his current album hit number one on the Billboard Jazz charts.

During the early part of my first year, Lorimar was extremely successful with its network TV shows still at top ratings. At the same time, Warner Brother's studios were experiencing some financial headwinds. Steve Ross, Warner's legendary CEO, and Merv Adelson were great friends. There was even talk of Lorimar coming to the rescue of Warners, in some manner. However, shortly thereafter, Lee Rich departed after a disagreement with Adelson. Adelson was tempted to enter feature film production and distribution, being lured in the same manner as my former employer, Lew Grade, and tragically, with the same disastrous result. Lorimar later joined forces with a successful producer of TV syndicated programs, Telepictures, to become known as Lorimar Telepictures.

In early 1988 a unique opportunity was presented from a very unlikely source. The music publishing catalog, owned by the notorious Morris Levy, longtime entrepreneur of music entertainment holdings, i.e., nightclubs, record stores, record labels, and publishing companies, (thought to be "fronts" for "mob" activities by some) was for sale. I had known Morris, referred to by many as "Moish," for many years, going back to my days at BMI, where I met him and lunched with his publishing representative, Phil Kahl. Moish was definitely a Damon

Runyonesque character who was thought to have various organized crime connections. Despite this shady reputation, he was one of the greatest fundraisers in New York. He was chairman emeritus (music division) of The United Jewish Appeal, raised funds for several hospitals and many other charities. I had attended a number of events presided over by Morris. The very mention of Moish in the music publishing community caused raised eyebrows and some fear. The major publishers wanted nothing to do with any assets controlled by Morris. At the time, the government, on suspicion of racketeering and extortion, was investigating him. I was very aware of the value of his flagship catalog, Patricia Music, (part of his "Big Seven" music companies) having dealt with it at BMI, and had always gotten along very well with Morris. In fact, in 1971, while at Beechwood Music, when we had just hit the charts with a song recorded by Tommy James and The Shondells, recorded on Morris' record label, Roulette, he called me.

"Sam, Morris... How ya' doin?"

I responded, "Morris, great to hear from you, and congratulations on your record!"

"That's why I'm callin'. I need half the publishin'."

I replied, "What? I can't do that Morris. This is a public company. I just can't hand over assets."

"Sam, I take half publishing on all singles I release."

My response was, "Sorry Morris, I just can't."

"OK, kid, so long."

The record had entered the charts at 65 with a bullet. (meaning it was hot) The next week I checked the charts and it was gone. That same day I received a call from Tommy James asking if Morris had called me. I told him he had, and explained the conversation. Tommy exploded, "YOU TURNED HIM DOWN??" I said I did, and he said Morris had simply pulled the record and discontinued distribution. Tommy was heartbroken, and I was stunned. I learned one lesson; however, Morris was a man of his word.

Upon learning of the availability of Patricia Music, I called Morris and told him of my interest on behalf of Lorimar. He seemed delighted, and invited me to meet with him in New York. Apparently, few players were interested in acquiring what they imagined to be a "tainted" asset. His asking price for the catalog was five million. I arranged for a meeting the following week, after discussing the deal with Jerry Gottlieb, who also would meet Morris. Jerry, who was instrumental in hiring me, oversaw my activities. Upon my arrival in New York, Phil Kahl, Morris' assistant who looked after Music Publishing, called and invited me to lunch, prior to our scheduled meeting. I questioned Phil about the condition of the publishing files, which he insisted was impeccable. After lunch he took me to Morris' office. Morris was his usual self and we got along very well. I told him that I could not commit to the offering price until I examined the files and had my accountants verify earnings. He said that was fine and that he already had accountants do a due diligence on his files before he justified the price quoted. This seemed unusual and added another notch to my interest in the catalog, and my assessment of Morris' business acumen. I spent much of the afternoon examining the files for myself, and was impressed with their condition and upkeep.

As it was a Friday, Morris suggested that I spend the weekend at his farm in Columbia County, New York, near the Hudson River. The farm was 1500 acres situated next to the heavyweight champion Mike Tyson's residence. Shortly after I arrived on a cold winter day, Morris gave me a tour in his pick-up truck. I had no idea that he had become an expert in horse breeding. I was overwhelmed at the size of his stables, which contained the horses of several famous entertainment celebrities. It was not just a stable, but a fully indoor track where the horses could work out. I was later to learn several famous horse breeders had been in touch with Morris seeking his advice. Apparently when Morris got interested in a subject, he became an expert.

Later, back at his home we were discussing many aspects of the music business, when he pointed to his telephone and said, "Did you hear that ring?"

I said I didn't.

He responded "No, and it hasn't since my indictment. It would ring off the hook when my services were needed for fund raisers, charities, and favors."

I said "Morris, tell me about the case."

He said, "I can't. It just gets too close to the top. But, when I get finished, I'm out of this country for good!" He went on to explain that he had already purchased a huge sheep ranch in Australia where he planned to live. He proceeded to set up a large screen and show me a film of that ranch and its possibilities. In the middle of the film the phone did ring.

Morris picked it up and whispered to me it was Polygram calling from London. He said loudly "No, I'm not interested your offer" and hung up. "There's no way I'd sell to those ex-Nazis!" It seemed that word was getting around of my interest in the company.

The next day I said my goodbye to Morris and promised to keep in touch. If our due diligence found no problems, we'd proceed to a contract, hopefully within a month, and I'd be back in New York to complete the deal. As I returned to the city I thought about what Morris had said about the case, and pondered why he was holding back—"too close to the top." I knew that not only was Roulette Records involved in the case, but also MCA Records, then a division of Universal.

Lew Wasserman was the chairman and CEO of that entire company. It was fairly well-known of his friendship and influence with President Reagan, whom he heavily backed, not only for Governor, but for president, orchestrating huge fundraising campaigns. Morris could truly be "in a box."

After about a month I had a contract drawn for the purchase of Patricia Music along with his other Big Seven affiliated companies, with the approval of management and returned to New York to finalize the acquisition. Morris had his lawyers go over the contract and we agreed to meet in his office the evening prior to the formal execution of the document. I arrived at his office to a smiling Morris. I sat across from his desk as he poured us a celebratory drink. Within minutes the phone on his desk rang.

He answered and said, "Sam, it's for you." I will remember what followed for the rest of my life.

The call was from Jerry Gottlieb. "Sam are you with Morris?" I answered that I was. He responded, "You have to kill the deal."

I was shocked, but managed to hide it from Morris's gaze, saying, "Oh really?" He then explained that the new public relations firm, we had recently acquired with Telepictures, found out about our deal and went mad! They told Jerry that Morris' Cleveland "mob" connection, Moe Dalitz, was the same connection Merv Adelson had early in his career in Las Vegas.

Morris interrupted asking who was calling. I told him it was Jerry Gottlieb and he said, "Oh, let me talk to him." I relayed this to Jerry who said "No Way!" I told Morris that he was in a hurry and simply couldn't talk. I quickly and nervously hung up when Morris broke the silence.

"The deal's fucked, right Sam?"

I said, "Why do you say that?"

"The man that authorizes you to give me 5 million bucks can't say hello? C'mon Sammy I know it!"

I sat back down in my seat almost speechless, and simply said,

"You're right Morris."

He inquired as to the reason, and I told him it was because of his connection to Moe Dalitz and Dalitz's past connection to Adelson. He said, "Dalitz, Dalitz? I never worked with him, he wasn't my guy!" At that point I was looking for a hole to crawl into. Morris could sense my misery and said, "Sam, forget about it. It's not your fault. Come on back tomorrow morning, and we'll have some coffee and pastry."

I returned to his office the next day with a plan.

"Morris, your company is worth the five million. I know you were counting on it, so I'm going to get it for you."

Later that day I called Chuck Kaye, longtime CEO of Warner Brothers Publishing, who had recently gone into business with the backing of a Japanese company. I told him about my deal but he was, at first, reluctant for reasons I previously related. I told him of my impression of the company and he said he'd look into it. Within about a month, Kaye acquired it for his new company, "Windswept Pacific." Morris got his deal.

Unfortunately for him, not long after, he was, in fact, convicted of extortion. He was sentenced to enter prison in 1990, but died of cancer just prior to that date.

By the end of 1988 it became evident that Lorimar was in trouble. In a reversal of fortunes Warners acquired Lorimar/Telepictures, effective the first day of 1989.

In late 1988 Merv Adelson called me to his office. He let me know how impressed he was with the work I had done for Lorimar. He advised that he would be calling Steve Ross at Warners to praise my work, and set an interview for me with him. I told him how much I appreciated working for him, and looked forward to my meeting with Steve Ross.

As luck would have it, a few days before I left for New York for my meeting with Ross, I learned that he was seriously ill and couldn't attend. Instead, he arranged for his temporary replacement, Robert Morgado, an accountant, to meet with me. Upon meeting Morgado I realized that shades of my RCA meeting with Menendez were recurring. It became quickly evident that Morgado in his new position, was full of himself. He immediately belittled my accomplishments at this "little company," reminding me that Warner's employed over 500 throughout the world. I acknowledged the size of Warners, but gently reminded him that aside from their vast catalog of valuable "standards" from years past, a majority of their current income was derived from songs that they administered but did not own. I also reminded him that the un-recouped balance of advances from such deals that were written off, were known to be in the tens of millions.

Needless to say, there would be no further meetings. Morgado was a disastrous choice to fill in for Ross, who tragically never recovered. The damage done by Morgado became notorious, even rattling the famous architect of Warner Brothers Records, Mo Ostin, who soon resigned. After a short tenure, Morgado was given an undeserved "Golden Handshake," and removed.

Warner Brothers Music Publishing was, of course, complete with a replacement CEO for Chuck Kaye, who had recently decided to leave. The replacement was, oddly enough, a former accountant of Warner Music. I was all too aware that the last person that CEO wanted to see come aboard was me.

In December of 1988, a Lorimar attorney called me to his office. He had an envelope he was told to deliver to me from Merv Adelson. When I arrived he told me to open it. I did, and to my shock, enclosed was a new contract for the year 1989. I said, "What's this?"

The attorney said, "Just sign it, and give to me."

I was dumbfounded and didn't understand. The attorney just said, "It's Merv's way of thanking you."

CHAPTER 53
Background Music To The Foreground

While my career in music was basically establishing songs, much of my attention was centered around background music.

At BMI I am probably most remembered as the person who first created background music crediting. In that process I also worked with background music library publishers who were largely overlooked by both BMI and ASCAP. The lack of attention to these publishers at that time resulted from the inability of both societies to identify works, either audibly or via station reports. Consequently, they were looked upon as second-class citizens in the world of music. These libraries were referred to as "canned music" or "music by the yard." However, they played an important part at local TV and radio stations. Small, guaranty payments were awarded to these publishers in recognition of their "nuisance value." However, in later years they grew to the point of greater recognition and value by both BMI and ASCAP. Capitol Records was an advocate of these libraries establishing the Capitol-Q and HI-Q libraries early on. When I was brought into that company to preside over Beechwood Music, I insisted that these companies report directly to me.

Later at ATV I was determined to develop a background music library and persuaded Robin Philips (son of famous UK publisher Jimmy Philips) to leave KPM Music, one of the world's most successful libraries and owned by EMI, and join ATV. Robin quickly established Bruton Music as a greatly respected on-going library. (ATV Music's office in London was located on Bruton Street.)

A company known as Regent Recorded Sound represented both the Bruton and KPM libraries in the United States. The music publishing of the Bruton entity was, of course, ATV Music. KPM's publisher was Screen Gems-EMI, headed by my good friend, and buddy, Lester Sill. Not long after this joint representation, the head of Regent, unfortunately, tried to play Lester against me and vice versa to improve his deal. A rather heated Lester called me complaining that I'd gone behind his back with Regent to get a more favorable deal. I shot back accusing him of the same. We then both realized that we were being "played."

Lester and I met and decided to get rid of our deals and form a joint venture for our distribution. We both came up with a figure to settle our contracts with Regent, but were turned down. Lester was particularly upset and decided to execute an audit. The audit produced numerous contractual breaches, which we brought to the owners attention, and once again offered a fair settlement. Again, the offer was turned down. We had no option but to sue. We eventually won and, in fact, put the owner out of business. Lester and I then got together and decided on a name for the company.

I suggested we use a bit of each. "A" for Associated, the first letter of ATV, and "PM" which stood for last two letters of Keith Prowse Music, the original name standing for KPM. However, the company would be known as Associated Production Music or APM for short.

In September of 1988, I was contacted by Dain Blair, an executive of HLC (Hicklin, Lubinsky, and Cansler) regarding Killer Music, a music provider for many top commercials and jingles. It became generally known that Lorimar was being taken over by Warners, hence the call from Blair. Dain explained that as a result of HLC's success, they now had a library of many tracks intended for commercials that never went final, and became their property. They also had additional tracks where the music reverted to them. Dain felt that these tracks, being fairly contemporary, would be suitable for production library purposes.

During the early days of APM, my daughter Jenny, a fine musician, worked for that company. After my departure from ATV, she took a position at the Lawrence Welk Publishing company, which had recently been purchased by Polygram.

In order to get some impression of the value of the tracks that Dain was representing, I asked Jenny to stop by HLC, after work on her way home, to listen to them. She did this routinely and gave me her thoughts. She reported that the production quality was good, and the material could have value if acoustical instruments could be overdubbed to add the melodies missing from the tracks. Overall, she thought it had real possibilities.

With this information in mind, I started to develop a plan for what would be needed financially to make this new venture a reality. While Ron Hicklin, now the sole owner of HLC, would contribute the existing tracks and studio time needed for sweetening them, I would need to find a way to pay personnel and other associated costs for the initial launch.

I decided to play a hunch, and called a Lorimar executive who had been in contact with Michael Milken in regard to some Lorimar activities. A meeting was arranged at Milken's offices in their very impressive conference room. I had prepared a 5-year business plan that showed a break-even and a small profit in the third year, and good profits thereafter. Four executives and Michael met with me at their conference table. After I explained everything and asked for questions, Michael asked if he could meet me for a moment outside the room. To my surprise, Michael complimented me on the presentation then went on to say. "Sam, you are only asking for five million; we simply don't get involved in any project for less than fifty, so this is just not for us, sorry."

I explored additional possibilities for investor interest with a New York investment group, as well as banks, to no avail. Once again, I contacted Owen Sloane to determine if he had any ideas. He felt it might be a good opportunity for one of his clients, Paul Anka. Though I had never met Paul, I had enjoyed dealing regularly with his uncle Andy, while I was at BMI, who represented his music publishing interest, Spanka Music.

I first met Paul at The Ivy, a well-known Beverly Hills restaurant that catered to many celebrities. Paul advised that he had appeared in the UK through the auspices of Lew Grade, so we initially had much to talk about. He seemed genuinely interested in my project, and felt he would have no problem raising funds for our needs. I had expected that he would be an investor, but it seemed that he would only act as an agent, for a piece of the company.

During that time MGM was going through a re-organization, and an Italian Investor/Publishing Magnate, Giancarlo Paretti, was making a play for the company. Paul claimed to be a friend of Paretti, who had taken space at the Dino Delaurentis building on Wilshire Blvd. Paul arranged a meeting for us and Paretti at his office. While Paretti was very gracious, I had the feeling that he really didn't understand the concept of the business I was proposing. Nevertheless, Paul assured me that he did, and that we would have no problems.

With Paul's assurance of funding, I made no further efforts to seek investors. As time dragged on I would call Paul to check on developments. He continued to assure me that everything was fine. This went on for weeks. Finally, I called Paul and told him that I must have a formal commitment by a designated date, which he again assured me was no problem. I continued to hear nothing. The final date arrived. I called Paul and simply told him that I had reached my limit, and he was eliminated from the deal. He couldn't believe it. I told him he was given every consideration, but failed to deliver, and hung up.

I went home, told Joan that the deal simply wouldn't happen. We had purchased a lovely small home in Carmel in 1986, where we planned to move when I retired, so with the unexpected severance salary from Lorimar, I said we could just retire a little earlier, sell our home, and move to Carmel. When we went to bed that night, I had left a copy of my five-year plan on our kitchen table.

At about 2:AM I awoke, and silently went downstairs for some warm milk, and noticed the plan on the table. I sat down and was leafing through it when Joan also arrived and saw me looking at it. She said, "You really wanted to do this, didn't you?"

I said I did, but again that it now looked impossible. She reminded me that my attorney, Owen Sloane, had said he'd like to join me as a partner, which I had disregarded.

She then said, "If Owen believes so strongly in you, why don't you?" I told her that we had no investors, and that we'd have to re-mortgage both of our homes to get started. It would be a huge gamble at our ages. She simply said, "If you really want it, go ahead."

I was about to "roll the dice" on the biggest gamble of my career.

CHAPTER 54
The New Venture

In early 1989, the foundation, of what would become known as Killer Tracks, was set in a small second floor office on Seward Street near Sunset Boulevard, leased by Ron Hicklin of HLC Killer Music. The initial employees who occupied this rather cramped space were Michael Sheehy, an ex disk jockey from CBS radio's local outlet, who had worked for Hicklin for some time, my daughter Jenny, who probably knew more about the available tracks than anyone, my former assistant/secretary from Lorimar, Diane Craig, a new office clerk, and me. From time to time, Dain Blair the person who engineered this venture for Hicklin, would spend time with us.

I had to take out second mortgages on both of my homes, and cashed in stock received from Lorimar to get started. There was no need for me to take a salary as a result of the gracious "severance" pay granted by Merv Adelson of Lorimar.

The immediate task was to convert the existing music available into 60, 30, and 15 second tracks, with "mix-outs"* for broadcast commercials. In addition it was also necessary to either extend these tracks, or create longer ones for usage behind action in films. Our goal was to have 30 CD's available within the year for distribution. Michael Sheehy, who had done some production for HLC, was in charge of this effort.

While Jenny was occupied with copyright, clearances, and proposed licensing, she would occasionally visit and observe production sessions done at HLC studios. She would also, from time to time, learn music editing from Ted Lobinger, a producer and editor for HLC's Killer Music.

Al Capps, veteran music composer for Killer Music, along with Jonathon Merrill composed new longer works for the library. I also commissioned John Hobbs and Steve Stone to compose country flavored cues to add a new dimension. Final editing was Michael Sheehy's responsibility.

The entire year was spent getting ready for our first release. Finally in February of 1990 we were ready. I was, of course, anxious since the entire year was spending with no income to offset the expense. PR articles were released to the music industry magazines, along with some substantial advertising.

Through Dain Blair's international contacts for Killer Music, he was able to pre-sell the newly named Killer Tracks library to a Swedish television network. He emphasized the quality of the music, which used more acoustic instruments than most libraries of that time. He also stressed the exactness of the timings of the works. The payment was to be fairly substantial and would go a long way in keeping the new venture solvent. So, with great expectations the library was shipped.

About a week later Dain received a call from his Swedish clients complaining that many tracks were not usable as they were not in accordance with the timings listed on the labels. They threatened to return the library. Fortunately, after some calming by Dain, and a promise to repair the tracks, the company retained the library but delayed payment until the corrections were made.

As the production of these first 30 CD's was by Killer Music employees, I was quite upset. I insisted that corrections must be made, prior to re-manufacture of these CD's. Naturally, this process added further delay and stalled the receipt of vitally needed income. When the producer responsible for the production of these CD's was confronted, he merely said he thought the timings stated were "close enough." He became the first casualty of our new company.

The biggest challenge we had to achieving success was finding the right salespersons to pitch this new library. The world was not waiting for an additional production music library. We had to prove that we were different, and hire the people who could get that message across.

Diane Craig, my assistant brought over from Lorimar, was an ardent country music fan, with an outgoing personality. I thought she would make a good salesperson and urged her to try sales. She was somewhat reluctant since she had no experience in that area. I expressed my confidence in her, and she decided to take up the challenge. Our initial offering contained some country music, which she capitalized upon, and brought in a major radio station in Nashville, almost immediately. She went on to become one of the steadiest, successful salespersons at the company.

Once again an obstacle, not of our doing, threw a roadblock into our path. Shortly after our debut in the U.S., a former HLC Killer Music writer filed a "restraining order," barring further distribution of the library on the grounds that Hicklin did not have the rights to distribute his music through Killer Tracks, among other complaints. The order was granted, and for several weeks, sales solicitation was again brought to a halt.

It was only through my friendship with Alan Shulman, a New York entertainment litigation lawyer, was this matter brought to an end, allowing us to continue in business.

In late 1989, Jonathan Zavin, our former legal policeman who took down illegal Beatles "look alike" shows for ATV Music, had called advising me that a Japanese industrialist client of a partner, in the new firm he had joined, was interested in getting into the music business. Jonathan had recommended our fledgling company.

Throughout 1990, sales were beginning to evolve, but not at the pace I knew would sustain the operation. New sales personnel were needed and were sought after. A better sales team was set up with Phil Spieller, a former APM executive and longtime manager of NFL Film's music department was brought in as Sales Manager. Phil had a lot of experience in dealing with Production Music Libraries.

New larger space became available at HLC, and my son Ben was brought in to design our offices that were now on two floors. James Frangipane, a former Killer Music employee requested a transfer to Killer Tracks and became a successful sales person very quickly. Additional writers were added, and new recordings produced, giving the library a wider choice of material.

We were just starting to jell when the next dilemma hit us, "Desert Storm." Sales throughout the entire U. S. economy almost came to a standstill, as history will attest. While we were experiencing some success at film production houses that took a chance on us, the large majority of these companies did still not take us seriously. Something dramatic had to be done.

I wracked my brain for something, and suddenly recalled a paper I had done in my Marketing class at Rutgers. The paper was a review of Walter Hoving's "Distribution Revolution." Hoving, in 1932, during the height of the "Great Depression," convinced Montgomery Ward to issue a mail-order catalog directly to farmers, granting them credit, despite criticism from several executives of the company. His mantra was that he had "faith in the integrity of the American farmer." By 1941, this gamble was a huge financial success. The amount of "bad debt" amounted to 2%. Could something like this work for our fledgling company?

I called Phil Spieller to my office and asked if he could prepare a list of the top film production houses that relied on pre-recorded music. He said he could, and reckoned that there were close to one hundred. I then told him of my plan.

We would ship our entire library, free of charge, together with a supply of licensing forms to each of them. A letter would accompany the shipment indicating that the library was theirs for a three-month period, granting them free usage from licensing fees for the first $300 otherwise due to us. If they wished to retain the libraries after the initial free usage, they would then have to pay fees in accordance with the rates stated in the license forms. If they didn't like the library, they could return it to us, COD.

Phil looked at me like I was crazy. He felt that we would be robbed blind. I then asked him if this was the best quality library he'd ever dealt with. I knew that he had experience with many libraries in his career. He assured me it was. I then told him if these were the top production houses, they'd recognize that quality as well. So far, they had expressed no interest. This would get the library into their hands. So, with baited breath the libraries were shipped.

*versions of the music, deleting the melody line, to not interfere with dialog.

CHAPTER 55
Ah, So!

While waiting and hoping for the right outcome of my expensive bet on the acceptance of our library by the major production houses, day to day work had to continue. Further investment had to be made in new music productions, requiring payments to new writers and the cost of creating new tracks. With no backing other than out of my pocket, and the implicit services provided by Ron Hicklin, we were barely surviving. The revenues we were now receiving from the licensing of the initial CD's helped, but were not yet enough to offset these expenditures.

At that time Japan had a booming economy and their industries were eagerly buying into U.S. properties and companies. One company bought the Pebble Beach Golf and real estate properties at an unbelievably high price. (which later proved unsustainable) Another group had purchased the famous Riviera Country Club hotel and golf course. Real estate in New York and others cities was being picked up by Japanese investors at unrealistically high prices.

In late 1990 Michael Braun (Jonathan Zavin's partner) and Jonathan contacted me advising that one of their clients, Sazale, an owner of a hotel chain in Japan, was interested in entering the music business. They would soon be closing on their acquisition of the Bel Aire Hotel in Los Angeles and would be in L. A. in the near future. I explained that we were not in the pop music business, but rather dealt in production music, and went into detail as to our operation. They said that they would relate that information to their clients, but also asked if I would rule out an expansion into popular music. I told them that it was not the aim of the company, and could only be done if it was fully funded. They promised to get back to me soon.

Shortly after our telephone conversation, they again called advising that Mr. Haneda, the principal owner and president of Sazale, and a group of his executives, would be in L.A. the following week, and requested a meeting.

Upon their arrival, I received a call from one of their executives inviting me to a reception at the Bel Aire Hotel, celebrating the close of purchase of that hotel. Late that afternoon a white Rolls Royce showed up at our offices, which were now located in much larger space in the main building of HLC, on Sunset Blvd. I was taken to the hotel where a celebration was in progress in a small conference room.

I knew this hotel well, since Joan and I stayed there with Thea Zavin and her husband and Ron Anton and his wife while working at BMI. The hotel was small, some 100 rooms, but in a spectacular garden setting of varied trees, with a pond containing swans, which was the logo for the hotel. The hotel had a fine restaurant, where I had entertained many overseas clients while at ATV Music.

I was welcomed by Mr. Haneda and seated at a central location among his executives. Dom Perignon champagne was literally flowing everywhere, and spirits were high. After the social amenities and small talk, an appointment was scheduled for late the following day at our offices.

Several executives including Mr. Haneda arrived on schedule and were given a tour of our facilities. After a thorough lecture by me on the nature of our business, John Ma, apparently Mr. Haneda's chief assistant, brought up the possibility of extending our operation to include popular music. He also mentioned Mr. Haneda's daughter, a vocalist whose recordings had been released in Japan. I emphasized that additional funding would be required to organize that kind of operation, and that it had to be considered a gamble. Ma assured me that it would be no problem.

When they left I was given Sazale promotion material. Their dazzling yearbook included a 100-year development plan for the company, with aerial photos of their planned geographic expansion. Also, included were recordings of Yukiko, Mr. Haneda's daughter. Oddly enough, to my surprise and enjoyment, I found her to be a quite talented jazz singer. While I didn't think she was suitable for the pop market, I felt she could make her unique mark in the jazz segment.

As they were quite keen on entering into an agreement, subsequent meetings were held to discuss terms of our association and the required necessary funds. Terms were generally agreed upon, so agreements were to be drawn by our attorneys. Owen Sloane represented our company. Monthly funding by Sazale was agreed upon, which became the "consideration" for Sazales's share of the company. The contracts were executed and our new expanded company commenced operations. New personnel were found, and office space was expanded, as well as budgets, to accommodate this Pop Music division.

Apparently, in discussions with John Ma it was learned that one of Owen's clients was Paul Anka. Ma requested an introduction to Anka by Owen, on behalf of Mr. Haneda. Owen complied and, Mr. Haneda was totally impressed with Anka, who could be very ingratiating. Before long, Mr. Haneda considered him a friend. My impression, however, based on my earlier experience with Paul, was that Haneda was more of an "opportunity." As a result of this "friendship," Haneda invited Paul to Japan as his guest. Haneda wasted no time in showing him off as his friend. Paul complied by performing at a well-known Karaoke nightclub. Naturally, Paul took great interest in Haneda's daughter's career and offered to produce her, to Haneda's delight.

When word came back to me of this situation, I cautioned John Ma, that Anka was all wrong as the producer for Yukiko. I felt her talent was as a jazz singer, where she would have the best chance for success. I was sure Paul was not equipped to handle that type of production, and would try to convert her to the pop market using current in-style songs, including some of his own. That was exactly what he did, the results of which were what I had anticipated. Worse yet, was the unbelievable amount Anka charged Haneda for his "production services," which could never be recouped. Mr. Haneda got his first taste, a rather sour one, of the Pop Music industry.

Meanwhile within less than two months after shipping of our "free" libraries to the top music production houses, licenses began to show up. This meant that some of these producers had already used their $300 free license credits, and were now paying for further usage. Gradually more and more of these licenses began to appear. By the end of the three-month trial period, only one library was returned. A week after it was returned, I received a call stating that the production company made a mistake, and would I please return the library to them. It became evident that my gamble was paying off. After a one-year period, these production houses accounted for over $900,000 in licensing fees.

Not long after the Bel Aire Hotel acquisition closed, the amount paid leaked, to extreme criticism of the deal. In excess of 100 million dollars was paid. This was a figure that could not have been justified or "penciled out" by even the most optimistic of investors. To make matters even more embarrassing for Sazale, was the story that after the closing Mr. Haneda said, "Tomorrow we play golf at our golf course." He was gently advised that the golf club was not included in the acquisition.

He then proposed a deal to buy out all members for a ridiculously high price to each member, which was immediately rejected. The Bel

Aire club members were, and are some of the wealthiest people in America.

Although the monthly funding was now in place for the creation of a Pop music arm of Killer Tracks, the foregoing situation became a concern for me as to the solidity of our deal.

CHAPTER 56
Financial Hara-kiri

Despite the detection of clouds approaching the Japanese Nikkei Stock Exchange, Sazale continued to expand in its now newly enchanted entertainment addiction. During this period a Japanese novel entitled "Strawberry Fields" became hugely successful in that country. The book told the story of two Japanese brothers immigrating to the United States, after the end of World War II, who founded a strawberry farm in the Salinas Valley of central California. It was a tale of their early struggles, their experiences with newly found <u>Nisei</u> friends, and the simultaneous slow recovery of the Japanese economy.

Sazale optioned the film rights and subsequently produced the motion picture. I was called upon to recommend and set up the production of the music to be used in the film. After reading the book, I decided that Fred Karlin would be perfect to score the film. Not only was Fred an experienced film scorer, but also a recognized songwriter, having written the music for the Academy Award winning song "For All We Know," for the film "Lovers and Other Strangers," later to become a hit by "The Carpenters."

The highly respected director Koreyoshi Kurahara was soon to visit Los Angeles to "spot" the film with Karlin for the placement of the music in the film. I was contacted and asked to greet Mr. Kurahara upon his arrival at the Sofitel Hotel in Beverly Hills. Unfortunately, the plane was delayed by some four hours, which I spent waiting at the hotel, as we were to have dinner together that night. When he did arrive, it was after midnight. The kitchens were closed so I had to prevail upon management to allow us to sit in the dining room and have coffee and pastries, the only food available, sent to us.

The director spoke rather good English. He immediately apologized, and thanked me for waiting so long for him. We talked about the film, but also many other interests we seemed to have had in common. It became obvious that he was a man of great learning and culture. He was proud of the Tokyo String Quartet that had gained fame for their excellence, and he was happy to know that I enjoyed them as well.

At one point, which I will never forget, he became silent and then said, "My people now think that they are giants, but I know that they have feet of clay. I shudder to think what may soon happen. "

He was not wrong. By the end of the year the Nikkei Stock Exchange suffered its greatest drop in history to 50% of its recent high-flying real estate and financial "bubble" rating. Savvy investors, at fractions of the prices paid by the Japanese, gobbled up their real estate acquisitions. Pebble Beach Resort was purchased for one half of the price paid by the Japanese by Marvin Davis, then owner of 20th Century Fox. Rockefeller Center was repurchased at a very reduced price, as were many other properties in New York and other major cities. And, alas, Sazale was forced to sell the Bel Aire Hotel for forty percent of the price they had paid.

Eventually, a great musical score was produced by Fred Karlin. Unfortunately, the film was later released in the U.S. to little notice or financial impact.

To create a separate pop music division, I had hired some 5 new employees, headed by veteran music producer and publisher, Brooks Arthur. In addition, budgets were created for writer advances, demo records, promotion and other incidental expenses required for such an operation.

The Japanese insisted on calling this new division Primat Music. To this day, I don't know what that term means. Budgets were set and approved and monthly payments were agreed upon to cover these costs. Income for Killer Tracks continued to improve, and it looked like we were right on track for the success I had forecast in my original projections.

The monthly payments to support Primat Music were sent on time at the beginning of the venture, but reminders from me were needed as time went on. Finally, at one point despite my requests, we received no response and no funds. In desperation, I called Michael Braun, the New York attorney who engineered this deal. After about a week he called back and sorrowfully advised me that Sazale were financially unable to continue payments. They had not returned my calls to "save face." It seems that on top of the Japanese economic collapse, their very popular hotel chain, Sekitei, was under government investigation for renting rooms by the hour, for executive "matinees." The scandal severely hurt their business.

As a result of this fiasco, income from Killer Tracks had to be used to meet these new expenses, which had yet to be offset by pop music income. Sazale, by breach of agreement was no longer a partner, but I was stuck with the accumulated overhead until I could unwind the new division as delicately as possible. Until that time Killer Tracks income, which had reached the "break even" point, now was the sole means of support for both areas, thereby throwing us into a deficit position.

I searched for a new partner to take over the former Japanese responsibilities, and thought we had found one when Leeds Levy, recently-appointed CEO of MCA Music (Universal) was determined to acquire a 50% ownership in the entire opoeration. We were told that the deal was a foregone conclusion, so I decided to relieve the pressure by taking my family for a holiday in Carmel, our favorite place for a long weekend. During our drive, we received a call from an MCA executive, advising the "deal was off." I later learned that a Universal executive, to whom Leeds reported, overrode Leeds decision, based on advice from a music consultant he hired, who had no experience whatsoever in production music. It was not long after, that Leeds left the company to take a position as CEO at a more enlightened organization.

I was left in the same struggling position, when a short time later I received a call from a well-known CEO of an international music publisher, whom I was aware of but had never actually met. He called to request a meeting with me at our offices.

CHAPTER 57
Also Sprach...Nick

Nick Firth, the CEO of the Music Publishing arm of BMG, was in the music publishing business, almost from birth, being the grandson of one of the famous Dreyfuss brothers, who created, perhaps, the most respected popular music publishing company of the twentieth century, Chappell Music. That catalog was built on the music of Broadway shows and was a treasure-chest of great writers such as the Gershwin brothers, Jerome Kern, Rodgers and Hart, and Rodgers and Hammerstein, and Cole Porter to name just a few. In time, Chappell was acquired by Warner Brothers. The company was, then and now, called Warner-Chappell.

BMG is a division of Bertelsmann, originally a German book publishing company that continues to this day with the acquisition of several important U. S. book publishers including Doubleday, Random House, Penguin and Alfred Knopf, among others. BMG (Bertelsmann Music Group) was set up as part of their expansion into entertainment production.

Nick had called me from San Diego, where he was negotiating for the purchase of Network Music, the hottest music production library at that time. Apparently, word had gotten around of my situation, so he decided to check it out for himself, while he was on the west coast.

It was odd that after all my years in the business, I had never come directly into contact with Nick Firth. I, of course, knew of him, and was aware of his position. Though he was certainly respected as a music publisher, I was aware of a number of stories that were uncomplimentary regarding his personality. I later realized that because of his many years spent in the UK, (his mother was English) his demeanor sometimes rubbed others as haughty, particularly when he used English pronouncements such as "shedule" instead of schedule, or referred to someone as "cheeky."

After a tour of our offices, we got down to business. There was no doubt that he was interested in getting into this area, as part of his expansion of BMG's music publishing. BMG, a few years earlier had acquired RCA Records including their music publishing operation. After our initial meeting, I visited his New York office, and found him sitting in the same office that had been occupied by the late Jose Menendez during our infamous meeting.

After several meetings, terms were agreed upon, which not long after appeared to me as much too favorable to BMG, since without the burden of Primat Music, Killer Tracks would quickly become profitable. However, at the time, I was not in a very good bargaining position.

BMG, unlike my experiences at ATV and Lorimar, was run like a military operation. Monthly, itemized management reports were expected, scrutinized, and critiqued. I realized that a more modern system for reporting was necessary, and brought in my son Ben, who had loads of accounting experience having worked so successfully for the accountants who handled all of ATV Music's financial matters. Ben also had graduated Pepperdine College with a degree in Business. The system he eventually set up was so successful that it was largely adopted by BMG.

With the acceptance of Killer Tracks by the industry, it was necessary to constantly add new music to the library in order to keep up with the latest trends. New writers were contracted and joint distribution deals were created with writers who were specialists in various contemporary styles. Accounting systems were enlarged as well as Management reports to accommodate this expansion. Ben handled these expansion duties with skill, though it elicited no praise, though due, from BMG.

Acknowledging the success of Killer Tracks, Nick set about acquiring additional production music libraries. He first concentrated mainly on British companies. Nick spent a great deal of his early career in the UK working for Chappell Music, (made famous by his grandfather and Uncle) in various capacities. His taste in virtually everything, knowingly or unknowingly, was obviously British. This extended to his taste in music. With the acquisitions of the UK companies Atmosphere Music, and Match Music, he decided to recommend that we try to create music more in the style of these British companies so that we could better serve the UK and international markets, his first big mistake. Gradually, he would interfere and make what I considered unreasonable demands on Killer Tracks, despite the fact that we were becoming highly profitable. I was beginning to understand why some of my associates were rubbed the wrong way by Nick.

Despite our differences in running the business, which became heated at times, Nick and I enjoyed a fairly good social relationship. We, and sometimes our wives, would often dine together. On a number of occasions he and I would play golf. I particularly enjoyed playing at his wonderful Bedford golf club, just outside New York City. Nick had obviously taken lessons, either in the UK or the US, and though we played with fairly equal ability, he felt compelled to coach me and point out my faults, which I'm sure were, and continue to be, many. The one that he constantly reminded me was "Keep your head down!" I think I still have to concentrate on that.

When he would receive our monthly management reports he seemed to feel that he must find, and point out even a small detail to reprimand me. On one such report he sent a memo pointing out an insignificant "line item" which was over budget for that month. I thought this item was ridiculous to cite, and shot back this short return memo: "Nick, let me give you some of the advice that you often give me: Keep your head down! That way, you'll get a better view of the BOTTOM LINE!" Upon receipt of my memo he was furious and immediately telephoned me shouting his displeasure and once again using his favorite expression, that it was "cheeky" of me to write such a reply. My retort to him was to remind him (with expletives removed) that I was still co-owner of the company, and in no way had to report to him.

I was certainly aware that in our agreement with BMG they had an option, after five full years, to buy out Killer Tracks shares at a multiple of net income, for which I was not exactly happy. To soften the blow, I was to be given a bonus for producing income above the amount projected in the budget for 1997.

I had felt that I would be ready for retirement by the time 1997 rolled around, so we continued our rocky but successful association. The company continued to expand and additional space was needed and found for storage and shipping, as well as for our new employees. Our sales-force had hit their stride and though competition among them over territories existed, overall they all seemed to be doing well, and no one wished to depart for greener fields.

By this time, my daughter Jenny had taken over production, having increased her skills by taking a course in control room mechanics. Jenny kept the company up to date musically by studying the top music trade magazines for musical trends. In addition, our sales-force would constantly keep her abreast of what our clients were looking for. Overall, the company was doing fine. I must mention the dedication of our constant sales team of Phil Spieller, sales manager, Jim Frangipane, Diane Lantz, Ann Jenney Burke and Marilyn Richards, all of whom brought in the steady sales through devices of their own creations.

Bertelsmann had a tenet to be adhered to by all affiliated companies. Each division of their company was expected to bring in a net profit of at least 15% annually. After our second full year with BMG, our net profits averaged 22%, so there was no reason for criticism of our operation. Nevertheless, we still had to contend with Nick's nit picking, which I had come to realize was simply his manner.

During my final year, I was invited to attend the BMG Music international meeting in Portugal. Nick and I once again had our round of golf, but with no critiques involved.

Nick continued acquiring Production Music Libraries in the United States and Europe, yet Killer Tracks continued to be the Flagship Library of the group. Though I was told that I was welcome to stay on as CEO after the final acquisition by BMG, I decided that I had had enough. I was definitely not interested in becoming part of the BMG operation. Nick, therefore, contacted a number of candidates through an executive placement service, and asked me to interview each one that he was considering. Finally, we both agreed on Gary Gross, a former executive of a large pharmaceutical company, as the best replacement. Gary was well mannered, into the new digital media systems, and had a temperament that would certainly not rattle Nick in the ways I had. A marvelous send-off dinner was arranged for me, full of humor and praise, which I will never forget.

Some time thereafter, when we were living in our planned retirement home in Carmel, I received a letter from Nick containing a sizable check. His note acknowledged the great year completed and the well-deserved bonus. I called him back to acknowledge receipt, but had to ask him a question that long nagged at me. Why had he not acquired the "hot" Network Production Music company in San Diego, and decide to take on our fledgling, struggling company instead? His answer astounded me. He simply said. "I thought it was wiser to bet on you."

CHAPTER 58
Retirement. Really?

On an insufferably hot day (112 degrees) in early August of 1997 we moved to Carmel, California to begin, what I had planned to be, my retirement. The evening we arrived it was 67 degrees in Carmel, and we were convinced that we made the right move. I instinctively knew that I couldn't stop all work immediately, any more than one could stop a fast freight train in its tracks. There were still Trust Music Management clients to serve, especially our own catalogs, Mandina and Rocksmith Music. Rocksmith became very active in fulfilling requests for the song "Majesty," from Jack Hayford's increasingly popular "Majestic Praise." Joan spent much of her time licensing this song internationally, while we retained CCLI (Christian Copyright Licensing, Inc.) to handle the flood of domestic church requests. BMG had put me on a one-year retainer to be available to Killer Tracks for advice when needed. So, we found office space near downtown Carmel. Little did we know, at the time, how busy I would become.

At roughly the same time, the ATV Music catalog was assigned to Sony Music by Michael Jackson. I received a call from Sony asking if I would be available as a consultant to them on a monthly retainer. I immediately agreed.

Just prior to our move, I received a call from the heirs to the Harry Warren estate requesting some help with their catalog, Four Jays Music, which contained some works of their famous grandfather, Harry. The main body of his works, however, remained in the Warner Brothers Music catalog, as he was a staff writer at that company for many years. They also suggested that I examine the status of his works in that catalog as well.

Harry Warren was a standout composer for Warner's, who was brought to the west coast as result of Warner's buy-out of the music publishing company that published Warren's successful works, while residing in New York. Warner's was among the first to realize the potential of sound in motion pictures, and to innovate the "Hollywood

Musical." Warren was their key writer, having composed all the music to *42nd Street*, one of the greatest shows of all time. Several songs from that show became standards in the Warner Brother's music publishing catalog; they included "42nd Street," "Shuffle off to Buffalo," and "You're Getting to be a Habit with Me." In addition to the hits from that show, other Warner Brother's musicals by Warren produced a virtual catalog of standards such as, "Jeepers Creepers," "We're In The Money," The Boulevard Of Broken Dreams," I Only Have Eyes For You," "There Will Never Be Another You," "September In The Rain." "You Must Have Been A Beautiful Baby," "On the Atchison Topeka And The Santa Fe," "Serenade In Blue," "I've Got A Gal In Kalamazoo," and "The More I See You," among others.

After assisting in reaching an agreeable resolution regarding the division of royalties from Four Jays Music amongst the three heirs, I was asked to look into the royalties they were receiving from Warners. My findings led to numerous discussions with Warner Music Publishing executives to iron out, what I determined to be oversights and shortcomings. With the assistance of my longtime attorney, Owen Sloane, an equitable resolution to my claims was worked out, to the satisfaction of the heirs.

Shortly after the resolution of the Four Jays problem, I received a call from a Century City attorney requesting assistance in handling the publishing, and appraisal of one of his clients' catalogs. The client turned out to be Doris Fisher, daughter of Fred Fisher, a famed early 20th century composer of such well-known songs as "Chicago," "Peg O' My Heart," and "Come Josephine In My Flying Machine." Doris, his daughter, collaborated with him on a number of other songs and became a respected songwriter and performer on her own, with the encouragement of Irving Berlin. Earlier in my career, I had met with her two brothers, in an unsuccessful attempt to acquire the Fred Fisher catalog.

Doris was about 85 years of age when I first met her at her Wilshire Boulevard penthouse apartment. She greeted me in her beautiful dress robe, but seemed somewhat wary of me until we sat down to chat. She learned that I was well aware of her era in the business, and loosened up when I mentioned common friends and contacts. She then invited me to her dining area for tea and pastry. This would become a regular routine in future visits. It quickly became obvious that she was depressed with the state of the music business, and her life in general. I asked her about the status of her publishing company, which she reported was being administered by Universal Music. She complained that she wasn't earning enough to live on. I told her that I'd investigate this situation and get back to her.

After my investigation, I called Doris to advise her that her catalog was in great shape and of real value to Universal. I further notified her that if she was in need of money, it was available as an advance against earnings. She commented that she didn't really believe me, and I assured her it was possible.

She then asked how much she could get and I answered, "Probably around $150,000." She was startled and declared that I was dreaming. I replied, I thought it was possible, and our conversation ended. Unknown to both of us at the time, was a pending single of one of her songs by Pink Martini, a very popular group. The Doris Fisher catalog had a number of hit songs over the years including a song she had written for Rita Hayworth entitled "Put The Blame On Mame," which she performed in one of her most successful films, "Gilda." The song became a hit and was covered by many artists. The catalog also contained a number of hits recorded by "The Inkspots," as well as other songs released by "known" singers of that period.

Within about three weeks of my telephone call, I had Universal deliver to her apartment the check for the amount I predicted. A week later I was in L.A. for meetings, in addition to my scheduled meeting with her. As she opened the door to welcome me she said, "Which planet are you from?" She was totally flabbergasted by the check. She already had tea and pastry ready, so we sat down and once again, and after some small talk the mood darkened. She recited a list of the recent deaths of some of her contemporaries and wondered why she was still around. I did my best to cheer her up, and scheduled another meeting. Before that next meeting, I happened to be in town with Joan, who had wanted to meet her. She insisted on taking us to lunch in Westwood, near her apartment. We had a pleasant lunch and I arranged to meet with her shortly thereafter.

In the interim, her daughter Fredericka, (Freddy) being concerned with Doris' state of mind and health, was visiting her. After my meeting with Doris, where she again listed the notables in the music business who had passed away, I met with Freddy, who told me of Doris' frustration at still living. On one occasion Doris actually checked into a hospital declaring that she was dying. The hospital and her doctor contacted Freddy to confirm that there was nothing wrong with the health of her mother, so Freddy picked her up and took her back to the apartment.

On my next visit Doris seemed happy about the success of the Pink Martini recording, but once again drifted into depression. I tried to bring her out of it by celebrating the success of the new record. She agreed, and decided that we should have a "belt" of whisky like they used to celebrate when she was younger, and in the prime of her career. She got up from the table, where we were having our tea and pastry, brought in a bottle of rye whisky, and poured out two shots. We clinked the two shot glasses as I shouted L'chaim! We threw back the drinks as was the style. Immediately Doris started choking, and I tried to come to her aid. I took the glass away, patted her back and eventually she calmed down.

The depression came back even stronger. "I can't even down a shot of whisky like I use to!" To keep her talking I asked her to tell me what she really missed.

After a pause to recollect she said, "I miss the big bands, I miss being with the musicians and writers, I miss the drinking, I miss--". I stopped her and asked what she missed the most, and will never forget her most candid answer. "I miss the cheatin'." I knew that she had led a very diversified life, and had been married four times.

Freddy had returned to her home in New York, but came back a short time later as Doris again threatened to go to the hospital. While Freddy was with her, she asked her to take her to the hospital because she was convinced that she was dying. Freddy refused. A few days later, while Freddy was shopping, Doris telephoned for a taxi that did take her to the hospital. Freddy heard from the hospital that she had checked in, and was upset. She was told by Doris's doctor that he would keep her there for a few days for observation. Four days later, Doris was dead.

We often hear stories of success based on the "will to live." We never consider the possibility of the reverse.

Several months later I was asked by Doris's attorney to prepare a report evaluating the worth of Doris Fisher Music, to be used to determine possible inheritance tax for the heirs of the estate, Freddy and her brother, who was living in Las Vegas. The report was completed and approved.

Doris Fisher was an artist, who simply lived for the industry and its excitement. When that excitement disappeared, so did Doris's zest for living. She will be long remembered by aficionados of, what was formerly known as "Tin Pan Alley."

CHAPTER 59
Not Quite Finished

The activity from my retirement date in 1997 to 2004 kept me almost as busy as my prior full-time employment. Phil Everly contacted me regarding the royalties he was receiving from The Everly Brothers early record company, Cadence. That company went through a number of subsequent ownership transfers since originally owned by Archie Bleyer. Bleyer was longtime music director of the Arthur Godfrey radio and television shows. He formed Cadence Records by signing Julius La Rosa, of that show, as his first artist. Other artists to join that label included The Chordettes, Johnny Tillotson and Don Shirley. The company was eventually purchased by the famous singer, Andy Williams, whose earliest recordings were also released on that label, which he renamed Barnaby Records. Bleyer, was at the time the Everlys were on Cadence, also Phil Everly's father-in-law.

Phil sent me whatever contract materials he had in his files. I had previously urged him to look into this matter with an audit, but once again as the relationship between he and his brother had deteriorated, Don refused to have any part of it. Don, in fact, had set himself apart and seemed to distrust everyone. Phil finally decided to take on the project himself.

The original contract, in 1957, accorded the boys a royalty rate of 3% against 90% of sales for the first year, rising to 4% in the second year, and 5% in the third year. There it stood after all the remaining years, which were subsequently spent at Warner Brothers Records. It should be kept in mind that Cadence, now Barnaby, had the original masters of the Everly's huge breakout years. At the time I commenced this study, new yet unproven artists were receiving 10 to 12% to sign to a record company.

After my initial findings, and with Phil's approval, an auditor with a great deal of record company experience was retained. The findings were substantial, so once again attorney Owen Sloane sent a demand letter claiming the amount of unpaid royalties due. After numerous legal claims and defenses were argued, we thought it best that Phil simply contact Andy Williams, his friend and fellow entertainer.

Andy was not aware of the situation, since he had merely retained an outside accounting company to oversee the administration of Barnaby, including royalty payments. After receiving Phil's letter, he was chagrined and embarrassed. To our surprise, he simply agreed to the claims, and instructed his lawyer and accountants to pay the past claims and 50% of every dollar received on their behalf thereafter.

While the recovery was in excess of $100,000, Phil was left footing the entire bill for the services leading to the outcome. This meant that Don received far more than Phil, who initiated and funded the whole project. Phil rationalized by stating that it was worth it since their royalty status, from that point forward, had greatly improved. With that proven success, it took little convincing to have Don share in the expenses of a Warner Brothers audit, which I convinced Phil to undertake.

During this period Phil was to celebrate his 60th birthday. His wife Patti, with the assistance of Phil's longtime buddy Terry Slater, put together a huge surprise party. Phil hadn't a clue. Patti asked me to come down earlier in the day of the party, since she told Phil that she was just having a little "get together" of his friends for the occasion. She had arranged, what appeared to be a small spread to confirm it to Phil. Phil took to dressing in a comfortable blue sweat-suit and white sneakers, which came close to being his uniform. I could remember him appearing in that attire a few months earlier at a luncheon date I had with him in nearby Toluca Lake.

The most potent market in the world for the Everly Brothers, as well as Phil as an individual artist, was the UK. The Beatles, in fact, were huge fans. Phil had recorded one of his own albums there and had a large number of British musicians and artist friends. Terry and he were in touch almost daily. Terry and Patti arranged one of the biggest surprises of the evening. Terry had convinced a number of UK musicians, as well as the ones who had accompanied the Everlys on tour, to fly over for the party. They all arrived at the party by bus, and as they got off the bus, a totally surprised Phil suddenly realized, to his shock, that they were all dressed in blue sweat suits and white sneakers.

The party immediately came alive and Patti opened up the backyard, which had been prepared for the added guests, unbeknownst to Phil. A joyous racket ensued as silly gifts were presented to Phil, the craziest of which was a walker containing a microphone and various other apparatus for the "elderly" Phil. Not long after, a Los Angeles Police helicopter arrived above the party with its spotlight directed upon it. A loud speaker in warning tones called out seemingly as a warning. "All you people down there, Enjoy yourselves! And, Happy Birthday Phil!" I later learned that this stunt had been arranged by Patti who, previous to her marriage, had worked for the LAPD. Needless to say, a wonderful, and memorable time was experienced by all.

After the Barnaby Records resolution, we immediately concentrated on Warner Brothers Records with the same team. We instinctively knew that there was much to recover. The audit, which became a huge undertaking, was handled by Fred Wolinsky's company, and the legal claims by Owen Sloane. Unfortunately for Don and Phil, the longtime bickering that occurred between them resulted in not getting the best management and accounting personnel to represent them during the height of their careers. Audits that should have taken place at regular intervals were never done. Hence, due to a lack of timely claims, statutes of limitation prevented us from recovering some of the flagrant income shortcomings that were found. Our total claims mounted into the high six-figure range, but due to the statutes of limitation imposed by Warners, only one third of that amount was settled upon. Fortunately, as part of the settlement, the royalty rate for the Everlys, which had been stagnant for years was increased. However, the years of their huge popularity and sales were in the past.

It was also during this time that the prices for music publishing catalogs were reaching their peak. The popularity of Jack Hayford's "Majesty" was now worldwide, as well as other music from his musical service, Majestic Praise. Steve Stone, my partner, and I had now owned the companies for thirty years. I was in retirement and Steve's position as a senior employee at Sony could be in jeopardy due to the youth movement craze in the music industry. We decided to let the industry know, in a subtle way, that we would consider an offer. To that end, we offered the job of getting this message to the right parties to Pete Carlson in Nashville. Pete was an independent music publisher, and general music business utilitarian who we both respected and trusted.

It took little time for Pete to find a candidate who could meet our price. Clive Calder was one of the bright lights in the music publishing and recording industries scoring successes in a number of areas. He owned a recording studio, anticipated the Hip Hop craze, created the Boy Bands, and managed and distributed them on his record label, and was just then expanding into Christian and Gospel music. His most recent acquisition was the Brentwood-Benson Christian Music Company in Franklin Tennessee. Mandina and Rocksmith Music companies were a natural additional asset for that company. The negotiations and final sale moved quickly, to all parties' satisfaction.

As could be expected, shortly thereafter, Calder sold his properties, including his music publishing holdings, to my former partner, BMG Music. Several years later, the whole of BMG's music publishing, including Killer Tracks, was purchased by the Universal Music Group. It seems that both of the companies I had created and owned, (Mandina/Rocksmith and Killer Tracks) were now part of the Universal Music Group. As destiny would have it, I would spend a good deal of my future working with that organization.

CHAPTER 60
Winding Down, And then...

With the sale of our publishing companies and the resolution of The Everly Brothers claims, Trust Music Management activities decelerated. I was still representing the publishing of Jorge Calandrelli, who was receiving much acclaim for his music in the Academy Award nominated,"Crouching Tiger," though he did not control the music publishing. I also represented the publishing ownership of one of the heirs to the Harry Warren Estate, and did some work as an expert witness, and writer of affidavits for various entertainment lawyers.

With more available time, I decided to become involved in the Monterey Peninsula music activities. I volunteered for membership in The Carmel Music Society and eventually became chairman of the booking committee. I was later accepted as a board member of the Monterey Symphony Orchestra. That situation ended in late 2007 when I received a telephone call from a lawyer in Los Angeles.

The lawyer, whose name I simply can't recall, told me that he had originally recommended me to Doris Fisher, and asked if I still gave appraisals for the value of music publishing catalogs. I told him that I did, and he advised me that he had a client soliciting a bid for the sale of a catalog seeking one million dollars. I asked for the name of the company and he replied, Daywin Music. I thought for a minute back to my days at BMI as head of Publisher Relations, and suddenly recalled the name. "Isn't that Doris Day's company?" He answered, "Why, yes it is. You know of it?" I told him that I did, and advised him that she was a popular resident of Carmel where I lived. I told him that I would be happy to appraise the catalog, but would need statements of income from all sources for the past five years. He assured me that they were available and could provide them for me.

Several weeks later I received the reports that I requested, and was contacted by Jim Loeb, Doris's manager, to introduce himself and have me confirm the receipt of the statements. I later learned that Jim was the longtime friend of Terry Melcher, Doris' son. Just before Terry died of Melanoma in 2004, he requested Jim look after his mother. Jim was extremely diligent in this task, and very protective of Doris.

I spent a great deal of time analyzing the reports before contacting him. I finally called him to advise that I had completed the analysis. He immediately asked if they could get a million for the catalog.

I responded, "No," then paused and said, "You should get 2.5 million."

He was somewhat shocked and said, "C'mon, don't kid me!" I said, "I'm not kidding, it's worth it " Jim skeptically said, "Really?" I responded, "Today is Wednesday, by Monday I can have you a bonafide offer for 2.5 million."

"What's the catch?"

"I'm in for ten percent."

Jim then said, "Let me talk to Doris and get back to you."

Three days later he did call from Doris's garden, where they were walking. Before we could start our conversation, Doris broke in asking Jim whom he was talking to.

"It's that guy named Sam who says your catalog is worth more than double what we were asking."

Doris said, "Let me talk to him," and took the telephone. However, she didn't talk. She started singing "Sam The Old Accordion Man," which I knew was from her great film "Love Me Or Leave Me."

When she finished I said, "Doris you got it wrong."

Somewhat surprised she replied, "What?"

"I'm Sam You Made The Pants Too Long."*

She laughed and said, "I think we should get together for lunch."

As I was a member of the Quail Lodge Golf Club, where Doris's home overlooked the 17th and 18th hole, I had often seen her lunching in the restaurant, and suggested we meet there. She was agreeable, so we met at 12 noon a few days later. Jim Loeb, of course, accompanied her and introduced me. Doris seemed somewhat wary until I said, knowing she was from Cincinnati, "Doris, wouldn't you rather be eating at Mecklenburg's?"

"How do know Mecklenburg's?" I told her that I was a student at the Cincinnati Conservatory of Music. That restaurant was just down the street. She said she loved that restaurant and the "ice" was broken. We talked about Cincinnati bands and bandleaders, then onto the Les Brown band, where I knew some of the personnel, then to great musicians, and arrangers. The conversation simply went on and on, as she realized that I knew the business.

Finally, Jim, who was more or less simply an observer, said, "Doris, it's almost three o'clock. We've got to feed the dogs." Doris stood up to leave and grabbed my arm as we walked to Jim's car. As Doris got in, I told her how pleased I was to meet her. Jim went to the driver's side and got in, but they didn't leave. He got out and came around to me.

I asked, "What's up?"

He said, "Doris doesn't want to sell the company, she wants you to run it."

Having spent a great deal of time analyzing Daywin Music, I knew what had to be done, and looked forward to the challenge. Finding and assembling all the necessary data, including domestic and foreign contracts and licenses, initially, turned out to be a full time job.

Terry, Doris's late son, had turned over the administration of Daywin to several companies over the years. At this time, BMG Music, a company that I was very familiar with from my experience at Killer Tracks, was in their fourth year of a 5-year contract as worldwide administrator. I also knew that BMG was in negotiations for the sale of their company to the Universal Music Group.

While Terry was an excellent musician and producer, I realized after going through the files, music publishing was not his forte. He would take large advance payments from BMG, but not realize their cost in terms of favorable deal points incorporated in the agreements, for the administering publisher. Some of these points in recent deals I found to be profoundly to Daywin's disadvantage.

I had been somewhat aware of the songs in the catalog that were used in Doris Day films such as "Please Don't Eat The Daisies," "Teacher's Pet," and "Move Over Darling," but was surprised to find, the now standard copyright, "I Write The Songs" included. Most people would naturally assume that the song was written by Barry Manilow, since he is most associated with it. It was, however, written by Beach Boy, Bruce Johnston, who was an Artists Music (ASCAP affiliate of Daywin) writer at the time. That song earned a significant portion of the Daywin/Artist Music publishing overall income.

By the time I was chosen to oversee this company, Universal had finally acquired the entire BMG Music Publishing catalog. Some time prior to the acquisition, Universal appointed Dave Renzer, a former BMG executive who I knew, as the new president of Universal Music Publishing. The Daywin/Artist music publishing administration agreement had one more year to run on the BMG contract, which was now assumed by Universal. A fairly significant unearned balance of the advances Terry had taken was still on the books. However, I had studied the statements rendered by BMG, as well as the terms of the agreement. I considered BMG to be "high-handed" to the point of possible legal actions. Those favorable contract terms had, in fact, accounted for the balance of "un-earned advances."

I called Dave Renzer to congratulate him on his appointment and advise him of my association with Doris Day's music publishing companies. He was aware of the catalog and very pleased that Universal was now the administrator. I then asked him if Universal had purchased the BMG Company or merely the assets** of BMG Music Publishing. He quickly and proudly assured that they had purchased the whole company. I paused a bit and said, "Oh! That's too bad! You just bought yourself a potential lawsuit." He was stunned and asked for an explanation. I was prepared with some of my findings that I showed him, and advised that if amends were not forthcoming, we might take legal action. I also reminded him that we were in the final year (1997) of the agreement. Dave acknowledged the problems and certainly did not want to lose representation of the catalog. He contacted several executives in Accounting and Legal to work out solutions to my claims.

After several weeks of haggling and negotiations, a final solution was agreed upon. We would terminate the current agreement and prepare a new 5-year deal. The existing unearned balance of advances would be wiped out, and new terms agreed upon. We would take no advance but would receive the best terms available for collection of both foreign and domestic earnings, on the "Most Favored Nations" basis. In exchange, we agreed to not pursue further damages.

The deal worked out well; publishing earnings have practically doubled over previous years as a result of this new contract. A good working relationship was also established, which was of benefit to both parties.

To paraphrase a principle of my former boss Lord Grade: "A deal is only a good one when both parties benefit."

---

*Popular novelty song of the 1940's possibly referring to a Jewish tailor in lower Manhattan. Also appears in Barbra Streisand's "Second Hand Rose" album.

** In many music publishing acquisitions the purchaser is advised to purchase the assets (copyrights) only, thereby protecting them from any existing liabilities. If it is a "company" acquisition they inherit everything.

CHAPTER 61
But The Melody Lingers On

While compiling information on Doris's publishing ownership and dealing with Universal, Jim Loeb and I were in constant contact, and got to know each other rather well. He would drive from his home in Los Angeles weekly to look after Doris. He'd oversee household help, assist Doris with the care for her dogs, take her shopping, and make sure she was in good health. I could see that he was under some strain and asked him a number times to come over to Quail Lodge, which was practically on Doris's premises, for 9 holes of golf. I knew he had occasionally played there with Doris's son, Terry. He would complain that he was too busy, didn't have clubs, and was lousy player, anyhow. I finally convinced him by bringing him a set of clubs, and insisting we play.

Jim met me around 3pm, and I had him hit some balls on the range to get used to the clubs. I could see he had a decent swing and after a short time took him to play the back nine. He started off well, to his surprise, and as we went along admitted that he was enjoying it. He was feeling quite good as we were approaching the 17th hole. Doris's home overlooked the 17th and 18th holes. Feeling more confident about his game he said, "I'm going to call Doris and have her watch us tee off the 18th." As we arrived Doris looking down from her deck, welcomed us. Along with Doris, however, was Betsy, who assisted Doris at her home. Betsy knew Jim quite well and shouted, "Jim, I'm bettin' on the other guy!" This must have shaken Jim because when he teed off, the ball went up in the air like pitching wedge. I was quick to follow and lucky enough to put one down the middle, though not far.

Jim said quickly, "Bad idea, let's get the hell out of here!" Despite that embarrassment he told me how much he'd enjoyed playing, and wanted to play again when I got back from a trip I was taking the following week to New York, for the Songwriters Hall of Fame event.

Joan and I had a wonderful time at the Hall of Fame dinner, where we met old friends and enjoyed the show. I even met with Anne Murray, who had my first giant hit "Snowbird," while at Beechwood Music, and reminisced about those days with her.

On our flight back we had to stop and change planes in St. Louis. While waiting for our flight my cell-phone rang. The call was from Doris's attorney at that time. "Sam, I hate to have to give you this news, but Jim Loeb died of a heart attack last night." I was stunned to the point of dizziness. The remainder of our flight was somber as I tried to grasp another tragedy in Doris's life, as well as mine.

When we got back I heard from Doris, who was as concerned about my reaction to Jim's death as I was to hers. Now there was a need to find someone who could take over the duties that were so ably performed by Jim.

After some consideration Doris decided to turn to one of the last remaining relatives of her family, Steven Stewart, son of her late brother Paul. Steven was a very successful real estate developer residing in Charleston, South Carolina, who had often visited his Aunt Doris as a child and young man. He had spent much of his life in Southern California before moving to Charleston.

After receiving the call from Doris, and understanding the situation, he decided to accept the invitation to help out, at least temporarily. It was not long before he contacted me to find out what I was all about. It seemed, that having no knowledge of the music industry, he was somewhat suspicious. I spent a good deal of time tutoring him on the business, which he seemed to grasp. Between that acquired knowledge, and Doris's praise, we began to get along well. He examined the increased revenues from my work in music publishing, and seeing the results, suggested that I look into other areas of Doris's entertainment income.

Finding and reviewing her recording contract was not a problem. Doris was a longtime recording artist for Columbia, which was now Sony. Later in her career she did a few independent recordings for Arwin Productions, a company set up by her late husband, Marty Melcher, for films, recordings, and music productions. There were steps to be taken to increase her income in this area that would successfully develop later.

The major problem was finding the actual contracts to her many film appearances that went back to the late 1940's. Steven went through Doris's house in search of these contracts. Through correspondence, I found the name of her accountants. I had a hunch that they might have copies. Finally, after numerous requests and written confirmation of our status by Doris, the accountants did supply us with copies of contracts in their possession. Between these two sources, and some cajoling of accountants at major studios, we accumulated almost all the needed documents.

As I had no experience in dealing with motion picture contracts, I had to do some fast studies regarding standard terms and terminology. It became apparent to me, early on, that no system was in place for tracking payment from studios, and that the work done on her behalf by her accountants left much to be desired. I felt that it was absolutely necessary to dismiss these accountants, and did so, with Steven's permission. All files were transferred to the accountants I had used since moving to Carmel.

Upon receipt of the files by the new accountants, I spent many days with them creating spread sheets based on the terms of these contracts. We listed original signing dates, terms and percentages of royalties, dates of payments due, renewal dates, and any other information which seemed constant within similar contracts. Armed with this information including the dates of the last payments received, I set about contacting studio personnel whose responsibility was submitting payments. Shockingly, I found no correspondence from one studio for over thirty years. I, therefore, had to do more research to find the correct party to contact at each studio. Each contract represented one film production, and so the search for information concerning some 39 motion pictures commenced. While deeply involved in this project I heard a variety of excuses for late or no payment, the most incredible of which came from the major studio that had not supplied an accounting for a very successful Doris Day film in 32 years. They stated that as of their last accounting, Ms. Day had a large unearned balance of advance, so they decided not to submit any statements until they were recouped. As forcefully delicate as I could sound, I reminded them that it had been 32 years and I was sure, by now, the balance had been earned out. I demanded an updated statement, reminding them of the terms of the contract. It took them nearly six months, with my constant badgering to bring the account up to date, but finally a statement was provided which included a check for some $110,000 and a promise to account semi annually in the future.

The above situation was not unique. Needless to say, after going through all film titles, a huge amount was recovered. Our spreadsheets now anticipated dates for payments due, and if not received, a notice sent.

At the same time, unbeknownst to me, Steven had examined Doris's home and guest quarters, and found initial faulty construction, which had resulted in rot in some areas. He alerted Doris, who had been unaware, but agreed to the repairs. Unfortunately, because of the inconvenience to Doris caused by the construction, and her not understanding the large costs entailed, a severe disagreement occurred between Doris and Steve, resulting in their parting of ways.

Once again, a personal manager was needed to assume the duties performed by Jim and then Steven. I again anticipated the questioning of my involvement, and the training of the new candidate in the mysteries of the music and entertainment business. However, as it turned out, I need not to have been apprehensive. Doris, in a relatively short time, selected a long time friend and loyal fan who had visited her often during his regular vacation trips to Carmel where he stayed with his wife at her guest cottage.

Robert Bashara was, and is a highly respected veterinarian residing in Omaha Nebraska, where he operates three well-known animal clinics. He has been involved in animal rights, rescue, and treatment even on the national level, all his life including in his tour of service in the U.S. Army. This match could not have been better for Doris and, as it has turned out, for me as well. Bob was a quick learner and acquired a real interest in all areas of the businesses in which I dealt on behalf of Doris. He, in fact, has come up with creative concepts for exploiting existing entertainment assets that previously had been prohibited, due to lack of understanding.

Quite often Bob and his wife Jan, would entertain Doris, Joan and me at a home where he was staying during his increasingly longer visits to deal with Doris's domestic, legal, and financial matters. Most importantly to Doris, Bob commenced overseeing and administering The Doris Day Animal Foundation, expanding its recognition worldwide.

One of the most successful ventures Bob and I set out upon was the release of a new Doris Day album in 2011, composed mostly of previously unreleased masters. This was the first new release of any Doris Day album in many years. The selection of songs to be used was made by Bob, me, and Jim Pierson, who had worked with Sony on several premium re-packages. The final approval was, of course, by Doris. Her taste in material proved to be excellent. Bob and I came up with the sequencing of titles that led it to become a "concept" album. The album was titled "My Heart " and though it was an Arwin Production, we offered Sony the distribution rights. To our surprise, Sony U.S., the company that now owned Columbia Records that had produced and released virtually all Doris Day records, had no interest, even though the album contained three Sony leased masters.

Fortunately, we had also submitted a copy of the album to Sony UK, aware of Doris's popularity in England, which had one of the most active Doris Day fan clubs. Sony UK was happy to have the album, and after some negotiations released it, not only in the UK but, with our permission, throughout Europe. Beyond even our expectations, the "My Heart" album quickly charted in the UK, and did quite well in Europe selling in excess of 100,000 CD'S.

Despite the UK and European success, and to the shock of Sony UK, Sony in the US again chose not to distribute the album, a move that speaks volumes concerning the current attitudes, and perceptions of major US recording companies.

Undeterred by Sony's decision, and in search of a US distributor, we found City Hall Records of San Rafael, California proud to distribute the newly created Arwin Records label through their independently affiliated facilities. Their good efforts, though limited because of their size, still resulted in an additional 35,000 sales.

While aware of Doris Day recordings, prior to my involvement, this activity put me in touch with her many and varied performances. It has led to my discovery of what a profoundly great vocalist and interpreter of songs she was. I've listened to most of her vast repertoire of more than 600 recordings which I now believe should be looked upon as one of the most significant contributions to the Great American Songbook.

After intensively listening to her album "Duet," recorded with Andre Previn, an album which happens to be my favorite, I said to her, "Doris, when I listen to you sing in that album, I think you're singing to me."

She smiled and answered, "When I was very young, and taking voice lessons in Cincinnati with Grace Raine, she said, 'Doris, before you sing a song, picture who you are singing it to.' I've always remembered that."

While I have been involved with just about every type, or style of music over my more the 50 years in the business, what a joy it is for me to represent a legendary artist who has sensitively recorded some of the most wonderful songs ever created.

The disappointment I received as a young man, which dashed my dreams of becoming a trumpeter in a major orchestra, actually turned out to be for the best. I recognized my limited talent, but discovered new abilities that kept me in music. I would encourage music students to look into the business of music, which through the diversity of new transmissions continues to add challenges. Perhaps knowledgeable music students can even influence and improve the quality of the music currently offered to the public, by becoming leaders of an industry now mostly directed by lawyers and accountants. Looking back, I must grudgingly admit that my conservatory training did often help me along the way.

In reviewing all that I have just written, I think I would be remiss if I didn't send a note to the New York Times which, while I was searching for work, plastered advertisements throughout the subway system boasting the many jobs resulting from their "want-ads." So, here's one, slightly modified, for them:

I GOT MY CAREER THROUGH THE NEW YORK TIMES

CHAPTER 62
Playing My Respects

I first met Mike Gould in the mid 1960's while at BMI in charge of Publisher Relations. He had come to New York from Hollywood along with another representative of Liberty Record's music publishing division to negotiate a publisher advance. Mike was then, I would estimate, in his early 60's and a veteran in the music industry. While the discussions were congenial, I detected a slight sense of condescension when addressing me, whom he must have viewed as rather young and inexperienced to be dealing with him.

When I moved to the west coast I would again see him at music publisher events, and struck up a more friendly and mutually respectful relationship with him. I learned that he had many positions with a number of publishers through the years. For reasons I can only speculate, these positions did not seem to last very long. I enjoyed my encounters with Mike and his sense of humor. Most of all, I enjoyed listening to the stories of his experiences in the industry over the years, and particularly his dealings in jazz, his first love and specialty. I could also detect a cynical edge to Mike's personality, possibly from what he might have considered his bad breaks.

I wasn't a golfer until I moved to the west coast, and out of necessity, knowing it was "the" industry pastime, started to take some lessons. Mike, of course, was a longtime player and in the late 1970's, after I was somewhat more proficient at the game, he invited me to join him for a round at the Calabasas golf course where he regularly played. At that time the course was only semi-private, and he could afford the green fees. I enjoyed the course, Mike's company and his stories. Any number of times he related how he was responsible for the hit song "Vaya Con Dios" performed by Les Paul and Mary Ford, while he was working at Capitol Record's early music publishing company.

At this time Mike was gainfully employed at Bourne Music, a New York based publisher that appointed Mike to promote songs from their catalog on the west coast. This association seemed to be a "natural" for

Mike as it contained many well-known "standard" songs such as "All Of Me," "Here's That Rainy Day." "Imagination," "Unforgettable," and "Willow Weep For Me," composed by crafted songwriters of the recent past who Mike could relate to. These were also the type of songs that were the most performed by jazz artists, Mike's specialty.

The company was headed by Bonnie Bourne, a Ziegfeld Follies girl, who inherited the company from her late husband, Saul Bornstein, a former top executive of Irving Berlin's music publishing company. When he departed Irving Berlin's company to start his own, Berlin as a gift, quitclaimed a large number of songs, not composed by him, as a starter catalog for this new company. Many of those songs were already top earners, and the basis for a great new catalog.

Unfortunately, when Bonnie passed away the company was taken over by her daughter Beebe who decided to "clean house," thereby costing Mike his job. So once again Mike faced hard times, and was forced to find work where he could. During that time we had moved to Calabasas Park and I joined the golf club. I frequently invited Mike as my guest, knowing he loved that course, but couldn't afford to play.

Mike, being experienced in all phases of music publishing, found some work as the U. S. representative of an established German music company run by one Joachim Neubauer. It was his job to find American hit songs to be sub-published by Joachim's company for Germany, Austria, and Switzerland. The job paid only a small amount, so together with Mike's wife's Nita's earnings from secretarial jobs, they survived.

Joachim was also an avid golfer, and when he visited the U.S. he and Mike would always play together.

Sometime in the early 1980's I received a telephone call, from a very emotional Nita, telling me that Mike had suffered a serious stroke and was in a nearby North Hollywood hospital. She requested that I go there as soon as possible. I went to the hospital immediately and found Mike in a coma. Standing next to his bed beside Nita was a gentleman I didn't know. Nita introduced me to Leonard Feather, perhaps the most famous Jazz critic, analyst, and journalist in America and obviously a dear friend of Mike. I was, of course, well aware of Feather and honored meet him. Nita encouraged Leonard and me to try talking to Mike even though he was unconscious, in the hope that he might hear us. This was, of course awkward, but we made an effort. Later that night Mike passed away.

The next morning Nita called again asking for my assistance with a problem she was facing. Mike had specifically requested that in the event of his death, he was to be cremated. The problem was that his brother was a conservative/orthodox Jew. According to Jewish practice, cremation was prohibited and the brother would be furious. I simply said, Nita, who do you wish to please?.... her husband's last wish, or her brother-in-law? Her decision was obvious, and she would make preparations for the cremation. She had one further request. She asked if I would pick up the ashes from the crematorium and, somehow, dispose of them at a golf course. She thought that would be a place Mike would have wanted. This presented me with a problem. I knew that it was illegal to do this, but I felt that, somehow, I owed it to Mike.

I picked up the ashes and was very surprised at the weight. It was much heavier than I anticipated. After much thought, I called Nita and suggested a plan. I would go out very early the next morning for a nine hole round on the back nine of the Calabasas course, before any other players arrived and distribute the ashes, if possible, on the 12th hole, a downhill par three of about 147 yards, which was a favorite of Mike's. I also suggested I play the round with Mike's clubs to make it more of a memorial. She was thrilled with the idea and brought me his clubs.

I arrived at the club at about 6:25 AM the next morning, hiding the ashes behind my bag and requested a cart, much to the starter's surprise. He knew that I usually walked, so I told him it was early and I was hardly warmed up; so off I went.

The tenth and eleventh holes were no problem, but when I arrived at the 12th, I looked down to find a maintenance man watering the green. He saw me, stopped and waved me to play through. It took a great deal of my shouting to convince him to continue watering, yelling that I was not ready. This was the hole that I intended to be Mike's final resting place, and I needed time. He finally finished and moved on.

I hurriedly lifted out the container of ashes and spread the contents along the newly planted flower-beds surrounding the tee, and placed a cardboard sign reading "Vaya Con Dios" against the post indicating the hole number.

I took out a 7 iron and prepared to swing, but stopped realizing that Mike could never have reached the green with that club. I pulled out his 5 iron, choked down, and hoped to land the ball on the green, since I felt this was the most important hole to par as it was Mike's favorite. Fortunately, it did land on the green and I parred the hole. I completed the nine holes with a score of 42, and signed the card, "Mike Gould as played by Sam Trust."

When I brought the card back to give to Nita, she was overwhelmed with gratitude and insisted on giving me two wonderful woolen sweaters that Mike had gotten in Scotland. She also brought me a set of Ping woods, that Mike had just had re-finished. I still wear those sweaters for golf on cold days. The woods, however, rest as a showpiece of when woodenheaded clubs were beautiful.

A few months later Joachim Neubauer unexpectedly stopped by our offices. He was shown to my office where we extended mutual greetings. He then talked about Mike's sad passing and wanted to pay his respects at Mike's gravesite. When he inquired where that might be, I will never forget the expression on his face when I said, "Did you bring your clubs?"

CHAPTER 63
Homage To The "Old-timers"

Throughout my career in music publishing, I've always been attracted to the "senior citizens" of the business. Every company in which I presided, I employed, what can only be called the "old-timers," who contributed to the success of our operations.

It seems a pity that as existing publishing and record companies get acquired by the large vertically integrated, mega-entertainment organizations, veterans of the acquired companies, who were so vital to their building and success, are usually not part of the acquisition. I can point out a number of situations where the acquiring company lost out in revenues, since they did not realize the assets they then owned. Further, they had no idea of the potential value of some of the items in these catalogs. The "old-timers" could have prevented this.

Warren Buffet seems to be the exception to the rule. When he acquires a company for his Berkshire Hathaway, he keeps the company virtually intact. He simply states that these people made the company attractive, so why would he spoil things.

Here are some of the "oldtimers" who contributed to the success of the companies where I worked:

GEORGE MARLO
Carl Haverlin, the first real president of BMI, was wise enough to keep George aboard BMI after the disposal of BMI's Publishing company, which George oversaw. His personality attracted writers who remained loyal, largely due to their love of this man, who was always available to them. Despite a mandatory retirement policy of 65 years of age at the time, he was kept on until his death at 86. He was that important to BMI, not only for his knowledge of the business, but for the morale of the employees.

219

CLIFFIE STONE

Cliffie was co-owner and manager of Central Songs, the company I acquired for Capitol Record's music publishing company, Beechwood Music, in 1969. Cliffie had hired all writers, some of whom became famous, and was already somewhat of a legend in country music. Without Cliffie, chances are that I would never have known of a contract he made some time previously with Gary Buck in Canada for the rights to works in Buck's publishing company outside of Canada. That knowledge led to my appointing Buck as president of Beechwood Music of Canada, and to the successes of "Snowbird" and "Put Your Hand In The Hand," with worldwide ownership of both. As soon as I resigned from Beechwood, Capitol's management dismissed Cliffie. The constant country chart success for Beechwood songs also ended.

Cliffie also took up office residence with me in the interim when I formed Trust Music Management. When I was appointed CEO of ATV Music, he was one of my first employees and was largely responsible in our acquisition of Bobby Bare's (a former writer of Cliffie's) Return Music, which brought Billy Joe Shaver to ATV Music. He was also very much involved in the acquisition of Brougham Hall Music that contained the now famous "Lucille," and the writers who wrote it. Cliffie stayed at ATV Music during my entire tenure with that company, and retired when the company was sold by Holmes a'Court. At the time, Cliffie had reached his mid 70's. A few years later he was inducted into the Country Music Hall of Fame, and given a star on the Hollywood Walk of Fame.

GERALD TEIFER

I first met Gerry when he was president of RCA's newly formed Sunbury/Dunbar Music Publishing in New York, while I was still at BMI. Previously, he had headed CBS's original music publishing entry April/Blackwood Music. After service as a paratrooper in World War II, Gerry worked in Nashville for Acuff Rose Music Publishing. He also served as a professional whistler in the Ted Weems band and performed as a whistler in a number of radio and TV spots. I can remember visiting him at his office to listen to a Tony Bennett test pressing of "Yesterday I Heard The Rain." The music was by Mexican composer Armando Manasero with sensitive English lyrics by Gene Lees. We listened in silence. Afterwards, Gerry discussed the song with me. It was a valuable learning experience.

In the mid 1970's Gerry was offered the job of heading John Kluge's latest venture in the music business, Metromedia Music Publishing, to be located in Hollywood. Gerry and his wife "Bundy" relocated to Los Angeles, and oddly enough, Gerry opened Metromedia's office on the same floor as ATV Music. After less than three years, John Kluge apparently became disenchanted with the business and disposed that operation, and his record company in Nashville, leaving Gerry high and dry. I knew that he would be an asset to our company and decided he would be perfect for our office in Nashville, an area in which he was well acquainted. As I was not impressed with the present performance of that office, Gerry was put in charge, and did a fine job. He stayed with us until the final sale, as did Cliffie. I took care to see that both he and Cliffie were under a defined pension plan, meaning that they would be fully vested when they left.

Gerry, and his wife "Bundy," retired to Clearwater Florida, but continued to correspond with us, furnishing us with his cartoon characters "The Krumpkins." It was only through his funeral announcement did I learn that he was a "freefall" parachutist who was dropped behind enemy lines during World War II. He was buried at Arlington National Cemetery with full Military Honors.

HAPPY GODAY

Happy was already a celebrity of sorts, having worked in New York for the Richmond Organization (TRO Music) for many years. He was instrumental in the promotion of the successful British musicals owned by that company, "Oliver," and "Stop The World, I Want To Get Off." TRO was, and is one of the most respected independent music publishing companies in the world, created by the late and great Howie Richmond. Happy's departure was a surprise to everybody in the business.

I learned that Happy was in Los Angeles and was instrumental in helping Barbra Streisand achieve an Oscar for the best song award, "Evergreen," from her movie "A Star Is Born." I decided that he would be perfect for ATV Music that was now going full speed in feature film production. I located Happy, interviewed him and hired him.

Happy was about five feet, four inches tall, at most. He weighed about 115 lbs. and always seemed to have a good tan. But his most distinguishing feature was his fast-talking and preponderance of malaprops. He seemed to be the Casey Stengel of the music business. I can remember a discussion I was having with him in which he kept referring to a "Phil Peters." I finally stopped him and asked him who Phil Peters was? He replied, "You know, our guy in England." I then

221

realized he was referring to Peter Phillips.

Happy got to work right away with one of Lord Grade's early films, "The Eagle Has Landed." The score was composed by Lalo Shifrin, which included a beautiful theme, most of which was, unfortunately, removed by the director. However, Happy listened to the theme and had an idea. He contacted Marilyn and Alan Bergman who produced a beautiful lyric. Happy had a demo created and pitched it to Barbra Streisand, whom he knew was working on an album dealing with rain as the concept. The song created from Lalo's theme was "On Rainy Afternoons." It was included in Barbra's album, which sold two and a half million copies. Happy also pitched the score to the Academy, which nominated it for an Oscar. In the following four years, ATV had either a song, or score nominated for an Oscar through Happy's efforts. During his stay at ATV Music, Happy pulled off another coup by getting the top 40 single "Calling Occupants from Interplanetary Space," originally from the "Klaatu" album for Karen Carpenter.

It seems that everybody of any importance had a Happy Goday story. I can remember having breakfast with Sammy Cahn and listening, most of that time, to tales of Happy. Why he was let go at TRO, I'll never know, and had no reason to ask.

So, it might be a good idea to consider the value of these "oldtimers" when acquiring a company. They must be considered a most important part of the "assets."

GLOSSARY

ASCAP, BMI, and SESAC: United States Performing Rights organizations that represent both writers and music publishers. The "performing right" is part of the US copyright law. The United States, however, was late in recognizing this right, which was enforced in Germany (GEMA) and France (SACEM) some 50 years earlier.

These organizations license and collect royalties from performances on Television, Radio, and Cable broadcasting, as well as non-broadcasting sources such as nightclubs and auditoriums. Credits are assigned for various types of these performances, and royalties are paid to their writer and publisher affiliates based on these credits. These organizations constantly police, and try to license all new forms of communications involving musical performances.

The oldest of the three is ASCAP, (American Society of Composers Authors and Publishers) which was founded by a group of composers including Victor Herbert, Irving Berlin, Sigmund Romberg and John Philip Sousa in 1914. Initial royalties collected were small, so the first royalty payments distributed weren't until 1921. With the advent of radio, performing rights income grew substantially, competing with, and soon overtaking the most dominant prior income,-sheet music.

As performance income grew, largely from radio performances, ASCAP was the sole purveyor of "performing rights." This put the broadcasting industry in a "no bargaining" situation. In 1939 ASCAP demanded a doubling of their rates. Broadcasters simply could not put up with this monopolistic situation, and much to ASCAP's disgust, formed a new performing rights organization, Broadcast Music, Inc. (BMI) in 1940. BMI represents writers and publishers in the same manner as ASCAP. Through the years, competition for writers and publishers between these two organizations became extremely intense. Both of these companies operate as non-profit.

SESAC was formed in 1938 by German immigrant Paul Heinecke. Very few know that it stood for Society of European Stage Authors and Composers. It has also operated as a performing rights organization, but for profit. Until recently it was hardly a rival to ASCAP and BMI. With new ownership it has attracted many significant writers, mainly artist-

223

writers, by granting them huge advances and guarantees.

AGENT: Usually referred to as a representative who deals on behalf of a client's particular needs. For example, the Harry Fox Agency represents the licensing of "mechanical rights" for the majority of U.S. music publishers. (see "Mechanicals")

BACKGROUND MUSIC LIBRARIES: (AKA Production Music Libraries) compilations of various moods of music often broken down to smaller segments which can be used in various films, promos, commercials, etc. Early on these libraries were derogatively referred to as "canned music" or "music by the yard." However they have lately gained respect due to the quality of their music and excellent recording techniques, and are now used by most of the top film studios.

BREAKOUT: refers to a song, i.e. recording, making a quick move up the national song charts or song suddenly appearing unexpectedly high when entering the charts.

BULLET: assigned to a song in the Billboard Charts predicted to move upward in following weeks.

CHECKER: term used to describe a person who identifies song titles from station reports of music usage submitted to BMI or ASCAP. At BMI they were sometimes referred to as "loggers." (see "Logging")

COPYRIGHT: a registration of a newly created work subsists whenever it is written down or recorded on audio or video tape. The copyright is then owned solely by the author or creator in accordance with the 1976 Copyright Law revision. When a writer enters into an exclusive agreement with a music publisher he, or she, is assigning that copyright and future works written during the term of his or her agreement, to the music publisher. The period of assignment may vary based on the status or leverage of the writer. The music publisher can then formally register the work(s) with the U.S. Copyright office for further protection to his claim.

A term oftentimes used as industry jargon referring to valuable song is, "Now, that's a copyright!"

CUE-SHEET or MUSIC CUE-SHEET: a record of the music used in

a film or video indicating the title or code number of the music, the nature of the usage, i.e., vocal, instrumental-background, or visual, and the length of usage. Crediting by performing rights organizations are dependent on these descriptions. For example, a visual-vocal performance of music would receive higher crediting than an instrumental background of the same duration, since it is the dominant focus of attention of the actors and audience.

DISTRIBUTOR: parties who actually provide retailers with product such as recordings. Oftentimes, smaller independent record producers retain distributors to represent and promote their product to retailers and the broadcast industry.

EXPLOITATION: a term used in music publisher's contracts meaning the promotion of the client's song(s). This is not used or intended, as what some might consider, a derogatory term.

HOOK: a repeatable phrase, usually in the chorus of a song that sticks to the listener's ear and memory. Oftentimes it is the title of the song. Examples: <u>Born Free.</u> <u>High Hopes</u>. However, in more esoteric songs such as <u>All the Things You Are</u> and <u>Stardust</u> the song title does not appear until the song ends, with the "hook" preceding it.

LICENSE: a document legally conveying rights of an owner to a licensee for usage by a third party. For examples: a music publisher may license the rights to quote a phrase from a song to a book publisher, or license a print company to reproduce sheet music for sale. The Harry Fox Agency yearly issues hundreds of thousands of "mechanical licenses" on behalf of the music publishers they represent.

LOGGING: The term used by BMI for the checking and crediting of all broadcast stations reports of music usage.

LOTOS CLUB: An exclusive club, dating back over 150 years, in which Sidney Kaye, founder and Chairman Of The Board of BMI, belonged. The club is located on Manhattan's upper 5th Avenue and lists many past and present notable members including Mark Twain, Andrew Carnegie, William Randolph Hearst, Orson Welles and Isaac Stern as members. The club is proud of their interest and promotion of the arts.

MECHANICAL RIGHTS: The U.S. Copyright Law requires a

statutory payment rate for the transfer of a song to any recording device. This law first applied to player pianos shortly after the turn of the 20th century. It is now most commonly used for recordings. The Harry Fox Agency is the largest purveyor of these rights on behalf of music publishers in the United States. The original rate, established in 1909, was 2 cents, and unhappily for writers and music publishers, remained in effect until 1978. Since that date the rate has regularly risen to 9.1 cents, with 1.75 cents for each minute in excess of 5 minutes. Rate increases are based on various economic standards.

MUSIC PUBLISHER: Essentially represents the musical compositions of songwriters and composers. He/she is entrusted to protect and promote (exploit) their compositions. The music publisher generally owns, and administers the copyrights to the material in their catalogs. In some cases, copyright ownership may be shared with the writer/composer, particularly if they are also the artist (singer/ songwriter) performing the work. Terms are usually negotiated for the percentage of copyright ownership between writer/composer and publisher based on past success of the writer.

PRODUCER: in the recording industry refers to the individual who is charge of, and actually oversees and supervises the recording session. The producer is usually accorded a significant percentage of royalties from the sale of the recordings, particularly if he has a record of past successful sales from his work.

PUBLIC DOMAIN: refers to musical works no longer protected by copyright laws.

The majority of these works have out-lived the duration of their protection in the territory in which they originated. Some are merely traditional works that were never copyrighted, and others may have fallen into public domain due to failure to renew their term of protection, in accordance with copyright requirements. In some cases, works considered public domain in one territory may be still protected in others, based on unique copyright terms in a given territory.

RINGER: a person considered as a "professional" being used to bolster the activity of a group considered amateurish. Example: a professional musician brought in to bolster a particular section of an orchestra.

SCORE: refers to the music composed for a film or musical. In classical music it is the term used for the actual printed music used by the conductor, showing what each musical instrument is intended to play.

SINGER/SONGWRITER: a recording artist who performs his/her original music. Prior to the late 1950's, this was relatively rare. Most recording artists received their songs from music publishers, who had stables of composers and lyricists who regularly ground out, and supplied singers, or their producers, with songs. With the advent of the singer/songwriter the industry seems to have resurrected the ancient "troubadours" who traveled from village to village, singing stories of recent events. Starting with writers such as Bob Dylan, this also seemed to be the pattern, breaking years and years of basically romantic love songs.

SONG-PLUGGER: usually employed by a music publisher to obtain recordings or usage of songs in films, and television, as well as performance on radio.

SUB-PUBLISHER: a publisher assigned the rights to act as the original music publisher's agent on his behalf, in the particular territory in which he resides and serves as a music publisher.

SYNCHRONIZATION RIGHTS: a license to apply music to film or videotape. While the "mechanical license" is largely based on a statutory rate, the synchronization license is freely negotiated, based on "whatever the traffic can bear." This leaves the copyright owner in a much stronger bargaining position. Until 1927 with the release of "The Jazz Singer," which introduced sound to film, very little if any revenue was garnered from this right. That phenomenon caused motion picture studios to quickly purchase some of the largest music publishers of the day. Today, in fact, the largest segment of the music publishing industry is controlled by Warner Brothers, Universal, Sony/ATV, Paramount, and Disney. Synchronization income is now near the top of income producers for music publishers as it encompasses not only films and videotape productions, but the extremely wide use of known copyrights in commercials worldwide.

TERM: in virtually all entertainment contracts defines the length of time an artist, writer/composer, etc. is contractually committed to exclusively serve the licensor.

For examples: a composer grants exclusivity to a music publisher for a period of five years. A recording artist grants exclusive representation for a defined period to a record company. A music publisher grants a "sub-publisher" a license to act as their representative in a defined "territory" for a period of time.

TERRITORY: defines the exact area contractually defined in a contract. A U.S. music publisher may be assigned rights by a foreign music publishing company for "The U.S. and Canada." A European music publisher may be assigned rights for representation of U.S. Company for Germany, Austria and Switzerland.

92353580R00133

Made in the USA
San Bernardino, CA
31 October 2018